The Pencil Case

by Lorraine Cobcroft

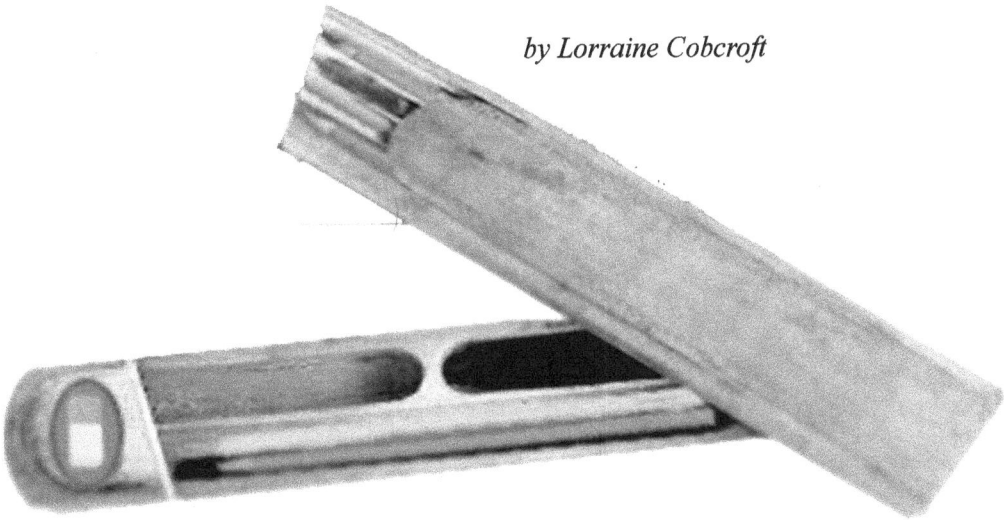

ACKNOWLEDGEMENTS

Little of worth is ever achieved alone, and what we do in isolation rarely brings much joy.

I owe a debt of gratitude to my editor, Robb Grindstaff, for his helpful advice and encouragement, without which I doubt this work would have ever been completed; to Barbara Scott of A Woman's Write, whose encouraging words motivated me to make yet another critical revision; and to Diana Hockley, who so generously gave her time and expertise to help me apply that all–important final coat of polish to the manuscript. Also to all my wonderful friends on Authonomy who have been so supportive.

Thanks are due to my wonderful family: my mother, daughters Suzie and Danie, son Garrick, sons–in–law, daughter–in–law (now, tragically, deceased) and adored grandchildren for their love, encouragement and support.

Most importantly, I owe a huge debt to my wonderful husband, Peter, who throws his untiring support behind my every endeavour, and whose love and companionship makes waking every morning a joy. Only his insistent modesty prevents me naming him as co–author. He is "the wind beneath my wings".

DEDICATION

This book is dedicated to the memory of Lesley and Edith Tuck, in humble recognition of their dedication, generosity and hard work loving and caring for homeless children.

I attended a reunion of some of 'their boys' a few years ago. One of those present proposed a toast to Les and Ede. It brought tears to my eyes when over two dozen men, middle aged and older, raised their glasses and, with no prompting, chorused "To Mum and Dad". There could be no more fitting tribute to the memory of a couple who gave so much to kids who had so little.

In the words of one of those who loved them, "If they aren't saints in heaven, they'll do me until some come along".

To be nobody but yourself in a world which is doing its best, night and day, to make you like everybody else means to fight the hardest battle which any human being can fight."

E.E. Cummings

"Nothing is more difficult, and therefore more precious, than to be able to decide."

Napoleon Bonaparte

BACKGROUND AND DISCLAIMER

Until around the mid–1970s, government policy across Australia was to remove children they considered to be "at risk" in their home environment. The story of "The Stolen Generation" is now well known internationally, but the whole truth hasn't been told. Children weren't taken solely because of their race. They stole white kids too.

Welfare legislation authorising the removal of children from poverty–stricken homes was enacted by people who were untrained and unable or unwilling to acknowledge that lack of money did not mean a bad home life. Children were removed to institutions where they suffered deprivation, abuse, separation from family and withholding of affection that scarred them for life.

Financial benefits accrued to welfare workers and churches through increasing the number of wards of the state. Increased government funding of welfare departments meant more jobs, and churches profited by keeping children on subsistence diets and dressed in rags, spending far less than the government allowances provided for the children committed to their care.

This is the story of one of the victims of this policy.

Although the story framework (the journey with the lawyer) is fiction, and details have been changed, most of the incidents related happened as described. To create a story — and because memory is sometimes unreliable, interpretations and perspectives vary, and access to detailed knowledge of some incidents is limited — creative licence has been taken in describing some people and places and relating details of events and conversations. Names of people and places have been changed, but some characters are named, or may be recognisable as known persons.

The story is told from diverse observations and fragmented and sometimes unreliable memories, including memories of individuals whose perspective was shaped by trauma and years of suffering pain, struggle and cruel injustices. There is no intention to defame or criticise individuals about whose life, other deeds, endeavours and deeper motives and intentions neither the author nor the protagonist has knowledge. Rather, the goal is to expose how their thinking and conduct in specific situations was influenced by a flawed system and the social prejudices of the day; and how it was perceived by, reacted to and affected the victims of society's failure.

7

The condemnation of those who continue, today, to misrepresent history, to discriminate based on race, and to deny victims fair reparation and assistance is, however, deliberate and made without apology.

The author endeavoured to be true to the protagonist's memories and representations, and to accurately reflect his thoughts and feelings, although her own experiences and emotions inevitably influenced the way this story was written.

PART I

1: COURTROOM BULLSHIT

OCTOBER, 1956

"Bullshit!"

Frederick Wilson thrust a handful of torn paper towards the bench and stormed from the courtroom. Outside, he spat in the gutter, wiped sweat and tears from his face, slung a worn coat over his shoulder and stumbled down the street.

Slumped shoulders reduced his height to a neat six feet. His tie hung loosely now, its knot slightly askew. A narrow belt drew shiny, oversized trousers in to fit a scant waist, but the creases were sharp. Despite its fraying collar, his shirt was crisply starched and snow white.

At the corner, he hesitated and glanced back uncertainly. Suited men emerged from the courthouse. His children must be still inside. He remembered how they looked as he passed them, leaving: little Jenny, tearful, trembling, gripped that grubby doll like a lifeline; Paul, white–faced, lips set tight, stood tall and glared defiantly at the judge.

"A chip off the ol' block," he thought with a surge of pride. "He'll survive. He'll take care of his sister too, if they let him."

Another terrifying thought ripped through his being. He faltered and almost fell.

"God, don't let them separate them," he mumbled.

Righting himself, he stared for a brief moment at the group congregating outside the courthouse.

"Bastards!" he screamed. "Curse you lousy bastards!"

He turned the corner and was gone.

JUNE, 2010

"It's been over 50 years now," Paul said, his tone more reflective than wistful, "but I remember me well. I was a bright, confident, happy–go–lucky kid — like my dad, Fred, if war and bullshit hadn't beaten so much of him

9

out of him. Like my brothers. Sure, they're bushies — a bit rough around the edges. But they're decent, hard–working, and smart in their own ways. Their skins fit comfortably, and they wear she'll–be–right–mate grins and answer 'You bet' to every 'Can you?' question. That was me, too, until I was eight."

Ern shot Paul Wilson a sympathetic smile as they bounced through the entrance to the desolate property. Paul parked by the scant remnants of the old shack, and they climbed out of the sleek Rolls–Royce Ghost, now thickly coated with powdery–pink dust and showing faint red sweat stains on its plush dove–leather seats.

This case was challenging Ern's allegiance to professional principles. Of course he was aware of the tragedy of the 'Stolen Generation', and some of the victims' stories had moved him. But interviewing the players in Paul Wilson's saga had affected him on an emotional level, and he struggled to maintain an acceptable level of detachment. Confronted, now, with a mental image of a black car transporting terrified children away from the familiarity of this bushland home and into a foreign universe, his intellect acknowledged the logic and valid intention of removal policies, but his emotions resisted. He took several deep breaths and ordered his stomach to be still, but it was miserably upset.

He sniffed the air and listened to the sounds of the bush, snapped a million images of nothing and scribbled copious notes. He felt and smelt the dust, the blades of grey grass and the eucalyptus leaves. Paul had told him how his dad predicted rain by observing the changing colour of tree bark, and now he peeled away the papery–white bark on the tree trunks to examine the red and yellow hues beneath.

He was thorough, but Paul had come to expect that of Ernest Stanley. He was the consummate legal professional. He'd become, over the past few months, a trusted mate. By now, Ern knew much of Paul's story, but he wanted to fill in the gaps in intricate detail. He wanted to understand the world Paul came from, and what drove him. He wanted to get to know the man Paul Wilson was, and the man he might have been.

The colours of the land had begun to soften and the shadows of the sparse scrubby trees lengthened as they started for the town, wheels crushing spiky, low, blue–grey grass flat against the hard, red earth. The sun's hot fingers painted streaks of burnt orange and brilliant red–gold over the distant horizon.

Paul pulled into the parking lot of the quaint little country motel, climbed out of the Rolls and thrust the keys in his pocket. Ern gathered his papers.

Paul phoned his wife, and Ern warmed in admiration as he listened to the one–sided conversation. In the area of relationships, at least, Paul had beaten the odds. He was resilient too. Ern had probed beneath his armour, seen the wounds and scars and the furious yearning for justice. But Paul presented, publicly, as a man content with his lot in life. He was equipped with a delicious sense of humour and a firm conviction that, one way or another, things would always eventually turn out all right. He was a survivor, not a victim, and that presented Ern with a challenge he embraced with vim.

They made selections from the mini–bar, switched the television on, and sank into the sighing depths of a worn cotton–covered sofa. In the morning, the reliving of Paul Wilson's saga would begin.

2: A BUSH HOME

1948 TO 1956

I guess the bullshit really started when I was about five. I was born in '48, so it would have been 1953. We were living in a bush town in western New South Wales. A toff came to visit us, demanding money.

The man wore a crisp white shirt and a dark tie and was clean–shaven, with oiled hair slicked back from a pale forehead. He held a zippered leather folio with gold embossing on the front in his soft white hands. He shouted at Mum until she cried.

My dad was thin, but muscled from hard work and his hands were big and rough. The man looked no match for him, so it shocked me to see my big, strong father tremble in his presence. Dad swore at the man, but the colour left his face, and afterwards he sat at our kitchen table with his head in his hands. Mum said for once she wished he had money to go to the pub and drown his sorrows.

Dad spent a good deal of time in the pub, especially in shearing season. All the shearers were heavy drinkers. It was punishing work in those stinking hot sheds, lifting and throwing sheep and bending over them with blades, pushing those heavy clippers as fast as their hands would move. There was no automation, and shearers were paid piece rates, so they went at it hard. Dad was a gun shearer. He averaged more than 200 sheep a day.

When he wasn't shearing he went droving, broke horses or helped with planting or harvesting on nearby farms. It was hot, thirsty work. A few cold beers at the end of the working day was a well–established tradition among Aussie workers, but Dad often had more than a few. Mum complained bitterly when he came home 'full', as she put it, but I liked that it put him in a cheerful, joking mood. He was often moody and glum when he was sober.

We lived in a little white cottage on the edge of town, close to the river. It had running water and electricity and a neat little garden edged with a white picket fence. I think it must have been the first home Mum and Dad ever shared. They lived there when I was born, and when Jenny arrived. They lived there when their first–born arrived too. He only survived a year. They laid him to rest under a mound of dirt on the riverbank.

When I was three, Mum brought Ian home to that house. She made a little bed for him in a drawer removed from the dresser. I was jealous of him at first, and annoyed that he seemed to cry all the time. My jealousy passed as he grew older and learnt to play. A year later, another brother, Robert, was born.

A few weeks before that toff came, Dad fell from a horse and hurt his back, so he couldn't work. A week after that visit he hitched his horse to the old wooden cart, loaded some stuff in it, and we left that house for ever.

He shifted us out to a shack on the edge of a big grazing property a few miles out of town. It used to be a worker's cottage, but a fire had blackened all the walls so there were hessian bags hanging where the windows used to be. There were only three rooms, and no bathroom. We washed ourselves, our clothing and the dishes in a huge tub outside the door that we filled with water dragged by bucket from a dam.

It was biting cold in the shack on winter nights and damp in the wet. When my brothers were old enough to sleep in a bed, I had to share with Jenny, because there weren't enough beds for four of us kids. I didn't mind really, because on cold nights we could cuddle close to keep each other warm. On hot nights, we put as much distance between us as possible, but everyone swam in sweat anyway and an extra body in the bed probably didn't make much difference.

Seemed like it was nearly always hot and dry out there. When folks weren't praying for rain, they were ploughing ankle deep in red–brown mud — the river cutting off access to town — and it would seem like the rain'd never stop. Then, for a little while, the paddocks would be all soft and green and the sheep would fatten and the river would run clean and clear, but it wouldn't last long. The sun was merciless, and it'd quickly burn the grass and lift the red dust again.

The dryness made it hard to grow stuff, and the dust made it impossible to keep a home clean, but Mum scrubbed the big black stove and swept the floors. She placed up–ended packing crates beside the beds, covered them with little cloths, and set treasured ornaments on them.

I helped her plant a vegie garden, and we picked berries and mushrooms in the fields nearby. We caught fish and craybobs. Sometimes she shot a pigeon or a rabbit. Now and again, Dad brought home a sheep or calf. "Road kill," he called them. Run over by a car or bit by a snake or something, he reckoned. We knew most were not.

I pinched fruit from local orchards. Got caught often. The owners would clip my ear and send me packing, but I don't think they minded really. Sometimes they'd give me fruit to take home to Mum.

14

After I started school, I scrounged cordial bottles and cashed them to buy bread. I loved the soft kissing crust, and I'd always pick at it on the two–mile walk home. I was nearly always hungry.

We had no money for several months after Dad's fall, but when his back started to heal, he started making whips and selling them. Everyone who bought them said they were works of art. I loved to watch, fascinated by the way he sliced and plaited the leather. I loved the raw smell of the cowhide and the coarse warmth of the leather between my fingers. I wanted him to teach me, and I dreamt of being a whip maker one day.

One time, before he started making those whips, he gave Mum a few bob. She gave some to me and asked me to walk to town to buy bread and cigarettes. We'd been living on thin onion soup for a week, so she was excited by the prospect of having bread to go with it. The thought of it had me salivating all the way on the long walk into town.

I passed the little white cottage that was my first home and thought wistfully that we'd never been hungry or cold when we lived there. Then I passed through the government housing estate. It was crowded with tiny fibro cottages with a single smoking brick chimney rising above each little tin hat. In their dusty, wire–fenced front yards, the screeches of frenzied mothers competed with yapping dogs and bellowing kids. There were about five styles of cottage, repeated in patterns across a dozen streets. I wondered why we couldn't live in one of those cottages.

At the end of the main street, I stopped at Petracca's newsagent to look mournfully at comic books and wish I could afford to buy such treats. I couldn't read, but I liked looking at the pictures. I continued on past Spiros' Milk Bar to Comino's General Store. All the stores seemed to be owned by Greeks. They always had plenty of money. So did the toffs who owned the grazing properties scattered around the countryside, and the shearing contractors. It was only the shearers and farm workers who were poor. Of course, the Aborigines were poor too. They lived in metal humpies in a settlement on the edge of town and wore clothes the toffs and shearers' wives discarded. The old men grew long beards and sat about smoking and drinking methylated spirits. The women sat in the parks with their legs crossed, watching snotty–nosed kids playing. Some of the younger men worked on farms and their wives helped out in the homesteads of the wealthy graziers. They were good workers, but they'd go walkabout for weeks or months on end, sometimes just when they were needed most. They were a friendly lot, but they didn't mix much with the white folks. Police would move them on when they sat about the street corners.

Mr Comino ladled some milk from a drum into a shiny tin billy, pressed the lid on, and passed it to a lady wearing a wide–brimmed sun hat and high–

heel shoes. She thanked him, placed sixpence in his hand, smiled down at me, then clicked across the floorboards and down the wooden steps, dangling her milk pail from a gloved hand.

"G'day, Mr Comino," I said, sidling up to a huge wooden counter and dropping my coins on it.

"Yez tiz," he replied. "Wadda I get for you?" His accent always amused me, but Mum said it wasn't nice to laugh.

"A loaf of bread, please. And Mum wants some cigarettes. She said you know which ones she likes."

He fetched a loaf from a glass cabinet and placed it on a sheet of tissue paper on the counter, wrapped it carefully, and put a piece of sticky tape across where the ends of the tissue joined. He pulled a packet of cigarettes from a high shelf, and I held out Mum's string bag for him to put the bread and smokes into. Then he pressed some keys on the cash register and it rang a bell as a drawer popped open. The drawer was filled with money.

How nice to own a shop and have all the bread you could eat, and sliced meat, and sweets, and ice cream and all that other stuff, and a drawer full of money as well!

He picked up the money, dropped it into the drawer, then passed me four pennies in change. As tempting as it was to spend it, I put the change carefully in my pocket to hand it back to Mum. It was hard to resist the sticky, sweet smells from colourful jars of jelly babies and caramels on the edge of the counter and the rich silkiness of the ice cream in the big, silver drums that cooled the front section of the store, but Mum would check the change carefully.

On the long walk home, I set the bag down and crouched to remove some burrs from my socks. When I stood, I noticed a dark–coloured snake slowly forming a wide circle around me. I froze. My heart pounded at the ground and my legs went woozy.

"Snakes'll bite if you annoy 'em, son," my dad had said. "But they're much scareder of you than you are of them. If you leave 'em alone, they'll get away quick as they can. If you see one near you, don't move. Movement frightens them. Jes' stay still an' it'll go away."

Somehow, remembering those words didn't reassure me greatly, but I was far too frightened to do anything other than follow his advice and stand stock still and silent. The scaly green–brown creature slithered through the dust, circling my feet. It raised its head slightly to look at me through beady black eyes, exposing a creamy underbelly. I was unable to identify it, but I was sure it must be a deadly variety. Any moment now I would feel its poison fangs sink into my leg, and its venom would surge through my veins. What should I do then? Movement after being bitten was fatal, but there was no–one within earshot to help. I was surrounded by vast grazing paddocks and the odd desert bush or gum tree. Behind and ahead lay miles of soft red–dirt road. Over a mile home, almost a mile to the first lonely cottages on the outskirts of the town, and at least half a mile through the paddocks to the nearest homestead.

I wondered if snakes regarded breathing or heart palpitations as movement. I was careful not to move a muscle, but I couldn't stop my racing heart or my nervous panting. I watched as the creature slithered around me, leaving a smoothly grooved trail to mark the path it travelled.

If Mum were here, she would shoot it. She often shot snakes that came too close to the house. Lucky she was a good shot, because she always took aim and then closed her eyes when she pulled the trigger. Hated seeing anything die. Always said "poor creature" after, but she was concerned for our safety. Both Mum and Dad disapproved of shooting anything unless it was to eat or for protection.

Occasionally young blokes on shooting expeditions drove near our house or over the paddocks of the station — shooting kangaroos or rabbits mostly. Sometimes ducks. Dad never objected to them killing for skins and meat, but if they left dead or wounded ducks or animals behind he would chase them and yell swear words at them.

"Live an' let live, son," Dad said. "There's an order t' the universe. Every livin' thing exists for a reason. We're meant to hunt for our tucker, and sometimes we gotta kill for safety, but killin' for sport's disgustin'."

He'd say it was OK to kill this snake, though. It was threatening my safety. Only problem was, I had nothing to kill it with. I didn't have a rifle with me, and anyway, this creature would inject its deadly poison before I could raise a gun, take accurate aim and shoot to kill. There wasn't a strong stick within reach. If there had been, stretching for it was movement that would invite attack.

Dad often slid a stick under a snake's belly, lifted it up, and tossed it away from him so that it slithered off in another direction. Not brown snakes, they were deadly. He'd do that with a tree snake. He'd whack a brown snake with a stick and break its back. I wasn't sure I could hit hard enough and in the right spot to kill a snake. If it survived an attack with a stick, it would certainly be angry and strike.

I guess it was only minutes that I stood there paralysed with fear, but it felt like an eternity. Eventually, the snake quietly slithered off to the side of the road and disappeared in a clump of long, grey grass. I stood still for a few moments longer, scared that movement would alarm the creature and cause it to return and attack. Finally, I plucked up courage to move slightly. I picked up my bag, stopped, looked around me, and listened for any hissing sound or rustling in the grasses. When I heard nothing, I took a few more tentative steps.

My progress for the next few hundred yards was painfully slow. I kept stopping to look carefully around me and listen for any hint of the reptile's presence. When I finally relaxed a little and convinced myself the snake had found another interest, I hastened to the inviting shade of a gum tree near the side of the road and sat down to rest. The strain of standing perfectly still and the terror of the moment had left me exhausted.

Sitting there, under scant shade, a savage sun beating down on me and powdery dust irritating my nostrils and making my mouth dry, I was aware of the fierce, stabbing pains of hunger. I could smell the fresh–baked bread — a warm, soft, comforting aroma. My mouth watered and my nostrils twitched.

A little pick at the crust surely won't hurt?

I reached into the bag, extracted the wrapped loaf and carefully pulled away the tissue. The loaf broke neatly at the crease in the middle and the deliciously soft crumbs tickled my fingers. I set one half carefully aside and began to pick at the half in my hands. There was a loud crunch as I bit into the delicious crusty shell, and then my tongue found the silky–soft white middle.

When I finally rose to continue my walk, snakes no longer occupied my thoughts. My mouth was dry, my palms were wet and my bag was a little lighter. A light breeze had wrapped the tissue paper around the tree trunk, pressing it hard against the bark. One half of the loaf was little more than a crusty shell.

I tried desperately to conceive a plan to persuade old Mr Comino to exchange the small amount of change for a half loaf of bread, which cost nearly twice as much as I had in my pocket. I knew he wouldn't. I toyed with the idea of going back to look for cordial bottles, but it might take several days to find enough to pay for a half loaf. I walked the rest of the way home very slowly, with a heavy heart.

"What happened to the bread?" Mum asked when I handed her the bag and change. I stood in our kitchen staring hard at my feet and didn't answer.

"Answer your mother," Dad said. He spoke softly, but I could feel his glare.

"I ate it," I whispered. "I was really hungry and I just started picking little bits off the crust, and before I knew it there was a huge hole in the middle.

"But I can go back and buy some more," I added, hopefully.

"If we had enough money to buy more," Mum said. "But we don't."

The thought occurred to me that we would if she hadn't insisted I buy cigarettes, but I didn't dare say it. I learnt early in life to always be polite and respectful to my parents, and never answer back. Anyway, Dad was already unbuckling his belt, so I settled for pleading "But I was really, really hungry".

It didn't help, and nor did relating my encounter with the snake, which I'm sure neither parent quite believed. I copped a flogging and a stern lecture about stealing being wrong no matter what the circumstances. I'm sure Dad pinched a thing or two when the chips were down, but he was big on the importance of honesty. He had no tolerance for thieves or liars.

#

There was a little shed at the back of the shack where Dad stored his tools and stacked wood to keep it dry for use in wet weather. He often took me down there and let me watch him clean his rifle and sharpen knives. He showed me how to split chips, start a fire and make a frame to hang a billy. He taught me how to make billy tea. He taught me to shoot a rifle, too, and he let me practise shooting tins off the old chopping block. One day, he brought a pocketknife home for me and taught me how to whittle. We made little wooden dolls for Jenny. Mine were queer–looking things, all bloodstained from nicking my fingers, but I loved copying anything Dad did.

I wasn't allowed in the shed when Dad was away, except to fetch wood for the stove. Every day, when he packed his tools away, he'd warn me never to touch anything when he wasn't around. But the first time he went droving again after his back healed, temptation exceeded fear of punishment. I was fascinated by the way he flicked his file like a knife after sharpening the axe. It would strike a mark in the timber beam above the shed door. The day after he went away, I climbed up on a wooden block to reach that file. I stepped back, took careful aim and threw with all my might. It missed of course. Flew right through the open doorway and glided neatly into the middle of a stinging nettle bush. I tried all day to figure a way to retrieve it, but to no avail.

In the afternoon, I filled the wood box by the stove, and then I took the bucket to fetch water from the dam and filled the tub outside the door ready for the evening wash–up. I helped Mum fetch the washing off the line. When Mum started the ironing, I fetched water in a jug for her to sprinkle on the pillowcases to damp them down. Then I helped her fold the underwear and shake the red dust from the towels. When she started peeling vegetables for dinner, I climbed on to the stool by the stove to watch her.

"When will Dad be back?" I asked her.

"Not sure. Four days. A week maybe."

I breathed a little sigh of relief. Time to find a way to fetch the file, maybe? I felt her watching me closely and I squirmed a little.

"What did you do, Paul?"

I studied my feet in silence for a minute. How come she always knew?

19

"Come on, son. Out with it. I should have known there was a reason you were being so helpful today. What have you been up to?"

I gave her a pleading look, hoping desperately that being helpful would earn her favour.

"I threw Dad's file and it landed in the prickle bush." I said. "Can you help me get it out, Mum? Please!"

She regarded me thoughtfully for a minute, then shook her head.

"Sorry, son. He's warned you often enough not to touch his things."

I slid off the stool and went outside to stare in desperation at that bush. I tried prodding at it with a stick, fishing for the file, but the nettles stung my hands and arms.

Mum made rabbit stew for dinner that night, and it tasted wonderful. After I helped her wash up, I sat on the stool watching the shadows from the kerosene lamp dancing on the hessian window coverings and thinking up stories to explain the file's disappearance. I pictured my father glaring at me as he unbuckled his belt. The only thing I was afraid of back then was the faint hissing sound that belt made as he slid it free of its keepers. It was a sound that made me cringe even when I knew I wasn't about to cop a flogging.

I often spent long, hot afternoons lying on my belly in patchy grass under a gum tree near the gate, listening to birdcalls and drawing pictures in the dirt with a stick. Dad's dog, Rusty, would lie there with me, his head resting on my back, panting hot breath over me. Rusty always went with Dad when he went droving. When Dad came back, he'd come bounding in ahead of him to find me lying there. He'd lick me all over and lie with me to wait for Dad to reach the gate. Then Dad would swing me up into the saddle in front of him to ride back to the shack.

I was lying there the day Dad came back from that trip, but for once I wasn't pleased to see Rusty. He sensed it and whined, but Dad didn't seem to notice. He pulled me up in front of him with a soft chuckle.

"And what have you been up to eh, Towser? I hope you were good for your mother while I was gone. I missed my little mate. One of these days, when you're a little older, I'll take you with me."

I knew I should confess what I'd done, and I was only postponing the inevitable by staying silent, but I was in no hurry to spoil the pleasant mood. He would find out soon enough. When we dismounted, I watched him remove the saddle and I helped him wash his horse down and give it feed and water. Then I followed him into the house and sat beside him while he drank his tea, and he told me stories. He told great yarns — exciting tales, but not always factual, I suspect — about the early explorers and how the country was discovered and settled. I'd often go down to the riverbank and pretend to be one of those explorers, coming back, exhausted, from a long trek — no food or water left, the only survivor from my party.

I sat there listening to him that afternoon, watching Mum roll pastry for a pigeon pie, trying to act as if nothing was wrong. I kept up the act after dinner when he sat outside under the eucalyptus trees and strummed an old guitar. He did that often, and I loved to listen. Sometimes Mum would sing. Dad would talk about his boyhood and his courting days, and months on the trail droving. Never talked about the war though. That subject was taboo. Mum mentioned it to me now and then, but she always told me never to speak of it to Dad. She said he had a real bad time and he often had dreadful nightmares and woke in a cold sweat.

Dad went down to the woodshed that evening, but the axe didn't need sharpening and I guess he didn't bother looking for the file. It was late the next afternoon when he came looking for me, black–faced, and beckoned me to follow him. He led me to the shed door and pointed at the beam.

"Where's my file?"

For a brief moment, I considered lying, but I knew that would only make things worse. Lower lip quivering, I pointed at the bush. He pondered the situation for a moment, looking first at me and then at the bush, and then at me again. Then he grabbed me by the scruff of my neck, lifted me high in the air, and dropped me right into the middle of those nettles. I grabbed that file and scrambled out of there that fast you couldn't blink, but it stung like hell for hours afterward.

The next day he came home with a pocket full of darts and started giving me lessons in the art of throwing. Taught me well, too! I got to be damn good at it. Used to play in the pubs all the time when I was in the army. Used to win a few quid. In different circumstances — free to travel the circuits — I could've played competition and made a motza, I reckon.

#

Despite the discomforts of that shack, I loved living there. I loved the bush. Except on school days, I was feral and free. When Dad was at home, I followed him around the paddocks and watched him working. When he was away, I played on the riverbank by day and lay in the grass after dark, finding pictures in the stars and dreaming of one day taking a swag and going droving with my dad, camping out at night and making billy tea and damper and sleeping in the open.

From the time I started school I hated the unwelcome restriction of my freedom, and I hated that the kids tormented me because we were poor. In my second year, it occurred to me that I needn't go, but I could roam the riverbank instead, seeking shelter from the rain and the authorities by hiding in the bushes under the bridge.

The river became my haven. I spent countless hours roaming the grassy banks — crackling twigs tickling the soles of my feet — pretending to be an explorer or fisherman. I lay in the sun on the soft, warm sand. Dangling willows on the banks dared me to climb and swing on their outspread limbs. On hot days, I stripped naked and dropped from the branches into the murky waters.

Dad found out about me wagging and punished me severely. For a whole week I wasn't allowed out to play or to go with him to the shed, or to sit outside in the evenings listening to his songs and stories. The punishment was enough to persuade me, for a while, to suffer long, boring days in a stuffy classroom, chanting times tables.

I wagged again and went down to the river one day in the spring before my eighth birthday. I was walking to school when one of the town kids came up behind me and hit me on the head with a heavy, wooden pencil case. I darted off to the riverbank to escape his bullying. Once there, I figured I might as well stay. Dad's explorer stories were fresh in my mind, and I felt inclined to retreat to my world of make–believe.

I marched up over the hills and across the endless flat expanse, keeping the setting sun always to my right to hold my course firmly south. The soles of my feet burnt. My pack weighed heavier by the minute. My throat burnt, and my belly rumbled. My supplies had dwindled to almost nothing. A pale moon peeped from behind a cloud to mock me. My heart pounded, and a giddy sensation overtook me. Despite the heat, I shivered.

I pushed on into blackness, summoning the last of my courage, concentrating intently on placing one foot after the other and staying erect. If I could reach the river, I could follow it almost all the way back to the camp. There would be water, and maybe fish. There might be some edible growth near the river.

My sides were grazed from numerous falls against rough–barked tree trunks. Pack straps cut into my shoulders. Weakness overcame me. And then, from a distance, came the glorious, rushing river song. On and on towards it, summoning the last reserves of my strength, until, in the blackness, I caught the reflection of a twinkling star, and then the soft shadows of the willows and the glorious sensation of sinking into sand. I fell face down on the soft bed, lips parted to feel the clear, cool water on my tongue. Gulping, splashing, gurgling, caressing aching limbs with soothing slaps of wetness. Tiny rivulets traced through body hollows, cooling and reviving. I crawled up the bank to drop in a sodden heap on the sand and sleep.

In a moment, bored with this pretence, I leapt to my feet, snatched a bough from the willow and ran to a steeper outcrop of bank to cast a line. The bough whistled as the line whizzed through the air and cut the water. I dragged the bait expertly across the stream, and into a quiet, sheltered bay below. Almost immediately I felt the jerk and gently eased the line in. Again and again the line whistled through still air, and I reeled in my imaginary catch. At last, tired again, I wriggled up the bank to nestle against the wide willow trunk and rest.

A sharp, demanding voice cut the stillness. "What are you doing here, boy? Come here at once!"

My heart sank. I sprang to my feet and tried to run, but the sand swallowed my feet. My chaser was barely three yards behind, puffing loudly. I tripped and fell. A firm hand gripped my upper arm, dragged me up the bank and propelled me into the back of a black sedan.

The man took me home, and I saw the look of contempt as we approached the shack. My stomach churned, and my head throbbed as I watched my captor stride towards the woodshed. I trembled, fearing my father's wrath and that dreaded strap.

They talked a while in hushed tones. I stared at my feet, waiting silently for that savage grip on my upper arm, the angry roar, the whistle of leather as a deft hand raised the belt, the flicking sound as it turned in the air and began its descent, and the fierce, burning sting as it cut across my upper legs.

There was no beating. The colour drained from my mother's face and her hands began to shake. She covered her face with her apron, pretending to wipe perspiration from her brow, but I knew it hid tears. My father raged sure enough, but not at me. He raged at the man. He screamed and swore, and the man trembled, face ruddy and eyes bulging.

In the end, it was clear the man won. My father slumped forward, leaning heavily on his axe, gasping. Mum ran into the house sobbing. My triumphant captor grunted, stuck out his chin, bid them good day, and departed in a cloud of dust.

#

Mum laid out my best clothes, scrubbed my face, slicked my hair, and twisted Jenny's locks into neat plaits, tied with frayed ribbons. Dad polished our worn shoes, sweating profusely as he spat, brushed and rubbed until he could see his reflection. Mum kissed us and hugged us tightly, and her tears wet my hair.

The black car came again. The fat man sat behind the wheel, silently staring straight ahead. He waited with pursed lips, white knuckles gripping the steering wheel as if, released, it threatened to take flight. Mum collapsed on the old stump Dad used to split the firewood as Dad lifted Jenny in his arms and seated her carefully in the back of the sedan. He shoved me gently, pointing to the far rear door, and he climbed into the front passenger seat.

The black sedan cruised slowly down the track, through the open front gate and on to the main road, where it picked up speed a little as it approached the town. The only sounds were the soft hum of the engine and the crackle of gravel beneath spinning wheels. Dad fixed his gaze firmly on the road ahead, fists clenched, jaw thrust forward and lips tightly set. I studied my shoes. They had never shone so before.

The car stopped in front of the local courthouse. A man with long, white, curly hair and black robes listened while two suited men took turns speaking and the fat man told on me for wagging school and playing on the riverbank. He said stuff about Mum and Dad — mean stuff. He said they didn't care for their kids properly. He said they lived in filth. I tried to tell the long–haired man that wasn't true. Mum worked hard to keep the little shack clean. They told me to be quiet. Then the long–haired man spoke and hit a little wooden hammer on the table in front of him. A man collected a piece of paper from the table in front of the long–haired fellow and handed it to Dad. The suited men and the fat man looked pleased with themselves. Dad ripped up the paper and stormed out, swearing. [i]

A woman led us outside. We stood watching the shoppers going about their daily business. Some of the faces were familiar, but apart from the odd curious stare from the window of a car gliding by, there was no sign of interest in our plight.

I heard the monotonous chant from the schoolroom across the street, and, for once, I longed to be there listening to the teacher's tiresome drone. I would have welcomed her sharp rebukes, and even the master's cane, if only I could erase the events of the past week and go home.

Raucous laughter drifted from the tile–fronted pub on the corner. Men lounged carelessly in the doorway. A tall, grey–haired man leant against the lamppost on the edge of the footpath, hands thrust deep in his pockets. A spent cigarette dangled from one corner of his mouth. I recognised him as a friend of my father. He shot a brief, unconcerned glance at me, shrugged his shoulders, and strode off in the opposite direction.

The early spring sun shone bright and warm that day, yet I shivered, standing there in the monstrous shadow of that old stone building. Behind me, two grey–suited men passed casual remarks on the events of the morning in a tone of official satisfaction. I felt sick. An image of my dad appeared before me, stiff and tense, fists clenched, face twisted with rage. His scream echoed through my head, again and again, weakening each time I heard it. I reached out, but my arms were too short. I tried to call, but the words stuck in my throat. A broken, tormented man faded from view, engulfed in a mist of fear.

The woman crouched and looked sympathetically at Jenny and me.

"You're going away on a little holiday," she said. "Soon you can come back and see your mum and dad again, and then your family won't live in a shack anymore."

I frowned at her and shook my head.

"It won't be long. I promise. And then you will have better clothes and shoes to wear to school so the kids won't tease you. And you'll have books and pencils and a ruler, like the other kids, so you won't get in trouble any more for not having the right stuff."

None of that mattered a jot to me now. All I wanted was to go home.

The woman led us across to the black car, opened the door and helped my sister in. I watched her crawl to the far end of the seat, press her frail body hard against the door and begin to bawl. Tears streaked her tiny face. Two watery streams poured from her nostrils. Now and again she lifted a grubby rag doll to wipe her wet face on its belly. She gripped it as though it, too, might at any moment scream profanities and leave us.

The woman motioned to me to follow, but I resisted for a while. I stood there trying desperately to conceive an escape plan. Then the woman pushed me in beside Jenny.

I must not cry.

I sat stiff and erect, eyes clamped tightly shut to hold back tears.

"Don't carry on so, lass," one of the suits said, his voice high and harsh. "You'll be all right. You'll be well cared for where you're going. Better care than you're used to. Far better."

The car door slammed. The fat man climbed into the driver's seat. I reached over and placed a reassuring hand on my sister's shoulder. Her sobs softened.

The engine kicked over. The car eased from the kerb. Down the main street, on to the highway, it picked up speed as the miles fell away and the safe and familiar was left far behind.

Taken: an artist's impression

A towering brick castle

3: A "HOLIDAY" IN HELL

ARMIDALE, OCTOBER, 1956

A heavy, grey blanket hung low over the town. Along the edge of the highway a welcoming guard of bare liquid ambers shivered in an icy breeze. The black sedan swung off the main road and headed up a steep, gravel road, past a graveyard. It revved a little as it climbed a steep drive and stopped at the huge oak doors of a towering brick castle that glared menacingly over the town below.

Geoffrey Simms heaved a deep sigh as he pulled the handbrake and reached for the doorhandle.

"It's only for a little while," he muttered, ushering us out. "Some nice people will care for you here for a while, and soon you'll be able to go back home again."

He led us up three broad, concrete steps to the heavy double door, raised a brass ring, and thumped it hard against its metal base plate. Once, twice, three times. Heavy footsteps. One door swung open to reveal two tall, black, human towers. I struggled to adjust to the darkness as my eyes journeyed from the flared base of the towers, up the vast expanse of blackness, to the white bibs, double chins, tight lips, ruddy cheeks and piercing eyes. A few thin wisps of hair escaped the stiff white bands fixed low across the foreheads, and from the top of the bands, black veils covered their heads.

"Sister Catherine, Sister Anne," Simms bleated. "Paul and Jennifer Wilson. You were advised?"

"Yes, yes. Thank you, Mr Simms. We are prepared for them."

"Paul, Jennifer, say good afternoon to Sister Catherine." He indicated the shorter tower. "And Sister Anne. These good ladies care for the children here at St Patrick's, along with Mother Emmanuel, the Mother Superior, who is in charge here, and Sister Agnes. You will be very happy here for a short while, until you can go home again, soon. Well then, say good afternoon, please!"

"Afternoon," we mumbled in unison, staring at the floor.

"Penguins," I muttered irreverently, half under my breath. "They look like penguins." Simms cuffed my ear.

"Good afternoon, children," said Sister Anne. "Do come in out of the cold."

A musty odour irritated my nostrils, making me want to sneeze. I surveyed the room carefully. High timber–framed windows, all closed, with thick, worn curtains tied back at the sides. High ceiling. A huge wooden desk angled across the left rear corner with two padded chairs facing it and a straight–backed kitchen chair behind. Several padded chairs and some pine dining chairs were arranged around a crackling open fire under a grey–painted timber mantel. Freshly cut logs were stacked on one side. A huge gruesome statue of a man nailed to a cross was fixed to the wall above the mantel. He stared down at me, pained face pleading for release.

Simms eased his weight into the deeper of the padded chairs. The shorter nun seated herself in another, facing him. The other beckoned to us, pointed to the dining chairs near the fire, then left through a rear door at the side of the desk. She emerged moments later with a lace–covered tray of clattering china teacups and large silver pot. A third nun followed her into the room and sat in the straight–backed chair behind the desk.

"Pleasant trip, Mr Simms?" the nun behind the desk asked. The voice was hard and demanding, but he didn't seem offended.

"Not at all, Mother."

My eyebrows lifted and my eyes popped.

Mother? This jowly hag with her dagger eyes and disappearing lips? My mum was gentle and soft–spoken, and real pretty, with chestnut curls and smiling hazel eyes.

"They seldom are, mind you," he continued. "But this one was worse than most. Girl sobbing constantly and that boy with his sullen, belligerent stare. He's going to be a handful, that one. Like his father. A nasty piece of work that man. Those kids are fortunate to be free of his bad influence. My, this cup of tea is welcome."

I glared at him. The sour taste of bile rose in my throat.

"So what's their story? What do we need to know?"

"Not much to tell, really. Boy a month off turning eight. Girl, five. Living in a rundown shack in the bush. Wagging school. Toddler and baby taking up all the mother's time. Not enough food for the family. Father a no–hoper drunk. No Aboriginal blood, at least not that we can tell."

"Father doesn't work?"

"Oh yeah, off and on. Farmhand, droving, shearing, that sort of stuff. Whatever he can pick up, I guess. Seems he's had some bad health. War veteran. Prisoner of war for three years in Changi. Copped a nasty leg wound that gives him a fair bit of strife. And then a horse threw him and he did his back in. But he's back working now. Just can't seem to get on top enough to fund his drinking and smoking and look after kids as well."

"Is he receiving a veterans' pension?"

"Don't know. Didn't ask. I'd presume not. Probably wouldn't know how to apply for one, if he knows such things exist."

"Pity. It might help them."

"The only help for that family is to rescue those little urchins from the bad influence and put them in a decent home. They are better off here, trust me. They'll get some schooling and be taught some discipline, instead of roaming all over the countryside making nuisances of themselves."

Why didn't he rescue our brothers, Ian and Robbie? There was nothing Jen or I wanted to be rescued from.

"The children will be looked after here," the nun said. "We'll teach them to fear God and obey rules. Send them to school."

"You do a great job here, Mother. You and the Sisters. These kids are fortunate that places like this exist. Otherwise, who knows where they'd end up?"

"Thank you, Mr Simms."

"How many do you have now?"

"Nearly 60 at the moment. Too many for four of us to manage, really, but we try. It's a thankless task. There's only so much you can do for children like these. You know… the sins of the fathers. They come from bad stock. Not much you can do about the blood that runs in their veins.

"Of course the boy will eventually go off to St Vincent's, in Sydney," the Mother continued. "The Brothers there are very strict. Even the most rebellious fall into line after a few months of the Brothers' discipline. But really, this one looks quite fragile."

"Looks can be deceiving, Mother. He needs a very firm hand."

"He'll find it here."

"Of course. As I said, Mother, you and the Sisters do a magnificent job."

"Shall we finalise the paperwork, then?"

He rose, walked to her desk, handed her a folder, and took one of the comfortable seats facing her. She opened the folder and read from it. Sitting stiffly on that hard upright chair, at the side of the fireplace, opposite my white–faced little sister, I tried to judge her expression as she scanned the page. My eyes were drawn, instead, to the worn leather strap resting across one side of the desk. It wasn't difficult to imagine what that was used for, but I prayed she didn't use it on little girls. I'd copped a few good hidings, and once, when I was jack–rabbiting across a paddock, hoping to escape a belting for disobeying, Dad flicked the tip of a stockwhip across my backside. It stung like hell. But Dad would never hit Jen with a whip or a strap. I glanced at my baby sister. I'd promised Dad I'd take care of her. I would not let this old crow beat her with that thing.

29

Jen and I tensed as Simms and those black and white apparitions discussed us in clearly audible whispers. I don't think I was actually meant to hear, but the events of the past week seemed to have sharpened my senses. Simms and the Mother periodically cast furtive glances in our direction as they perused paperwork, fixed rubber stamps to pages, and carefully applied signatures with steel–nibbed pens dipped in a deep inkwell.

The tray had been deposited on the end of a large sideboard, and two cups were filled and placed on delicate china saucers on the oak desk. A platter of biscuits passed between Simms and the nuns, bypassing us. They offered us nothing.

Finally, our captor took his leave. Tipping his hat, he strode back into the daylight. His exit allowed a weak stream of light to penetrate the room for just an instant, before it was plunged back into dreary half–darkness. A nun rose, smiled at me, and lifted Jenny gently from her chair. Taking her hand, she motioned me to stay and led Jenny across the room, through a creaking rear door, and down a concrete–floored hallway. Sister Catherine beckoned to me to follow and we trailed along behind them. Near the end of the hall, two creaky timber staircases climbed at right angles to the hall in directly opposite directions. Jen was led up one. I climbed the other.

At the top of the stairs, a long, open passageway passed several distantly spaced doors, each leading to huge dormitories. Unpainted dark, brick walls were lined with neatly made steel–framed beds and tiny bedside lockers. Small windows admitted little light and no fresh air.

I was struck by the austerity and absolute conformity of the place. The beds were placed equally tiny distances apart, separated by identically sized bedside lockers, creating a small sterile square of territory for each occupant. Every bed was perfectly made. Covers were pulled tight. Corners were tucked in perfect triangular folds. Floors were scrubbed. Furniture was brightly polished. There was not a toy, book or personal item of any kind in sight. There was a pervasive disinfectant odour: The smell of fear.

The leather–faced Sister led me to the end of the passageway and opened a wide, tall cupboard. Inside, a collection of roughly folded underpants, discoloured singlets, shorts, shirts, jumpers, socks and shoes jostled for space. She tugged at the corners of some garments and they tumbled out. She rifled through piles to assemble a collection of items that seemed to satisfy her and she thrust them at me, screwing up the remaining items and shoving them carelessly back.

"Off with those dirty rags. You'll wear clean clothing here. You'll wash now and change." She motioned me to follow her back down the stairs. Under the stairwell, a thin trail of water oozed from under a door. She opened the door and pointed inside.

"Toilets, washroom. I'll wait here. Put your soiled clothing in the bin there." Then she turned her back and stood, guard–like, across the doorway, arms folded firmly across her chest.

I relieved myself at a long steel trough, then washed my hands and face in icy water at a metal basin, drying them on a rough towel hanging above.

None of the garments were new. They were darned, worn and shabby. The shorts were too large and patched at the back. Jumper sleeves stopped inches above my wrists. The shoes were just a little too tight, but I supposed they might wear in. The singlet and underpants were scratchy. The shirt collar was badly frayed and the threads irritated my neck.

The clothes I had worn here were better, and Mum had made sure they were clean. She scrubbed them with red hands in an old tank cut in half and laid on its side on four big stumps of wood that Dad had levelled with the axe. She would light a fire under it after filling it with an old galvanised iron bucket, fetching water from the dam 20 yards away. When the water heated, she would dump the clothing into bubbling water, leave it simmer a while, then let the fire go out and lean over the steaming tub to scrub each garment, in turn, until the frayed–collar shirts were snowy white. Sometimes, I would help her peg them out on the wire line Dad had strung between two trees. They would hang there, flapping in the breeze, until nearly dry. Mum always liked to take them off when they weren't quite dry. Then she would take them inside and lay them on a worn blanket on the kitchen table and iron them with two big black irons that she heated on the stove, alternating between them so that one was heating while the other was in use.

If there was a dry wind, sometimes she would shake and brush the shirts as she removed them from the line, and she would curse the red dust that seemed to coat everything. But my clothes were always clean and neatly pressed when I put them on in the morning, and although Dad returned from droving trips covered in red dirt and stinking with sweat, he always left wearing a clean shirt and trousers and with a clean pack.

When I was done dressing, I stood for a moment staring hesitantly at the massive black back with its stiff veil ending just above the waist. Fear wrapped itself about me, anchoring my feet and binding my tongue. Finally, she turned to appraise me, nose upturned and lip curled. "Red hair," she sniffed. "And no doubt the ugly temperament that goes with it. Well, you'll lose the attitude quickly. I shall see to that."

She asked had I ever made a bed. I shook my head.

"We'll find an older boy to teach you," she barked, and seemed to hesitate a moment to think. "Colin," she said decisively. "Colin will show you around and teach you how things work here. You can meet him later."

She led me back up the stairs to the dark dormitory and across to one of the beds on the far side. She ordered me to open the drawer of the bedside table where I found two handkerchiefs, a toothbrush and a small black comb.

"We bathe before breakfast. Wash every night. Clean handkerchief in your pocket each day. Teeth cleaned and hair combed morning and night. And make sure your toothbrush and comb are returned to that drawer immediately after use."

Then she led me back down the stairs and out to a barren, chain–wire fenced paddock.

Boys ambled about, hands in pockets, expressions sullen, sending up clouds of dust as they kicked the dirt. Here and there, a few kicked a ball back and forth. There was not a single item of playground equipment. Apart from one or two balls, the yard was devoid of toys. Beyond the side fence, another identical playground was inhabited by girls, carefully segregated from the opposite sex. A couple of the girls hugged shabby rag dolls. On one side of each playground a nun stood guard, watching every move with a stern expression.

There was no point in making friends. I would be leaving soon. I stood quietly in the corner of the playground and watched the others curiously. Shortly, Jen emerged from under the stairs. The gate to the girls' playground creaked open, and she was nudged through with a gentle push from behind. The gate closed behind her. I made my way quickly to the dividing fence and beckoned to Jen. The girls' guard approached and explained firmly that boys and girls must stay in their own playgrounds and were not allowed to mix.

"But I want to talk to my sister."

"Girls and boys do not talk over the fence," the voice commanded. "It is not allowed. Off you go now."

I shrugged and returned to the corner of the field. My baby sister huddled against a chain–wire gate, clutching that dreadful rag doll, sobbing violently.

A gate squealed and clanged and a Sister charged towards the tank stand.

"Phillip Robertson," she bellowed, as she reached for some object and turned to stomp across the playground. Startled, I turned to stare in the direction she was heading. A boy — about my size — stood, white–faced and trembling, watching her approach. He was clad in an oversized white shirt with half its frayed tail dangling over short, tight serge shorts. One sock hugged his ankle in thick rolls of grey wool. The other struggled to hang on halfway to his knee, sagging in generous wrinkles. His skin was dark, and straight black hair was kept short with a blunt cut, as though a mixing bowl had been upended on his head and its rim used as a cutting guide.

Reaching him, she grabbed his upper arm, spun him around to face away from her, and proceeded to pound his buttocks until, with the fourth slap, he began to blubber and moan. With a satisfied 'Hhrmmph" and a click of her tongue, she returned to the tank stand and replaced the mystery object with meticulous precision.

Save for the odd disinterested glance, there was no reaction to her outburst from any of the boys. I was tempted to go to her victim and try to offer comfort, but instinct cautioned me to follow the example of the others and ignore him. I had no idea what sin the poor boy had committed — if any — and I trembled a little considering the possibility that my inadequate knowledge of rules and expectations might result in me suffering the same fate.

I had assumed, seeing the strap across the Mother's desk earlier, that the Mother would deal with misbehaviour as Dad had done — with a stern lecture and two or three stinging swipes across the backside. I was shocked at the cold brutality of the Sister's attack and alarmed that it seemed to elicit no reaction from the other children.

A whistle sounded as the sun began its descent and the Sister beckoned me to join a line forming at the playground gate. As I stood waiting for her instruction, I glanced sideways at the huge, old, wood–plank platform that sagged under the weight of a slightly rusted water tank. On the corner of the stand a large scrubbing brush rested, its wooden handle worn and whitened.

"Ain't never used fer scrubbin'," the boy behind me whispered, obviously noting my curious stare. "Pity it don't give her splinters."

Although tempted to ask if it was used often to beat children, I was afraid to speak. My unspoken query was answered, though, when I looked down at the legs of the boys ahead of me in the line. Angry welts blazed crimson and bruises ranged from deep purple–black to faded green–grey.

Bleached by summer sun and coated with frost on cold winter nights, the giant scrubbing brush rested for years on the corner of the tank stand. It was moved only when an angry penguin flew into a rage, or coldly and calculatingly targeted a child to vent her frustration, or maybe just to amuse herself. The only time Sister Catherine's obvious boredom was relieved, it seemed, was when she held that monstrous device. The brush was worked frequently, and with astounding energy, to beat the devil out of every evil urchin who had the misfortune to enter that ugly abode.

At the sound of a second whistle, I trooped behind the other kids into a huge dining hall furnished with long trestle–style tables and hard bench seats. Girls stood in rows behind the benches on one side and my line marched to stand behind benches on the other. A sour–faced sister stood in one corner and some older girls stood beside the cook at a servery at the far end of the hall.

Table by table, kids moved silently to the servery to swallow a dose of vile Epsom salts, then wait while their plates were filled, returning in military formation to their place. When all of us had filled plates before us on the table, the nuns ordered eyes closed, hands joined under the chin and heads bowed, while an older child recited the 'Grace'. Finally, the order was given to sit and eat.

I was surprised to find I had no appetite, and there was nothing to tempt a reluctant palate. Besides, by now the food was stone cold.

"Eat everythin'. Say nuthin'," came the hissed advice from the boy beside me, "less o' course ya want a sore arse!"

After the meal, we marched with military precision to the end of the hall to stack plates for the older girls to wash. The march continued to the playroom, where a small collection of tattered books and toys — mostly broken — were provided to amuse us until bedtime.

I stood in sullen silence in the corner of the playroom, studying my feet. Colin approached.

"Can't find anything to play with?"

"Don't want to play," I replied without looking up.

"You'll get used to the place soon enough."

"Won't be 'ere long enough," I mumbled. "Goin' 'ome soon."

"Yeah. Right. Aren't we all?"

I wondered what he meant, but I didn't ask.

Yet another whistle was followed by a summons to the youngest children to line up at the door, and a nun led them off to bed. Another group followed some time later. Then my age group was called to assemble at the door and march up the stairs to the dormitory to fetch toothbrushes and combs, troop back down to the bathrooms to wash, clean teeth, don scratchy striped pyjamas, and march, once more, up the stairs to bed.

Sleep wouldn't come on my first night there so I heard the shuffle, sometime later, as yet another age group performed the bedtime march. Eyes squeezed shut, I tried to think happy thoughts, but I kept seeing the long-haired man with the hammer and hearing those awful men. My sister was calling my name, begging me to come and take her home.

I spent the following days engulfed in a lonely mist of fear and desolation and the nights drifting from sleepless torment to horrific nightmares. My cheeks burnt with poisonous rage. My hands trembled. The nuns left me to work through my terror and misery alone. For three days and nights I cried inside, but never allowed a tear to fall.

I woke in the mornings trembling from nightmares about suited men in a courtroom and angry penguins. I sulked over the meals they placed before me: Lukewarm, tasteless, unattractive dishes served with the inevitable slice of stale bread. In the playground I stood afraid and aloof, kicking the dirt at my feet in angry resentment, and at night I tossed, turned and cursed under my breath until my tortured body collapsed into sleep.

On the fourth day I steeled myself to accept my fate and began to scheme to make life there bearable.

"Treat everything in life as an adventure, son," my dad had said. "Whatever challenge you face, plan to beat it and enjoy the journey. No matter what life throws at you, there is always something good in it: A lesson, an experience, a victory, a chance to be kind to someone, a reason to get up tomorrow and try again."

There were fruit trees out back, along with chooks and milking cows. A resident handyman did carpentry work and tended the gardens and animals. Sister Anne, the plump, comely faced cook, seemed quite nice. If I made friends with the right people and showed interest in the right activities, just maybe there were ways to make being here not quite so dreadful.

On the fifth day, I felt Sister Catherine's wrath. As I leant against the fence, kicking the dirt pensively, a group of boys approached and began to torment me. I ignored them for a time, but when their persistence began to irritate, I lashed out. My kicking foot connected lightly with a shin, causing several boys to scurry away while my maliciously dramatic victim shouted a curse, contorted his face, and dropped to a crouched position to nurse his wound.

Sister saw. She saw everything. She stood at her post, day after day — grudgingly, sour–faced, watching every move, waiting for any excuse to pounce. Like a monstrous magpie in nesting season, she flew across the yard to my corner, black robes flapping about her like massive wings, working vigorously to propel her forwards and keep her feet in the air. Gripping the bristled side of the scrubbing brush, she landed whooshing and swishing in a giant cloud of dust that stung my eyes and filled my nostrils and coated my tongue.

The Sister grabbed my upper arm in a vice–like grip, spun me around and pushed me face–first against the wire fence. Taking careless aim, she whacked my buttocks and legs. Again and again. My lips and eyes ached from being forced tightly shut to prevent the smallest sound or tear escaping. Every fibre of my being throbbed and burnt.

When the witch was done, I pressed against the wire of the fence, shrivelled into a small ball, rocking gently from side to side. The Sister might have noticed I moved neither arm nor hand to wipe away snot or tears. Later, in the line–up, she saw no sign of redness in my eyes and no tell–tale tracks on my cheeks to suggest tears had flowed.

Colin had warned me, on my first day there, never to cry. Any sign of emotion invited much more savage beatings. So I had made my resolve on

35

my first night there, lying, terrified, in a dank, cold dormitory, listening to the breathing of a dozen sleeping boys and the creaking of cot springs as some tossed and turned. As I stared at the peeling paint on the high ceiling, wondering if sleep would ever come and silently begging my mother to come for me soon, I made a firm promise to myself. No matter how brutally they beat me or how cruelly they tormented me, I would never, ever cry. Whatever they might do to me, they would not break my spirit.

4: GAMES AND MAKE–BELIEVE

NOVEMBER, 1956

Ben Carmichael stared at me with contempt.

"That new kid must be a bit of a dope, I reckon," he muttered to Jimmy Phillips. "Always standin' in the corner kickin' the dust. Never joinin' in games and stuff."

"He's angry 'cause they won't let him near his sister, is all," Jim replied. "I heard him talkin' to Sister. Said he had to look after 'er, but they won't even let him talk to 'er."

"Well, 'e may as well get used to that, cause it ain't gunna change, is it? If 'e wants 'er so bad, 'e shoulda bin a girl. Acts sissy anyway. What we gunna do 'terday, Jim?"

"I dunno... Maybe we could go an' make friends with 'im?"

"What, with a dumb dust–kicker?"

"Well, maybe 'e's lonely."

"Well, all he has t' do is git out of that corner 'an act sensibul."

Jimmy regarded me cautiously for a moment, realising I had heard. Finally, he approached me, smiling.

"Ben wasn't so tough when he first come here neither."

"Didn't stand about kicking dirt for days," said Ben, following him.

"Didn't ya?" Jimmy's tone was one of admiration. "I think I bawled for days."

Ben dropped to the ground and sat doodling with his finger in the dirt. I surveyed the playground. I was standing in a single small patch of shade provided by a large gum tree in what would have been the right–hand corner of the enclosure, if the fence line hadn't been altered to cut off the corner, placing the tree just out of bounds — a safety precaution to ensure against tree climbing. In the centre of the ground was a concrete pitch used on rare occasions for cricket practice. A few assorted balls had been placed just inside the gate. Off to the left, an identical enclosure provided play space for the girls. They were privileged to have, in addition to some balls, a limited supply of skipping ropes. I learnt later that ropes had been available to the boys too, but it was quickly realised that boys were not inclined to use them for their proper purpose. A few groups of boys played chase or ball games.

"I remember Sister shouting at me," Jimmy continued, unaware that Ben was deep in his own recollections. "'They're dead, Jim. They can't ever come back again because they're dead and gone and no one will ever see them again.' Must've got sick of me bawling. She was real angry. But I never even knew what 'dead' meant then. Weren't 'til last year when 'ol Harry the handyman kicked the bucket I found out was death was all about."

"Are your parents dead?" He addressed the question to me, but added without waiting for an answer, "Reckon I'm near the only one here that hasn't got anyone."

"How come ya never wanna play?" the swarthy–complexioned Ben said suddenly.

"Don' feel like it," I replied. "Anyhow, won't be 'ere long."

"How long?"

"A little while. That's all. Then I'm goin' home again. Could be tomorra' even."

"Fat chance. What's your name anyhow?"

"Paul. What's yours?"

"Benny Carmichael. An' this 'ere is Jimmy Phillips. He's my best friend. We always play together."

I shrugged and kicked the dirt again, disinterested. My companions looked an unlikely pair: tall, gangly Ben with his spiky, black crew cut; and little Jimmy with his basin–cut, sandy hair and prominent cowlick in the centre of his crown, questioning eyes, and fair skin flushed from too long in the sun.

"How old are ya?" Ben asked.

"Eight."

"Me too."

"Wanna play with us?"

"Depends."

"On what?"

"What ya playin'."

"I always decide what we'll play. I'm the oldest." Ben smacked his chest.

"Not older than me," I challenged."

"Bet I am."

"Bet ya not."

"OK, when's your birthday?"

"Ain't sayin'."

"Cause I'm older an' ya know it. You're stupid. You don't even play. Just stand there all by yourself all day."

I rushed forward then, knocking Ben over. In seconds, the squawking magpie was descending, brush in hand, and Jimmy was running like a scared rabbit with Ben pulling himself up to follow.

They left me alone for a while, but a little later they approached again.

"You all right, mate?" Jim mumbled. I suspected he knew exactly how I was.

"Why wouldn't I be? You think that witch could hurt me?"

"'Course not!" said Jimmy, trying to sound confident. "Always layin' into someone with that thing. We didn't mean t' get y' int' trouble. Honest. We just wanted to make friends. Ben shouldna' called y' stupid.

"Anyways," he continued thoughtfully after a brief pause. "Might be older. Might be younger. Doesn't matter either way, does it, Ben?" He shifted his gaze to stare at his mate.

"No reason why a newcomer shouldn't be allowed to pick a game for once, is there?" he challenged.

"OK," Ben mumbled good–naturedly. "Pick a game."

Within minutes, Jimmy, Ben and I were kicking a ball back and forth, with Ben demonstrating the fine art of dribbling. Only to Ben's intense frustration, I mastered the skill instantly.

"Like this?" I asked, tapping the ball with the outside of my foot and then the inside, maintaining complete ownership as I eased it across the paddock with Ben following in an in–and–out weave, kicking at air in repeated failed attempts to take it from me.

"Wow!" said Jimmy. "He learns quick, Ben. He's pretty good at it, eh?"

I was beginning to enjoy the game.

"Done it before," said Ben, in a matter of fact tone that dared me to argue. "Can't learn that quick. Played before, haven't you, Paul? Just pretending not to know how so you can show off!"

I shrugged, grinned, and proceeded to dribble the ball back across the paddock in the other direction, yelling, "Take it from me if you can," and laughing gleefully at the two boys running at the spot where the ball had been a second ago, kicking at fresh air while I deftly executed the next move.

Before long, Ben and Jim had given up and fetched another ball. The three of us practised dribbling back and forth across the paddock, occasionally pulling back to execute a heavy kick, then catapulting across the paddock to retrieve the ball before another boy took possession, and dribbling it back to the starting point.

#

Sister Anne exited the girls' playground, brushing the dust from her habit, to intercept the departing Mother Superior. The Mother had just escorted a six–year–old back to the yard after administering a belting. Earlier that morning, Sister Agnes, who had less affection for the scrubbing brush than Catherine, had marched the girl off to the front office for a spanking with the worn leather strap I'd observed on the corner of the desk the day I arrived. She returned sporting bright red welts on her upper legs, her cheeks streaked with tears and her eyes swollen.

The Mother turned to observe the youngsters at play. Her black–veiled head nodded with satisfaction.

"The two new ones seem to have settled in, Mother," Sister Anne remarked.

"Thank the good Lord," replied the Mother. "It's so much easier to manage the children after newcomers have adjusted."

But I was anything but 'adjusted'. I was imprisoned — a most unnatural condition for a bushman, a champion big–game hunter, expert fisherman and famed explorer. The games the boys played bored me. The discipline and routine were intolerable. The food was tasteless, and never enough to satisfy. They had invaded my childhood world of adventure, uprooted me from the places and people I belonged with — stripped me of my identity, just as wild Aborigines might have captured explorer heroes and held them in bondage in a hostile, foreign land. There was no escape except to my land of dreams.

I was bodily imprisoned, but they could not contain my mind. When the freezing dormitory and barren playground were intolerable, I felt the blistering outback heat, plunged naked into the clear, cool, caressing waters of the river, and waded, stick in hand, through the shallow depths, exploring the watercourse. With wood grubs picked from the rotting timber of fallen willows for bait, I stood knee–deep in the chill, rippling waters and threw lines for yellow–belly or catfish. Quick, skilful hands baited the hooks, threw the lines, then reeled them in, one by one. Perfect timing, perfect skill, perfect control. I sieved the mud on the bank for craybobs, washed and broiled the tiny delicacies, and fried the fish on glowing coals. Then I lay, cooled and refreshed, in the soft lush grass near the water's edge, staring dreamily at dancing flames licking crackling twigs and savouring the rich, sweet after–taste of fresh–fried fish.

I scanned the clear, summer night sky to find pictures in the stars and conversed with the gnarled old willows whose drooped branches shadowed the light from old man moon to create ghostly images. They told me the legends of the river, the stories of those who explored it, fought it, and made their homes by it. And I climbed them and swung on their patient branches. And then I slept, exhausted and happy, on the soft, sandy riverbank.

When the boredom of childish games became intolerable, I recalled my dad's graphic descriptions of hunts and armed myself with a strong stick for a rifle to seek out wild pig. I stalked the bushland quietly, senses alert, the hunter waiting for prey. Oink. Oink. Followed the sound until the swine was in view; drew up the rifle, focused and fired. As the sow fell, the boar charged, thundering towards me. Fired again. Missed. It kept coming. Closer, closer, only a few yards away. I tensed, my sweat–beaded body rigid with fear. A third report from the rifle and the animal lunged earthwards, tusk gouging the dirt at my feet, dust flying and settling as light red mud on the sweaty black hide. The bullet made a neat wound just in the centre of the beast's forehead.

We'll eat well tonight, Pop. This one'll make us a real nice feast.

In the dining room that evening, sumptuous roast pork with crisp sweet crackling took the place of a single miserable sausage.

5: DREAMS OF HOME

MAY, 1957

Days passed. Endless, monotonous days of sameness; marching in lines to a breakfast of tasteless sticky porridge and a single slice of stale buttered bread. Standing for hours in the dusty, barren playground. Eating stale peanut butter sandwiches for lunch. Marching at the sound of a whistle into the long dinner hall, then queuing to march to the bathroom and up the stairs to bed. Every day I rose with a heart filled with hope that today would be the day Dad would come, or the black car would arrive and a government man would knock at the door and ask Sister to fetch me to be taken back home. And every day ended in crushing disappointment.

At night, brief haunting silences were broken often by a nun's screeches and that dreaded swishing sound, and then the piercing screams.

When sleep finally came, my dreams took me back to the comfort of the shack. I smelled the bush. Dead leaves tickled the soles of bare feet, and the river lapped rhythmically against its banks. I felt the exhilaration of swinging on the willow branches, skimming the water with my toes, sending splashes of icy–cold water dancing up to wet my trousers and the dangling hem of my untucked shirt. My 'old man' came striding across the paddock at the end of the day to where Jenny and I played. He thrust one of us up on to each shoulder, then made like a horse galloping home, clicking his tongue as we bounced. I dreamt my dad came to fetch me from the hard bed, lift me on to his back, and jog — tongue clicking — all the long way home to the shack.

While chanting times tables in the classroom, or copying letters on to a slate, I tried to do something Mum said had helped Dad through the awful wartime days in prison. I forced my mind to leave my body. While my physical being marched down bleak corridors or shivered through wet afternoons spent in a dingy brick play hall, my spirit rode the tractor with my dad and followed him over the paddocks on a pony. I felt the excitement of catching fish and shooting rabbit. And in the dining hall at night, while the others swallowed greasy stewing chops with watered–down gravy, I feasted

43

on fresh–fried fish and pigeon pie and rich rabbit stew. When they had lamb roast here, it was cold and tasteless and there was only ever two tiny slices. But I would recall the times Dad brought a sheep home and we dined for a week on mutton chops and roast.

I relived a thousand times the day Dad came home with an airgun. "Jes' look what I found in the paddock today while I was ploughin'. Jes' the thing a boy your age would like, I reckon. A real stroke of luck that was, eh!" And with a huge grin and a soft chuckle, he had passed me a shiny gun.

In the early mornings, the nightmares came again. I fled in panic from the panting fat man, felt the savage grip on my upper arm, saw the ruddy, bulging, sweat–streaked cheeks, popping eyes; the wet beads on the pulsing red forehead, the tight disapproving set of the thin lips and the huge Adam's apple bouncing in the thick, red neck. I was in the black car again, trembling. My little sister was sobbing softly, her crumpled face buried in the belly of her dirty rag doll. The bare liquid ambers shivered in the icy pre–spring winds and the ominous grey sky hung heavily over the drab brick tower with its heavy wooden doors. The doors opened to reveal squawking penguins who sipped tea and ate biscuits with the fat man and discussed my family as though we weren't even there. A voice told me it was only for a short while — a few weeks — then I could go home again.

It was after one of those regular dreams of swinging on willows that I realised, to my horror, I had wet my bed. The urge to pee woke me regularly in the early hours of the morning. It was cold in the building at night, and we had to descend the stairs and cross an open courtyard to the toilets. The stairs creaked and the doors moaned and the wind whistled through the dark, open corridors, so the place had a ghostly air. I was afraid, so I would lie and wait, enduring the agony of an overfull bladder, hoping to hold on until the first light of day. Once, I dared to ask a roommate to go with me, but he laughed and teased me. And then I suggested that perhaps I should wake Sister.

"Yeah!" the lad replied. "If you want a thrashing. You don't wake Sister for nothin' 'less ya dyin'. And then only if ya sure ya can't wait 'til mornin'."

I knew many of the others here did it, and I thought it a disgusting habit. When I woke in soaked sheets for the first time I was overcome. The horror of it; the humiliation; the disgrace. It seemed somehow fitting that I should be forced to join the morning parade of shame, shivering on the veranda in wet pyjamas through the Sister's angry tirade, waiting my turn to be beaten. I nurtured a vague but doubtful hope the punishment would somehow prevent a repetition.

I knew the morning routine well. I had witnessed it daily through the summer months. While Colin helped me tuck sheets and blankets tightly under the mattress and form perfect mitred corners at the end of my bed, the bed–wetters queued for their public scolding, then waited silently for the Mother's arrival or for the Sister to fetch the strap from the office. With the others whose beds were dry, I had watched, filled with pity as, one by one, the pathetic waifs stepped up and took a whack or two, then returned to stand miserably by their beds while an older boy stripped their bed, rolled the smelly sheets and made his way to the laundry.

I crawled from my bed, soggy flannel pants hanging heavily about my legs and the strong stench of urine annoying my nostrils. I pulled back the covers to expose the tell-tale yellow stain on the bottom sheet and stood expectantly at the foot of my bed, awaiting the Sister's order to queue on the veranda. Then I marched dutifully, wet flannel pants slapping at my legs, out on to the slippery frost–coated boards of the veranda to shiver through an interminable wait for the Mother's arrival. The cold burnt my wet legs and backside and turned my bare toes blue. Although I shuddered a little, anticipating the pain of the strap, I looked forward to reaching the top of the line and hearing the command to turn and bend, so I could finally shed my wet clothing. I silently apologised to Colin, who would have to wash my pissy linen, frowning in expectation of the older boy's sympathetic chiding.

Side verandah of St Patrick's Orphanage

"Filthy, disgusting, stinking dogs!" the Mother shouted, wrinkling her nose and turning down the corners of her lips. "Look at them, boys!" she commanded, turning her attention to those remaining in the dormitory. "Look at these dirty uncivilised creatures. Still not toilet trained!"

A few boys sneered and giggled. Most, I knew, silently wished they could stop the brutal ceremony that began each miserable day.

She passed the strap to Sister Catherine. "This disgusting behaviour must be curbed, Sister. These urchins will thank us, one day, for the training they receive here."

As Sister Catherine called the first in line to step forward, the Mother lifted her long black habit and stamped to the end of the veranda, then turned and stood smug–faced and akimbo to watch as Catherine raised the belt and struck her first young victim. I bit my lip hard and steeled myself for the expected pain, vowing for the thousandth time that however hard the blows, I would show no sign of suffering discomfort. I would march away tall, proud and defiant, giving no hint that under my breath I was praying fervently I would never wake in a wet bed again.

On occasions, the punishing Sister would bypass a regular bed–wetter in the morning line–up, but for any child who might actually be able to control his night–time bladder functions, the embarrassment of exposure and the seemingly interminable wait shivering in wet clothes on that freezing veranda was a far more effective incentive than the most vicious beating. I was still waiting to feel the lash, but I had already suffered a penalty far worse than any I could have imagined possible, and I was cold with dread of inviting such punishment again.

6: BIG BROTHER

NOVEMBER, 1957

"Nine years old, Paul. You are a senior now," the Mother said. "Seniors are expected to look after charges, the way Colin took care of you."

The singing of the birthday song followed grace on the morning of November 8th, 1957. The usual breakfast of lukewarm sticky porridge and stale bread followed. There was no cake, no gifts, no concessions, no treats. Save for the singing, it was just another day, except that when the morning meal was done, I was summoned to the Mother's office. After long mornings of painful practice, plenty of harsh words of ridicule, and regular bruising swipes with whatever object the Sister spied to hit with, I could make my own bed now, with perfectly mitred corners and the cover pulled so tight you could bounce a coin on it. I could tie my school tie and polish my shoes to the satisfaction of the penguins. I no longer needed Colin's help or supervision. Now it was my turn to play the big brother role.

"I'm going to assign young Sam Parry and Robbie Barker to your care. Unfortunately, both are bed–wetters. Starting tomorrow, it will be your responsibility to change their beds and wash their sheets, and your own. Hopefully, that will provide an incentive for you to stop your filthy habit.

"Of course you will make sure they wash, clean their teeth and comb their hair, and you must help them get ready for school in the mornings and supervise their wash at night. And make sure they obey the rules. It's a big responsibility, taking care of charges."

"Yes, Mother," I said, noting that there had been no birthday greeting, and that she had assigned me two charges, where most boys had only one to care for. I was certain that assigning me two was the Mother's way of making me pay for the extraordinary privileges I enjoyed. I had won the cook's heart and was allowed to go to the orchard to fetch fresh fruit. I lingered in the trees for ages, sucking sweet lemons and crunching crisp, tart apples. When I returned with a little harvest, cook rewarded me with a warm smile and a sweet biscuit.

The Mother took care to assign bed–wetters as charges to boys who also wet their bed. It had nothing to do with expecting the older boy to show kindness and understanding. Rather, it was a further form of punishment for the older lad—and quite severe too, considering the obligations placed on a nine–year–old.

"The beds must be made and the linen washed and hung on the line before breakfast, Paul," she continued, "and you will be expected to be on time in the dining hall for breakfast. Do I make myself clear?"

"Yes, Mother."

"Sister Catherine will ask one of the older boys to help you tomorrow morning, to show you how the job must be done. You may go now."

Sam Parry was a half–caste Aborigine. Aged five, he had fuzzy black hair and olive skin and a broad nose that constantly oozed thick, yellow snot. His mum died in a fight of some kind when he was three. His dad visited occasionally. Actually, he came often, but he was mostly turned away at the door because he reeked of stale grog and slurred his words. When he was allowed in, he brought Sammy a toy that was promptly confiscated the instant his dad left. Sometimes, he would take him out for the afternoon and Sammy would come back with wild yarns about his dad's claimed heroic exploits. He would tell me how his dad would soon take him home for good. It never happened.

Robbie Benson was six, and a rich kid. His mum was killed in a car accident and his dad reluctantly left Robbie and his sister at the Home temporarily until he could arrange alternate care. He came to visit every week, but the nuns despised him and resented his interference. He complained endlessly that Robbie wasn't wearing his own neat clothes, or his favourite toy had been taken from him, or he wasn't practising piano.

Both Robbie and Sam were given favoured treatment because their dads kept check. I only took care of Robbie for about a year. One morning, the handyman left a hoe by the wall near a garden bed he'd been weeding. Robbie took the hoe and began, quite expertly for one so young, to chip away the weeds. He was obviously quite practised. He told me he often helped his dad tend the gardens at home.

The neat results he achieved failed to impress the Mother, who flew into a rage and railed endlessly about the danger of a young child handling such a tool and spanked him.[ii] Two days later, his dad took Robbie and his sister away for good.

#

My new daily routine began the morning after my birthday. An alarm sounded at five a.m. and I rose and joined my charges in the morning line–up to be punished for wetting my bed. Then I accompanied my charges to their dorm to strip their beds and roll up their pissy sheets and pyjamas. I remade

48

their beds with clean linen, taking care to ensure the covers were tight and the corners perfect. Then I left them to dress while I attended to my own bed. And then I carried three sets of pissy sheets and wet pyjamas downstairs to the laundry room.

Colin showed me how to wash the linen by hand, in ice–cold water. I had to stand on a stool to reach into the huge concrete tubs. When the rinsing was complete, I squeezed as much water from the linen as I could, then struggled to the clothes line under a load twice my own weight. I had to run back to fetch a stool to reach the lines. It was sheer agony moving it up and down the line, stretching the sheets out and making sure they were straight and pegged firmly.

With no help on the second morning, I was late to breakfast. Grace had been said and the children were already slurping cold, sticky porridge when I reached the door of the dining room. Sister Agnes was waiting for me.

"Late, Paul Wilson," she snapped.

"I'm sorry, Sister. I — "

"No excuses, young man. It is the height of rudeness to arrive late for a meal."

"Yes, Sister," I mumbled, a simmering stew of resentment bubbling in my gut.

"No breakfast for you, boy. Go to the front of the hall. You will stand and watch the others eat."

I marched to the front of the hall and turned to face the other children, concentrating intently on maintaining a poker–face and deadpan stance.

"You see this rude boy, children? He has not the good manners to present on time for his meal, so he must suffer hunger until the next meal. That is the punishment for tardiness. We must all learn good manners, mustn't we?"

"Yes, Sister Agnes," the children chorused. My belly rumbled and rolled and my parched lips and tongue ached for a taste of the vile, sweet, weak tea the senior girls poured from big enamel pots each mealtime. I silently cursed the Sisters for their unfair expectations, but resolved to complete my morning chores more quickly in future.

JUNE 2010

Ernest Stanley checked his watch, stowed his digital voice recorder and climbed back into the Roller for the drive to town.

"Did you miss breakfast often?" he asked Paul.

"Only once, luckily," Paul replied. "Either I was a fast learner, or depriving me of food was an exceptionally effective punishment. But I washed pissy sheets in cold water nearly every morning for three years."

Through the summer, that washing task was onerous. In autumn, fierce icy winds burnt eardrums and wrapped soggy sheets around the children, tying them in twists that took forever to untangle. In winter, the taps froze. The older children filled the tubs and water buckets at night. In the morning, little children had to peel off sheets of ice to get to the freezing water below. For six months of each year we laboured across frost–coated paddocks and our hands were raw and covered with agonising chilblains.

Ern struggled to retain his composure. He'd declared himself prepared for this. He'd researched, interviewed, recorded and listened for endless hours to stories of life in children's homes. But it was apparent Paul's story was tearing away at the fabric of his reality — destroying his confidence in the system that governed and gilded his world.

"Kids suffer much worse in war–torn countries and the Third World," Paul said, shrugging off Ern's disquiet. "In Australia, we get it far too easy. And kids are amazingly resilient. We are born with strong survival instincts. Children cope because they have no other choice."

Pain lines creased Ern's brow as he battled to dismiss horrifying images of children running from gunfire and limbless children in makeshift hospitals in Third World countries. But that was there. This was Australia, in a time of peace and prosperity.

"I finally stopped wetting my bed about the time Robbie left," Paul continued, "so I only had Sammy's linen to do. Sometimes, he'd wet early in the night and it'd pretty much dry out by morning and we'd cover it over and pray the nuns wouldn't smell it. If a Sister found out what we'd done, she'd tell Sam to always demand clean linen and pyjamas. And I'd get a belting — a much less dreadful punishment than washing sheets in freezing water in the false dawn."

#

Paul wasn't assigned any other charges after Robbie left, but he had cared for young Sammy until he left that place. Despite the hardships, he had loved him. He told Ern how he ran to comfort him when he fell in the playground and skinned a knee or bruised an elbow, and how he ached for him when he was beaten, wishing he could intervene and take the thrashing for him. He said he would have done almost anything to protect him. The hurt in his eyes as he spoke of the boy confirmed his sincerity.

"I ran into Sam Parry years later, in a pub in Sydney," he said tonelessly. "He told me about being transferred to a home in Westmead, run by priests. One would take him to his bedroom in the evenings and molest him."

A little gasp escaped as Ern's chest heaved. Revulsion creased his brow.

"He ran away when he was 14," Paul continued. "Robbed a servo to get money to buy food. Did four years in juvie. When he got out, he was alone and destitute and he broke into a grocery store. He was awaiting trial when I met him. I asked him why he did it. It was a rhetorical question. He gazed at me for a while, shrugged his shoulders, took another sip of beer, and said, 'I was hungry. Nobody wants to give an ex–crim a job. How else was I to get money to buy a feed?' "

Paul told Ern he had read Sam's name in the paper some years later. He'd shot a guard while robbing a bank and was sentenced to life in prison.

"Poor bugger," Paul said, "I felt a pang of guilt. He was my little brother and I should have taken better care of him. But they separated us. They sent me away, and thank God I didn't go to Westmead. As shitty as my life was, I was lucky! I drank a toast to poor little Sam. While uttering a quiet prayer for his soul, I renewed my vow that I would exact revenge — for Sammy, and for all the others, as well as for Jen and me."

7: FATHER JOSEPH

JUNE, 2010

"You located Father Joseph?" Paul's wide eyes swam with delight. "I loved that man. He parted the grey skies and let the sunshine into my world."

Ern had located the elderly and infirm priest in an aged–care facility, and was pleasantly surprised to discover that he was still alert and coherent and his recollections of St Patrick's were vivid.

"That place must have seemed like a prison to the children forced to live there," he wrote in his reply to Ern's introductory letter. "It presented as a huge, austere, cold fortress perched high on a hill, just far enough from town that the children could not readily mix with town folk, but could watch — noses flattened against freezing window panes — as the lights of the town came on, chimneys puffed their thick grey smoke, and cars, reduced by distance to barely matchbox size, slid down gravel driveways bringing fathers home to children's hugs and wives' kisses.

"They couldn't see the people, and perhaps it was a blessing. But in later years they mixed with the town kids at school and in the grounds of the church on Sunday mornings. They passed them as they marched with military precision to their allotted pews, Sisters barking threats to keep them silent and ensure none forgot to genuflect to the altar and sign the cross with appropriate reverence."

Ern donned his solicitor's hat and quizzed the frail old man diligently, but when the priest showed signs of tiring, he helped him on to his bed and made him tea. Then the old Father obligingly bundled Ern into a time machine and took him on a tour of the Dickensian world he had toiled for 25 years to reform.

JULY, 1958

Father Joseph had just turned 40 when he arrived in the country town on the New South Wales tablelands. It was the middle of a bleak, icy winter. Pine trees shivered, their peaked tops tipped with a thick, white, frosty coat. Thinning white carpets made small slippery spots on bitumen roadways and the concreted paths that ran beside them. The massive dark–brick steeple, with its shiny brass cross on top, punctured the clouds, rising above them as a beacon to welcome the newcomer to his cathedral home.

Brother Charlie went with him to St Patrick's the first time. He introduced the Father to the Sisters and they served him tea with homemade Anzac biscuits, little cakes with fresh cream from their own cows, and sweet, fresh fruit from the orchard out back. They sat in the richly furnished front room, warmed by a blazing open fire, thick drapes over the high, narrow windows, and a plush carpet square on the floor between the deep leather armchairs. Afterward, Charlie and Sister Anne showed him around the building, explained management policies, and related the children's stories.

"Some of the children stay only a short time," Charlie explained. "Parents leave them while they recover from illness, sort out financial problems or find suitable living quarters. Some are children of widows, widowers, unmarried mothers or divorcees, surrendered voluntarily to care because the parent can't cope alone. Many of those only stay until their mum or dad remarries. They are the hardest to manage, because a parent or relative might visit from time to time and interfere."

They were also the lucky ones. The nuns were much kinder to those whose relatives made regular checks on their welfare, especially when their attention includes donations to the Home.

"Most of the children here were removed from family homes because of alleged parental neglect," the Mother told him. "Social workers look for signs of neglect and issue orders to place kids in State care, and the courts send them here or to one of many other homes like this, mostly run by churches."

The Father learnt that each social worker might move a dozen or so kids each year to homes like St Patrick's. All were told it was only temporary and promised they could go back home soon, but most would never be permitted contact with their parents again.

Being 'neglected' was a crime, and kids charged would carry the shame of a 'record' through to adulthood.[iii] Along with the shame, they carried the stigma of being a 'home kid' and the belief, instilled in them through countless cruel reminders, that they were society's burden. A high percentage of kids moved from institutions like St Patrick's to juvenile detention centres and jails.

"Not much anyone can do about it," the Mother Superior said. "Bad blood!"

The Home was a strong profit centre for the Church. The Government paid an allowance for every child in care there and parents were generally required to pay maintenance as well, although few actually met that obligation. Community donations were generous. Cases of fruit from local orchards; cakes, pies and bread from the town bakery; meat from the butchers and the surrounding cattle stations; and clothes kids from local families had outgrown, plus from stores who sent their shop–soiled stock and the surplus left at the end of each season.

The clothes were stored in a big basement room on racks and in cartons. Volunteers sorted them by size and mended tears and broken zips. The volunteers took the good stuff home for their own kids. Most of the rest remained in storage, it seemed, until deemed sufficiently moth–eaten or mildewed for urchins to wear. The Mother seemed to think most of the clothing was too good for children who would likely only soil it or scuff the knees and elbows until holes appeared. Clothes that were allocated were typically far too large for the wearer and, unless they disintegrated sooner, were worn well after the child had outgrown them.

Brother Charlie pointed out the cows and chooks and told the Father they produced an abundance of eggs, milk and cream. He didn't tell him that the cream was given to the volunteers. The milk was heavily diluted to make a sickly-sweet, weak tea, or watered down for use on cereals.

"Once, a stand–in cook used the milk and cream to make a big, creamy rice pudding," Charlie reported. "The Mother was furious. She said such food was inappropriate. The children's diet is bland and Spartan. Rich food would make them all sick."[iv]

Charlie took the Father to inspect the orphanage school — a single oversized classroom where nearly 60 children aged five to 14 laboured, supervised by the same nuns who guarded the playgrounds. Untrained as educators and unmotivated to teach, they strutted up and down the rows with rulers, rapping the knuckles of anyone whose attention appeared to lapse. They seemed concerned with little more than maintaining silence and compelling the children to persevere, with heads down and chalks gripped, in copying symbols on a slate.

Like the dormitories, the classroom walls were dark unpainted brick and the windows were high and small. There was a pervasive stench in that musty, airless old building, created by the combination of human odour and the disinfectant with which the floors and furnishings were regularly scrubbed. In the summer, the heat was savage. Thick, stale air hung heavily and perspiration soaked necks and poured from foreheads. Sweat soaked the backs of white shirts and caused rough serge pants to stick to skin, making thighs itch, until an irresistible urge to scratch exceeded fears of retribution and a child's persistent fidgeting enraged the Sisters. A nun would then relieve the itch, temporarily, by applying a leather strap or a ruler to legs or backside.

On the day of the Father's visit, the unheated room was freezing. The nuns were heavily clad, but the children wore only thin jumpers and, save for short socks, the girls' legs were bare. They shivered through the winter, fingers and toes swollen with angry purple chilblains that burnt and itched.

"The children don't go to school in the town?" the Father asked Mother Emmanuel.

"Oh no, Father!" she replied. "It would create all kinds of problems to compel the children of decent families to mix with the likes of these."

Later that day, Father Joseph shocked the Sisters by entering the playground and talking — crouched on one knee with his robe dragging in the dust — to some of the boys. He asked them if they might invite him to play cricket with them when the spring came.

"We got a pitch, Father," Jimmy Phillips replied. "But ain't got no proper wickets or good bat to use on it."

The Father stood and reached down to ruffle the lad's hair.

"I can fix that, young fella," he said, grinning radiantly. "You just get me an invite and I'll bring all the gear you need. Bet I can teach you some tricks too. I've hit a few sixes in my time, and I can bowl to strike out champions."

#

The following Sunday, Father Joseph witnessed an act of brutality that confirmed his conviction that God had sent him here to instigate reform. He came to conduct an early morning service in the orphanage chapel. The nuns invited him to breakfast after, in the parlour. A girl, aged 17, was employed at the Home as a kitchen-hand and charged with carrying his breakfast tray. She was one of several girls who had grown up in the Home and stayed on, after she turned 15, as hired help.

The Father's tray was generously laden with fried tomatoes and two fried eggs resting on thick buttered toast. On the side, a little bowl of fresh fruit salad was topped with a scoop of cream, and beside the cup of steaming tea, a glass brimmed with freshly squeezed orange juice.

The girl left the kitchen with the tray, started across the courtyard to the parlour, then paused a minute, gazing at the meal. She looked furtively about her, then balanced the tray edge briefly on a narrow ledge and reached for the juice. Her eyes darted about warily as she drew it to her lips and took a tiny sip. She set it back on the tray, licked her lips, glanced about her again, then hastened into the parlour to set the breakfast before the Father.

Father Joseph had already wiped the grease and runny yellow yoke from his plate with the last piece of toast and leant back in the armchair to sip his tea when he heard it. The girl's shrill screams were punctuated by thin whistles, followed by sharp slapping sounds. He lurched forward, alarmed. The Mother raised her hand to signal stop and smiled at him graciously.

"It's quite all right, Father," she assured him. "The girl who served you was seen stealing. Sister Agnes is administering her punishment. She will be done in a moment. The girl must learn to live by God's rules. Sometimes it requires harsh measures to teach these children. They have bad blood running in their veins."[v]

Father Joseph shivered as another slapping sound preceded another sharp scream. Then the slapping and the screaming stopped and he was aware of soft, sobbing sounds drawing closer. The girl stood before him, head bowed, face streaked with tears, trembling.

"Forgive me, Father," she mumbled. "I stole a sip from your juice glass."

"And why did you do that, my child?" he asked gently.

"Because I... you see... I didn't mean to. I knew it was wrong. It was just that..."

"Just what, my child?"

"I ... I have served it to the Sisters and their guests so many times. I just..." She broke off and stood staring miserably at her feet.

"Is it not served here with your breakfast?"

"Oh, no! Not to the children, Father."

"But you are no longer a child? You are grown now and just work here, yes?"

"Yes, Father."

"And do you earn a wage for your work and pay some to the Sisters for your keep?"

"They keep my pay in a bank account for when I leave. Some of it they take to pay for the food I eat and my lodgings."

"Then why…" he turned to the Mother, "Why should the girl not have orange juice? Why not the children, in fact? There is an abundance of fruit on the trees out back and I know the local farmers bring cases of fruit."

"There are things you do not understand, Father," the Mother replied. "We do our best here, but there are good reasons not to provide certain luxuries. We have 50 to 60 children to feed and our budget does not stretch to indulgences like orange juice for breakfast."

"Not even for those that are grown and paying their own way?"

"It would not be wise, Father. The children would want what they see the older girls have. It is a question of management, you see. In any case, we are dealing with a thief here, Father. What matters is that God's child learns to obey His law."

The Mother bellowed at the girl. "You will apologise now to Father Joseph, for taking what was his. And you shall ask for penance at confession."

The Father couldn't see why any further penance ought to be required after what the lass had suffered, but the nuns taught the only way to atone

57

properly for sin was via a voluntary self–punishment. The punishment they administered was merely to ensure the children understood they had sinned and penance was required. What they gave them to understand, in fact, was that they were so filled with sin that no amount of penance would ever redeem them. They were all born bad and could never ever be capable of good.

"But I saw the good in so many of them," the Father told Ern. "They shone when I praised and encouraged them. Brand a child bad, he might grow to fit that brand. Many did. They were taught to hate, and that adults were entitled to be violent when offended. They suffered such hurt that many of them, like Paul, grew up determined to exact revenge."

8: SPORTSMAN AND THIEF

FEBRUARY, 1958

Ouch!

Brother John's nicotine–stained fingers pulled hard at the hair of my sideburns. I gritted my teeth and squeezed my lips. The stink of nicotine irritated my nostrils and the side of my head throbbed. The Brother snatched the adventure book from my lap and thumped his finger on a page of the math book on the desk.

I hated math. It was the only subject I struggled with, so I retreated to reading as often as I thought I could get away with it. At the orphanage school, I'd never learnt to recognise more than a few simple words. No–one bothered to teach me, so I was left to try to make out words in the dull "Tom and Mary" reader by word–picture association. I had stared blankly at the pages until a child was called on to read aloud, then struggled to memorise the words I heard so I could make a passable pretence when called on later. But at the start of the 1958 school year, a Sister had called the children to line up and board a bus, announcing the orphanage school was closed and we would now attend school in the town. I was ecstatic. For a few precious hours each day there was a semblance of normality in my life. Taught by Brothers who had chosen teaching as their vocation, I learnt easily, and loved learning.

"You have 10 minutes to finish those sums, young man," Brother John said sternly. "Or you'll be sitting here doing sums through your lunch hour."

I turned my attention reluctantly to the required calculations, battling frantically to complete them. My mouth watered, thinking of the broken pie that might replace the stale peanut butter sandwich in my lunch box — if I could just get out of the classroom in time.

Done! The bell rang and I raced out to join a little group drawing straws to select a boy to stand watch while we crept down the back alley to the rear of the town bakery. The baker was generous with his 'staffies' — broken pies and flopped cakes that weren't suitable for sale. The Brothers knew the orphanage boys regularly snuck out, but they turned a blind eye. They hated seeing growing boys go hungry.

Returning with my belly full, I fished in my pocket for marbles. Rolling my precious taw between my fingers, I waited for the other boys to choose a game, find an adequate drawing stick and draw a ring in the dust. I'd had to borrow a few little balls to join the first tournament of the season, but I won consistently. Today was no exception. Started with five, and by the end of the lunch hour I counted eight round gems into the little biscuit tin Sister Anne had found for me. There were some real pretty cat's eyes among them. I'd even taken a steelie from that smug little Keith Woodrow, the mechanic's son. I left the ring jubilant, mates congratulating me and mourning their losses, and trooped off for an afternoon session of reading in the library.

I'd discovered a passion for reading. I devoured boys' adventure stories and they consumed me. I joined big game hunts and white–water rafting expeditions. I was the only surviving hero of dangerous exploratory treks across deserts and through jungles. I climbed the highest mountains; crossed the wildest rivers; fought Indians, bears and lions; mined for gold and ventured into dark coal mines. I read and re–read favourite volumes, hanging on every word.

#

"Sports Carnival tomorrow, boys," Charlie announced brightly to the little group waiting at the bus stop that afternoon. I was wrestling with another lad. Charlie cuffed our ears lightly. "Keep that up and you two will find yourselves in the office getting six of the best while the others are walking to the fields," he warned.

I stepped back, pressed my hands against my thighs and shot the Brother a wry grin. I'd felt the sting of the Head Brother's thin cane more than once. The day before, I had slunk back to class with both burning hands tucked up in my armpits after receiving three hard whacks across each open palm. But missing sport was a punishment worse than death. It was my greatest love — even more so than reading — and I excelled at it. I could run fast and swim strongly. I had quick reflexes and a sharp eye. Within weeks of starting school in town I'd found myself dreading holidays and living for sports days.

#

"Next event: Backstroke. Under 10s," the inter–school swimming carnival co–ordinator announced. "Swimmers, please assemble at the northern end of the pool. The race will begin in 10 minutes."

A shivering group in wet togs gathered around Brother Charlie to hear him announce despondently that the junior backstroke champion had contracted measles. There was a chorus of groans.

"But we need him. We're behind on points. We need to win this race," Jimmy Barnes protested.

Charlie shrugged. "We'll just have to select a replacement and hope for the best. Geoff Harrison?"

"Booo. Nooooo!"

"Phillip Coussa?"

"Noooo."

"Dennis Mitchell?"

"Nooo."

"Paul Wilson?"

I didn't swim much. St Patrick's kids were rarely permitted to go to the pool, but our class trooped off to the senior school once weekly in the summer months for swimming lessons. I'd learnt to swim when I was very young, and I swam strongly, but I knew only one stroke — a somewhat ungainly imitation of the standard Australian crawl. I'd never attempted any other.

A dozen questioning faces focused on me and something in my belly turned over.

How hard can it be? I silently considered my lack of knowledge of the stroke. *They just turn on their backs and wave their arms about.*

I nodded at Charlie. There was a despondent collective sigh from the boys surrounding me. Charlie patted my back and wished me luck. With the lump in my belly still somersaulting, I strutted to the assembly area at the end of the pool.

"Ready, boys?"

I swallowed hard. Foam danced as twelve young bodies hit the water. Unfamiliar with the starting procedure, I waited for the others to take their crouched positions, then mimicked them, tense fingers and toes gripping the wall and body rigid. Remembering Charlie's instruction, I inhaled deeply and tried to relax. Chill ripples caressed my thighs. A tenacious white sun beat through thick haze, and I feared that despite the chill, overcast day, my face and bare shoulders might be burning. My heart thundered so loudly I feared I wouldn't even hear the starting signal.

Froth bounced and sprayed. Twelve sleek young bodies glided through the water, arms slapping the surface in rhythmic rotation and fluttering feet disturbing the surface just enough to create a delicate dance of bubbles. At the halfway mark, I tried to look to the sides. No foam. No splashing bodies. I must be way behind. A wave of despondency washed me, but I kept up a valiant effort anyway.

At the finish line, I glanced about, confused, trying to identify the subject of the applause. It took several moments to realise I was yards ahead of all but one of my competitors, and a few clean feet ahead of the runner–up.

Paul Wilson, backstroke champion, school hero, stood on the little dais, glistening beads on my white belly, back and limbs and wet curls pressed flat against my head. Trickles ran from the hem of my togs down the insides of my legs to pool at my toes. Cheers and clapping almost deafened me. My cheeks glowed, my eyes danced, and my proud heart threatened to burst right through my chest wall and float away.

We didn't get to keep personal possessions. There was no provision in the tiny squares of dormitory space we were allocated at St Patrick's, nor in the cupboards or on the shelves of the vast halls below. Anyway, the other boys would want, and fight for, anything another had and they didn't, and the Sisters had enough to cope with without breaking up fights over possessions.

I went home from the carnival that afternoon elated, proudly carrying a little trophy. It remained on top of my personal table for just one day before it disappeared, never to be seen again.

MAY 1958

"David Simpson, Brian Hutton, James Griffen..."

A hundred and twenty–two boys shivered and fidgeted in the convent courtyard at morning assembly as Brother Charlie read the names of the boys selected to play in the under-elevens rugby league team. As each was called, they proudly took their place beside the Brother, their short procession to the front of the crowd accompanied by cheering and applause.

I was paying scant attention to the proceedings. The list was predictable. Everyone knew who the good players were. Having paid careful attention to Brother Charlie's instruction and the examples of the seniors, and practised moves for endless hours, I was among them. But Home kids didn't make sports teams. The Sisters would never allow us to stay after school for training, let alone to travel to weekend matches.

"Kevin Anderson, Colin Davies, Paul Wilson..."

The calling of my name didn't register.

"Paul Wilson," the Brother repeated, slightly louder this time. I shook with disbelief. My name rang in my ears as though it were the name of a stranger. The boys on the dais blurred and floated about the Brother, passing a football between them. I saw me up there trying to catch it, but they kept snatching it from my grip and pushing me aside. I shouldn't be there. I didn't belong. Some of the boys had clenched their fists and wore twisted sneers. The cheering was subdued and reluctant.

"Hey, Home kid! Yeah, well, stay stumm," a sixth grader muttered, just loud enough for me to hear. "Of course ya can't play on the team. Brother made a mistake. He'll wake up in a minute."

I'll deal with him later.

Father Joseph stepped up behind me and lightly tapped my shoulder.

"You made the team, Paul," he said. "Wow! Congratulations! Go on, lad. Get up there."

I knew I was something of a favourite with the Father. He was kind to all the orphanage boys. He often said he was sure, despite our disadvantage, with a little effort we could make something of ourselves. He said he knew I tried hard and he predicted I would do well. He liked that I was mostly obedient and respectful. When he saw me in the hallways he would ruffle my curly hair and call me 'skinny' or 'mischief', but he told me often I was a 'good lad' and the Mother should be proud of me.

At the Father's prompting, I straightened my back, lifted my shoulders and marched through the lines. Twice, a boy stepped sideways to try to obstruct my path. I paused to say "Excuse me," in a loud, clear voice and then turned slightly sideways to push through, bumping the obstructer just hard enough to unbalance him. Only a handful of boys cheered as I climbed the dais, and there was far more grumbling than applause.

"Enough, boys," Charlie roared, then, more softly, "Well done, Paul. You've earned your place on the team."

After assembly, I approached the Brother to mutter in a quivering voice, "Thank you for choosing me, Brother Charlie. I really want to play on the team, but I doubt the Sisters will let me go to weekend matches, sir."

The Brother frowned and nodded gravely. "It's unusual, I know, for a St Patrick's boy to be selected on a school sports team, but you've earned your place. And it will be good for you, son. I think we should ask the Sisters.

"Perhaps Father Joseph can talk to Mother," he continued, turning to face his senior. "He seems to have reasonable success getting her to see his point of view."

"Thank you, sir," I said, staring despondently at the toes of my shoes. "But maybe you'd better plan for a replacement. Home kids don't play on school sports teams."

Father Joseph patted my shoulder. "We'll see. I'll talk to Mother Emmanuel this afternoon. We'll decide then, eh? For now, you are part of the team and that's quite an achievement. Congratulations. Now off you go to class."

In the end, the Mother Superior gave in, reluctantly, to the Father's persistent arguments. She battled valiantly to convince him of the unwelcome complications it would cause to have a child stay late at school and go away to sporting matches on weekends. There was the matter of uniforms and boots, too. Well, yes, of course Brother Charlie would find a kind family willing to pass down clothing their son had outgrown, but the uniforms would need to be laundered too.

"And Paul can't manage that?" the Father challenged. "He seems to manage to wash smelly sheets and his charge's soiled underwear."

The Mother shot me a mortified what–are–you–doing–here–hearing–such–remarks look and glared at the Father.

"Father, you will need to lecture Paul about making sure his schoolwork doesn't suffer, and he meets all his responsibilities at home. There can be no further concessions," the Mother Superior warned, not yet conceding completely. "Any slacking off or disobedience and he will be off the team immediately. That must be understood."

"I'm sure Paul's behaviour will be beyond reproach. This will be good for him, Mother. You'll see."

Finally, in response to the Father's promise to convey me home safely from every training session and to collect me and transport me to and from the weekend matches, the Mother yielded. Every Saturday in football season I was fed early, then transported to the football field seated in the front of Father Joseph's smart white Falcon with its plush red–leather seats. I felt like a king perched there beside him in the front seat. For one precious day each week of the footie season, I was a normal kid.

Proud of their little sporting star, Sister Anne charged herself with the task of making sure my diet was appropriate for a sportsman. She took me to the kitchen where she served me fried eggs and sausages or bacon and freshly buttered hot toast. I washed it all down with freshly squeezed orange juice and she packed a lunch box with tasty sandwiches with slices of devon sausage or cheese and tomato fillings for midday snacks. She would often sneak a sweet biscuit or two into the lunch pack. There was always a juicy half–orange for half–time refreshment and a flask of fresh milk that I drank before the match began, so that it didn't sour in the hot sun.

Making the team changed my status at school too. I was no longer the first suspect when a pencil case or lunch money went missing. Home kids were always being accused of theft and were quite often guilty. Denied replacements of lost pens and rulers and refused learning aides like coloured pencils and stencils — and punished by the Brothers when the lack of such devices rendered us unable to perform required tasks — we did what you might expect kids in such circumstances to do.

Some of the Brothers, and most of the parents of the town kids, expressed the view that this behaviour was to be expected, considering what we were and where we came from. We were the children of no–hopers. We naturally inherited our parents' defects. We were tolerated, even treated charitably by some who heeded the Christian instruction to suffer the little children, although with the stated opinion that we would mature to layabouts and criminals regardless of any kindness or help. But as a member of the team, I wore a new brand. The shabby uniform no longer defined me. Now, it was my sporting talent that identified me.

JUNE 1958

Father Joseph perched on a long bench beside a young family whose eldest boy was captain of the under 10 team. It was a sunny Saturday and the frost on the fields was thawing quickly. The crowds had gathered early, filling the grass slopes and grandstand. Families assembled on the thin, hard benches around the perimeter of the field or laid out picnic rugs to rest on.

The Father had collected me early from the orphanage kitchen, arriving before I finished my bread. He waited patiently for me to swallow the last mouthfuls, then clean my teeth and comb my hair in the washroom out back. Sister Anne was on retreat and the Father seemed disturbed that her stand–in served me porridge and bread instead of eggs. Instructed to prepare porridge and bread for 60 children, she said she could see no reason why I should be treated differently.

The Father frowned, noticing bruises on my arms and legs. He would have guessed I'd copped a fierce beating a few days before, but he didn't inquire or comment. Had he asked, I would have told him harsh treatment only made me more determined. But I would have dutifully confessed to misbehaving and acknowledged the beating was deserved. It didn't matter that I didn't believe it. I would say what was expected.

Our game was on home ground. We played well and won. Our team's skill was impressive and our trainer was good. Several of the boys showed talent. The coach said I shone. The Father smiled broadly as I left the field, basking in the admiration of my teammates and the cheers of the crowd.

Father Joseph joined Brothers John and Charlie to set up a little folding table by some benches under a shady tree, open a sandwich box and pour strong, warm tea from a thermos. My teammates hovered around the canteen, spending their two shilling coins on hot pies and sausage rolls with lashings of tomato sauce, and ice creams in wafer cones. I retrieved my little lunch pack from the Father's car and went off happily with them, wrestling playfully. Brother John passed us, heading for the canteen.

It was the smell that got to me, and hunger. The lunch the stand–in cook had packed was scant and unappetising. I had only a single Vegemite sandwich, while all the other boys were biting into juicy mince wrapped in crisp, flaky, brown shells with big red dollops of sauce on top.

I knew it was wrong to steal and I remembered Dad telling me sternly that hunger was no excuse, but when all the other boys were focused on their pies and the pie man had disappeared below the counter, temptation won. I snatched a pie and ducked behind a parked car to eat it. Hearing my name called, I wiped my lips carefully and struggled to reduce the tell-tale bulge in my cheeks by swallowing the last oversized mouthful.

The heavy, musky odour of nicotine. I felt John's fingers grip my sideburns and pull hard. I stumbled as he dragged me back to the table where the Father sat. When he released me, I looked up to see that his cheeks blazed.

"One of the boys saw him stealing a pie," John roared. "Stealing, Father, stealing! Now what do you think about that?" He laid a strong emphasis on the word 'that'. "A fine way for a boy to thank you for all the favours.

"And Brother Charlie," he added, turning, "now do you think it was a good idea to include him in the school team?"

I slumped my shoulders and hung my head. The aftertaste of the pie was suddenly foul. My mouth and throat burnt. I felt Father Joseph studying me, planning punishment. I pushed at a mound of grass with the toe of my boot and gulped hard. The tattle–taling fifth grader had followed Brother John and was peeping from behind a nearby tree, grinning maliciously. The Father beckoned to him.

"Did you see this boy steal a pie from the pie stand."

"Yes, Father," he said, gloating, "and I told Brother John, because it's a very bad thing to do, stealing."

"That's true," said the Father, "but I think this boy might have been very, very hungry. You see how skinny he is? And you have a nice round belly and full cheeks, and I suspect your mother gives you plenty of good food to eat. Yes?"

The boy nodded. "But —"

The Father raised his hand to silence him. "It was wrong to take that pie and Paul must be punished. I will help him learn that stealing is wrong, however hungry he might be. But you must promise me you will say nothing to anyone about this. Not a word, do you hear?"

"Yes, Father."

"Good. Now run along please."

The boy looked mildly disappointed at not witnessing at least a fierce lecture, but he shrugged and darted off in the direction of the ice–cream stand.

"I'll deal with him, Brother John. And please, the Sisters do not need to hear about this. The punishment I administer will be quite enough." Father Joseph was standing now, towering over me and gazing down at the top of my head, watching my foot kicking softly at a tuft of grass.

"Come with me, boy," the Father commanded, striding off in the direction of the pie stand. I followed obediently. He stopped a short distance from the pie stand.

"What did you have for lunch, lad?"

"A Vegemite sandwich, Father."

"Just one?"

"Yes, Father."

"Nothing else? A biscuit or cake? Fruit?"

"No, Father. Only a sandwich."

"Hmmm. And after that pie, are you still feeling very hungry?"

I ventured a cautious upward glance and noted, with surprise, the Father's thick neck. Although appearing uncomfortably constrained by his stiff cleric's collar, it showed no redness or pulsing to suggest rage. His shoulders slumped a little. Creased brow and bushy eyebrows hung low over pitying grey eyes and slender fingers tugged at the oversized lobe of his left ear, as though opening it to better hear the Almighty's advice.

"Yes, Father. I'm very sorry, Father. I know it was wrong to steal. It was... I was just…" My voice trailed off and I resumed kicking tufts of grass.

Beat me, please. I deserve it. I'm really sorry. Just don't stop me playing football. I couldn't bear it.

"Hush, son. I know," said the Father. "Hunger can be very hard to resist, and those pies really do smell good, don't they?" He walked resolutely to the counter and reached in his pocket for some coins. He placed one on the counter. "One nice juicy pie, please, with plenty of sauce."

He dropped another coin on the counter. "And this is for the pie the boy took. I forgot to give him lunch money. He was really hungry and he couldn't find me to ask. He is a good lad and he knows that next time he must come and find me, or remind me earlier to be sure to give him his money."

The pie man thanked him and passed across a soggy–topped paper bag. The Father passed it to me, smiling.

"Next time, son, come and tell me they didn't give you a decent lunch, eh? You can't play football on an empty stomach, but the pie man has a family to feed. If you take his pies without paying he won't have any money to pay his bills and look after his children. Do you understand?"

I nodded silently, disbelieving.

"Go on, then. Get that into you and enjoy it. But don't tell anyone about this, right?"

I nodded gratefully, slid back the soggy brown wrapper and bit eagerly into the crisp, brown pastry. My head was spinning. Doubt. Fear. Suspicion. An unidentifiable expectation.

Surely this can't be the end of this? Why doesn't he punish me? Because he's planning to tell Mother. That's why. He knows she will punish me harshly. He knows she will stop me playing football.

Two hours later, Father Joseph urged his white Falcon up the steep orphanage driveway and into the kitchen courtyard. He had been chatting idly

67

about the afternoon games, asking me what I thought of that player's moves or this team's chances of making the finals. Not a word about pies or stealing. I sat on the edge of my seat, one hand on the doorhandle, my eyes focused hard on the grey mat beneath my feet.

The Father reached across and laid a big, soft hand on my head, waving lightly to ruffle my curls. "Well, an away game next week, eh? I'll have to get here bright and early. Will Sister Anne be back to give you a proper breakfast?"

"Yes, Father."

"Good. I won't have to remember to give you money for pies then. But you be sure to tell me any time you don't have enough lunch. The Sisters don't play football, so some of them don't understand — like I do — how much energy a young fella needs to run and kick. You let me know if you are hungry, OK? Now off you go. I've got work to do."

"Thank you, Father." I lifted the chrome handle, pushed on the door and slid out of the seat, landing with a gentle thud on the asphalt.

The Father grinned knowingly at me as I slammed the car door and ran to the playground.

#

Three weeks later, on a Friday, Father Joseph came to take me to a late–afternoon training session, but a solemn–faced Mother had told me I couldn't go today. I worried that perhaps, after all, he'd told on me for stealing a pie, but there had been two games since and several training sessions, and he'd shown no anger or desire for retribution. Anyway, why would he come if he'd told and knew she wouldn't let me go? The puzzle was quickly solved when the Sister lined us all up and marched us up the stairs to the dormitory.

"There's a prowler," she said in a conspiratorial whisper. "A peeping tom peering in at the windows and trying to force the doors. We must keep you locked up here for your safety."

The Sister was moving from door to door and window to window checking locks and glancing furtively outside to see if the intruder was still stalking. She locked the dormitory door and ordered us to sit quietly on our beds. I guess we ought to have been frightened. Perhaps the smaller boys were. I wasn't. I couldn't conceive of a reason why a peeping tom would want to hurt small boys, but the Sister said he might be a violent criminal or an escaped prisoner on the run. She seemed quite terrified.

We remained in lockdown for over an hour. The Father was in the parlour, sipping tea and chatting. He told me, later, he saw the man head towards the orchard out back and return munching an apple. He lay down on the lawn to

68

take a rest, and then he shook his head wearily, turned, and walked down the long driveway towards the cemetery, where he turned and was lost from view.

The Father said the man looked harmless, but very weary. He didn't tell me then, but I learnt some 18 years later, the man had knocked on the door and introduced himself, asking to see his son and daughter. He said he'd been told this was where they were sent when they were taken a few years before. The nuns said he was misinformed.

No Paul or Jennifer Wilson had ever lived here.[vi]

9: MY SISTER'S DEFENDER

MELBOURNE, JUNE 2010

A sporty white Merc coupe with the Hertz logo emblazoned on the number–plate frame eased into the Melbourne cul de sac. Paul and Ern left the Roller in Dubbo and flew to Melbourne for their meeting with Jen.

Ern parked the rental car in front of a stylish Cape Cod with two small dormer windows on either side of its dominant red–brick chimney. A carved green hedge edged a pocket-handkerchief front garden in which a sprinkler pulsed, spraying glistening streams to soak the path to the front door. The spit caught Ern, painting a dark, damp smudge on the outer left leg of his jeans. A slightly embarrassed Jennifer Wilson — now Schwarzer, and showing a single streak of grey in the wave over her forehead — answered the doorbell offering a towel. Ern declined.

She cut a svelte little figure, dressed casually in tight–fitting blue jeans and sky–blue cashmere sweater, hair a veil of silk hanging loose to well below her shoulders, and a clean, clear complexion with finely carved, classic features. Paul embraced her, but it seemed insincere — dutiful, but reserved. Ern was mildly disturbed by the greeting, for he knew Paul adored her.

Jen was reticent. Paul had warned Ern she would be. She had married well and left her childhood far behind her. The memories were buried deep, denied. The past had never happened. But when Paul reminded her of an incident when she was barely eight years old, Jen's eyes clouded, her lips twitched, and her hand crept to her throat.

"The piano," she whispered. "Sister Cecilia said I had talent. She wanted to teach me to play and she told me I should practise. I was playing 'Twinkle Twinkle Little Star'. I didn't think I was doing wrong. Sister Agnes came in and stood for a few minutes to listen, then she strode across and slammed the lid down. It caught my fingers and I screamed. She ordered me to stand there and not move until she returned. I didn't know where she went. It never occurred to me to fear a beating. Not until the Mother appeared in the doorway holding her strap.

"It affected me. The... the purposelessness... the irrationality. Beatings were common, and often brutal, but not like that one."

71

A hesitant smile played at the corner of her lips and her eyes warmed a little as she turned to look at Paul. "My big brother exacted revenge. He was my protector. They hardly let us speak to each other, but I always knew he was there, watching out for me. Doing what little he could. Loving me."

Paul took up the story then, and her eyes grew cold and distant listening to him. She was fighting the memories down, pleading with her subconscious — and her brother — to allow her to forget.

"I threw the strap down the well," he laughed. "I remember it was the belt off a Singer sewing machine. They'd used it for years. It lay on the corner of the Mother's desk and the Sisters would send us into her office to advise her of our misdemeanours and tell her we needed help to mend our sinful ways."

The laughter ceased and a shadow fell across him. "Now and again, she would emerge from that office dangling it by her side, and our little world would freeze under a stifling blanket of fear. Time would stand still until she barked a name. Then she'd make a ceremony of beating someone publicly. She seemed to enjoy inflicting deep humiliation as well as physical pain. I'm sure she delighted in the scared faces of those compelled to watch the awful scene.

"I remember one time, not long after I went there, she had a real party humiliating me after early morning church. They often made us go down to the orphanage chapel in pyjamas. Apparently some idiot senior girl reckoned I exposed myself. I guess maybe my pyjamas didn't cover me up very well when I moved in certain ways. I was a little kid… uninhibited, I suppose. Certainly not yet conscious of any ability to offend females by exposure. The Mother called me a filthy pervert and made a big ceremony of thrashing me in front of all the girls. I think that was when I first decided those nuns were perverted — even insane, perhaps. I remember repeating 'You stupid bitch' over and over under my breath while she was thrashing me."

NOVEMBER, 1958

She beat Jen on a steamy afternoon in November. I had been out in the paddocks with Bill, the handyman. I relished opportunities to help him with the gardens or the animals. He worked me like a slave, but it relieved the awful boredom of the playground.

I think I was taking fruit or vegetables to the kitchen. I remember coming around a corner near the laundry and seeing a black–faced Mother, her precious strap dangling from a tightly gripped fist, striding towards the main hall. Sister Agnes was beside her, ruddy face twisted in malicious anticipation. Several of the older girls lingered near the laundry door. I saw one push a wayward curl from her forehead with the back of a soapy hand. A cloud of white froth decorated the bobby pin dangling near her left ear.

My sister was cowering near the door of the hall. I was hanging back in the shadows, so I didn't even notice her until I heard the Mother shout her name.

"Jennifer Wilson. Come here at once."

The Mother waved the strap menacingly. A lump rose in my throat, blood rushed to heat my cheeks and my forehead throbbed. I wanted to lunge forward and come between the monster in black and my baby sister, who was inching slowly forward, trembling violently. But I stayed back, pressing against the wall to avoid being seen.

"This disobedient girl presumed to enter the main hall without permission and touch the piano," she announced to her small audience. "Now, we all know, don't we, children, that we are forbidden to touch the piano?"

"Yes, Mother," the other girls chorused dutifully.

"And we all know, don't we, children, the penalty for disobedience?"

"Yes, Mother."

"Jennifer?" she demanded, having observed that my sister had not joined the chorus.

"Yes, Mother," Jenny stammered meekly, "but Sister Cecilia is giving me music lessons, and she told me I should practise."

"Indeed?" the Mother frowned. "I shall have to speak to Sister Cecilia, but she doesn't make the rules here. I do. And I have made the rules very clear. And I have also made it very clear what happens to children who disobey me, have I not?"

"Yes, Mother," she stammered again, barely completing the response before the first sharp blow fell across her lower legs.

I gasped as Jenny screamed. I pressed my lips together, clenched my fists and squeezed my eyes shut tightly. Hot, sour vomit rose in my throat and I swallowed in panic. I wanted to stop the witch; to snatch the strap and flog her; shield my baby sister. I should gladly take the flogging for her, but like a coward, deeply ashamed, I stood stock still and listened as the strap whistled through the air and snapped against her legs, buttocks, back and arms.

Again, again, again and again.

Jenny's screams gave way to pathetic broken sobs. She was lying on the ground, curled in a ball to try to shield herself. Deep red grooves on her upper arm marked where the Mother's huge hand had gripped it, fingernails digging into the flesh to draw traces of blood.

The witch was finally done.

"Anyone else who thinks of disobeying me can be assured of similar punishment," she declared in a stern voice, glaring at the girls in the laundry doorway. "Jennifer! Get up and go up to bed immediately. Get back to work, girls, unless you want a lesson in diligence."

The girls scurried. The Mother stood akimbo, wearing a satisfied smirk, while Jenny struggled to her feet and limped up the stairs to her bed.

I saw her later in the dining room, at tea time. Her eyes were red and swollen and there were scald tracks on her cheeks. Her legs and lower arms blazed with thick red welts. Here and there, a thin line of recently dried blood marked where her skin had broken open.

Cold rage gushed through me like a torrent, making me choke and gag on my food, causing me to unbalance when I stood. I fought to look away as I left the dining hall. Hate bubbled up inside me like simmering lava in an about–to–erupt volcano.

I lay awake for hours, plotting revenge.

The next morning, I watched and waited until certain the nuns were all in the kitchen taking morning tea. I crept out of the playground, across the courtyard, down the hallway and into the front office, pleading with the door not to creak as I pushed it open just far enough to squeeze through. The strap was in its usual place on the corner of the desk. I took a firm grip on it and ran as fast as I could down to the back paddock and the brick–rimmed well, dropped it in, and watched with pleasure as the monstrous device somersaulted its way to the deep, black bottom. Then I turned, dusted my hands, and walked resolutely back to the playground to seek out Benny Carmichael and pretend we had been playing together all morning.

The old handyman saw and told. I had really liked Bill until that day, and I was hurt by his betrayal.

There was no mystery, for me, in the Mother's angry entry to the dining room at lunchtime. I saw the looks of surprise on some of the other boys' faces and I noticed some of them cringed, no doubt examining their conscience for hints of any sin committed that might have been detected. I knew my sin. I waited expectantly for my name to be called and looked curiously to see what device replaced the strap. The witch had removed the thick leather belt she wore around her habit.

I tried to close my ears to her angry tirade. And then it started: the swishing and slapping noises and the heavy burning swipes as the welts rose red and angry, promising deep blue–black bruises.

"Cry!" she commanded. It took every ounce of courage and determination not to.

"Cry, you worthless scum!" She brought the strap down hard on the small of my back. I winced, but gritted my teeth hard.

"Your defiance will bring you to a sorry end, boy, just like your worthless father and mother and all the other filthy vermin they might produce to contaminate the world of decent people!" She spoke staccato, punctuating each phrase with yet another savage lash. I lifted my feet from the ground, but when she felt my weight, she released her savage grip on my upper arm. I fell to the ground and curled in a ball. The blows did not cease.

Breathless, she dropped the strap at last. Exhaustion overcame her so she could not stomp regally back to her refuge. She struggled to the door and leant against it, panting. The Sisters commanded the children to march back to the playground. Sister Anne helped me up. With tears in her eyes and tenderness in her voice, she gently guided me up the stairs to bed.

Pain gripped and mauled me, sinking its fiery sharp teeth into every muscle and joint. It exploded in my brain, the physical seizures and aches competing with the knifing pain of public humiliation, and the deep gut–wrenching torment of the Mother's condemnation of me, and of the parents I adored and so desperately craved to return to. I would not allow myself to cry. I would not let her break me. I would show her — that vicious, devil woman.

Tomorrow, I would begin my plan to exact my revenge.

10: FOSTER CHILD

BINGARA, DECEMBER, 1959

Marion Bennett stood just four feet 11 inches tall when her hair was up and her high heels on. She was barely adequately curved to be recognisable as a woman when she wore her gardening overalls and tucked unruly ginger hair under her husband's old hat. But her arms were long enough to hug five children all at once, and her heart was big enough to love as many as she could squeeze into the tiny cottage she shared with her gruff six–foot–one truck–driving husband and their own three offspring.

Marion Bennett chose me to spend Christmas, 1959, with her family. She picked me up from St Patrick's on a blistering afternoon in mid–December and took me to her little house on the edge of Bingara, in the north–west. There, I shared a bedroom with her two sons, while Connie Lewis, a five–year–old St Patrick's girl, shared a bedroom with her six–year–old daughter.

"Best clothes on tomorrow morning, children," said Mrs Bennett cheerfully as she gathered up the empty dinner plates on my first evening in her home. "We are going shopping for new clothes."

And after a pause, "You were very quiet at dinner, Paul. Is everything all right?"

"Yes, thank you, Mrs Bennett," I replied, taking care to enunciate my words clearly and display my best manners. The Sisters had warned me that invitations to holiday with good Christian families weren't issued lightly, and my behaviour and manners must be perfect or I would never be allowed to go again. Not with this family, or with any other.

Dinner at the Bennetts' house was a noisy affair. There was no 'silence at mealtime' rule here. Mr and Mrs Bennett quizzed the children about activities and friends and what they had learnt today. When they ran out of questions, there were jokes and riddles, and Mr Bennett told tall stories. I wasn't accustomed to being permitted to speak during meals and was mindful of the risk that I might unintentionally speak out of turn, or say something that displeased. Anyway, I was busy enjoying the delicious food. We dined on beef stew and dumplings, followed by cold rice pudding with homemade ice–cream. I couldn't remember the last time I had eaten so well.

"Dinner was delicious, thank you, Mrs Bennett," I said, hoping she had not thought my silence rude.

She replied with a beaming smile and Mr Bennett chimed in with "You'll be well fed here, my boy. Mrs Bennett is a wonderful cook".

I slid cautiously from my chair and began collecting cups to carry to the sink. "I can wash up for you, Mrs Bennett. "

"Why, thank you, Paul." She gave me another beaming smile. "Maybe tomorrow. We can't have you doing chores on your first night here. John will help me tonight, and Brian can show you where he keeps his books and toys. Eight o'clock is bedtime here. You can play or read until then."

In the morning she served piping–hot porridge with honey on top, and fresh, hot buttered toast. Then she ordered us off to the bathroom to wash, clean our teeth and comb our hair ready for a trip to town. "And no jostling or fighting, please. Wait quietly for your turn at the washbasin."

Despite the caution, the Bennett children shoved one another and trampled on each other's feet and shouted argument about whose turn was next. I stood still and silent at the end of the line, wishing the others would be quiet and fearing any moment now Mrs Bennett would get angry, or Mr Bennett would appear with a grim expression and a strap in hand. But Mrs Bennett was still smiling broadly when we reassembled in the kitchen and Mr Bennett was humming cheerfully as he polished the last in a long row of leather shoes.

There was plenty of jostling, shoving, laughing and tripping on the way to the store too. It didn't seem to bother Mrs Bennett a bit. Connie and I tried to march, silent and sedate, in line, but the Bennett children teased us. Eventually we began to relax a little and join in the fun. By the time we reached the Thrift Shop, I was convinced almost nothing could displease this cheerful little mother. Still, I wasn't taking any chances. I wanted desperately to be invited back again.

"New clothes for Paul," Mrs Bennett announced brightly to the Thrift Shop attendant. "Neat fitting, with no sign of stain or wear. Nothing scratchy either. He must be comfortable. His Sunday best is acceptable. He'll need play clothes and pyjamas. I'll get him some new underwear across the road. We'll need pyjamas and sun frocks for the little girl please, the best you have."

They outfitted me with smart–looking shirts with no fraying on the collars. The shorts didn't sag about my knees and the pyjamas didn't make my skin itch.

On Saturday, Mrs Bennett packed a picnic basket and we children all piled into the back of Mr Bennett's truck. It rattled and bounced out to the river crossing where Mrs Bennett spread old blankets and laid out sandwiches and fruit, while Mr Bennett roasted sausages over an open fire. We swam and floated in inner tubes from old tyres and scratched near the banks for craybobs. Then Mr Bennett organised a game of rounders. Mrs Bennett hit a home run, but I scored best. Mr Bennett took me aside part–way through the game and asked if I could pitch a little more gently so the younger children could make a hit and not be struck out every time they took a turn to bat.

Mr Bennett cut down a tall pine tree and loaded it into the back of the truck. We rode rather uncomfortably home, crowded around the tree, trying to avoid being pricked by the needles. We forgot our discomfort quickly when the tree was carried to the corner of the living room to stand in a bucket and Mrs Bennett brought the box of Christmas decorations from the garage and asked us to help string tinsel and hang baubles.

On Christmas Eve, Mrs Bennett rolled out shortbread dough and we cut star, tree and Santa shapes. When the biscuits emerged from the oven, I helped spread white and yellow icing on the stars and green icing on the trees. Then I painted Santa faces and coloured baubles with brushes dipped in food colouring. I was even allowed to lick one of the icing bowls.

The next morning, five rowdy youngsters rose early to find two identical dolls in prams under the tree and three identical red tip trucks with their trays filled with sweets. One of the trucks had my name carefully printed on a piece of cardboard and stuck where the number plate should be. I was overwhelmed. Home kids didn't get Christmas gifts.

Five children dressed in their best to walk with Mr and Mrs Bennett to the chapel on the next corner. We sang Christmas Carols, heard the Christmas story, shook hands with the Priest and wished all the neighbours a merry Christmas. Five children whooped home with expectant bellies and tastebuds to feast on roasted chicken and vegetables, plum pudding with brandy sauce and fresh whipped cream, and thick slices of rich fruitcake.

Shortly after breakfast on Boxing Day, Mr and Mrs Bennett sent the other children outside to play and asked me to join them in the parlour. I found myself shaking and I felt the blood rush to my feet. I feared perhaps I was about to be punished for some unintentional misdeed. I fought desperately to remember every word I had spoken and any act that might have raised objection. I was sure I'd obeyed every instruction, and certain I'd never forgotten my manners — not even for a moment. I'd worked very hard at always speaking respectfully. Whatever could I have done to anger them? What punishment would they hand out?

I'd seen Mr Bennett clip the boys behind the ear once or twice. Mrs Bennett waved a wooden spoon at them now and again, causing them to run outside or to their bedroom where they would remain quietly for a few minutes before returning laughingly to a woman who invariably greeted them with a hug and a smile, seeming to have forgotten completely that moments earlier she was threatening them. I'd never heard either of the Bennetts raise their voice in anger or order a child to their room; never seen either take a strap to any one of their kids, or even spank them with their bare hand, for that matter.

There was never any indication in the other boys' behaviour that they might have suffered a stern reprimand, let alone a beating. But right now I hoped fervently that they would settle for administering a thrashing, rather than sending me back to the orphanage. I'd rather take a beating every day than suffer the shame of being sent away.

There was no punishment. Mr and Mrs Bennett met me with wide smiles, kind eyes and outstretched arms. They praised my manners. They thanked me for my obedience and for being helpful. They said it was a great pleasure to have me in their home and they were happy that I got along so well with their sons.

"We've grown very fond of you in the short time you've been here, Paul," Mr Bennett said. That made the blood rush to my head. My chest puffed out and my shoulders lifted and a warm glow enveloped me.

"We wondered if you'd like to stay with us permanently." Mrs Bennett said softly, with a hint of caution in her voice, as though afraid I might decline. "We'd like to foster you, Paul. Do you know what that means? It means you would become part of our family — our son."

Paul Frederick Bennett! The name repeated over and over inside my head. It sounded good. I would go to the little village school down the road with their two sons, help Mrs Bennett tend the vegetable garden, and take turns with the boys chopping wood and mowing lawns. I could help Mr Bennett wash the truck on Friday afternoons. I would sleep in a cosy bed in a bedroom shared with two boys near my own age and eat wonderful, hot, home–cooked meals at a kitchen table with a family who enjoyed chattering and joking over their dinner. I'd never again have to queue in silence for lukewarm hash and stale bread, and never again wear shabby ill–fitting shorts and shirts with frayed collars. I'd never again be called 'home kid'.

Paul Frederick Bennett. Third son of Mr James Bennett and Mrs Marion Bennett. Wanted. Liked. Chosen.

"But," I hesitated a moment, terrified of seeming rude or ungrateful. I could hardly believe I was daring to speak, let alone spoil this moment with an objection. They stared at me, curious, concerned. I struggled desperately to force the words past the lump in my throat. I couldn't stop the tears welling.

"What about Jenny? My sister? My dad said I must take care of her. I can't leave her." I stared at my feet.

"I... I'm sooo ss... ooo... ry," I stuttered, drowning in wretched remorse, then surfacing to burn in the blistering flames of desire. "You are wonderful people and your offer is so kind. I would give anything to live here permanently. But...," I broke off with a pleading look, uncertain precisely what it was I begged for. I didn't really expect them to take Jenny too, but I couldn't leave her.

Mr and Mrs Bennett considered me for a moment, then turned to silently converse with each other. When they spoke, it was in unison, and neither looked even mildly surprised.

"I suppose there is no reason why we couldn't take Jennifer too, if she is happy to come."

I wanted to scream with delight. I wanted to whoop and cheer and hug everyone, and run up and down the street shouting to everyone who would listen. I wanted to run all the way back to St Patrick's to tell my sister and the nuns and Father Joseph. But the parlour mat held my feet firmly and would not release them, and the Bennetts' kind gaze held my eyes. When I tried to speak, the words stuck in my throat and only soft sob–like sounds escaped.

Mrs Bennett seemed to understand. She moved slowly towards me, wrapped her arms about me, kissed the top of my head, and muttered "Welcome to our family, son".

Mr Bennett warned her not to get 'all soppy now'. "He's a boy, love. You know how boys are about women carrying on all emotional like." He grinned at me. "Now don't go thinkin' jes' because yer one o' the family now yer can git cheeky. I'll clip your ear if you misbehave, lad. Make no mistake about that." He ruffled my hair affectionately. "An' you'll be expected ta' pull ya' weight around here. There's plenty o' chores ta' be done."

"Of course, sir," I said.

"An' none o' that 'sir' business, please. I ain't no 'sir'! Jes plain ol' Jim'll do."

"Oh no, sir. I mean, Mr Bennett. I could never call you by your first name. That's disrespectful."

"Hmmm. Then I guess it'll hafta be 'dad' or 'pop'. What d'ya reckon?"

I thought for a moment. Mr Bennett was nothing like my dad, but then, if I was to be their son, why not? I would sure like to call Mrs Bennett 'Mum'.

"That's settled then, I guess," said Mrs Bennett. "Next week we'll go to see the Mother Superior and make the arrangements, and bring Jenny home."

The following Tuesday, James and Marion Bennett went to see the Mother Superior, and they brought Jenny back. For three glorious weeks, Jen and I were part of a wonderful, loving family. She and I could talk and hug, and I could protect her the way I'd promised my father I would. We were inseparable, and our joy at being together surpassed even our delight at being part of a real family. Everything was a wonder to us. Our eyes sparkled and our cheeks shone.

I was nervous and hesitant at first, terrified of displeasing, but as the days passed I relaxed. Eventually, Jenny and I even dared to join in the Bennett children's innocent little acts of mischief.

#

An icy chill tiptoed down my spine when I spotted a sleek black sedan parked in front of the house one Monday morning.

I crept inside.

The lounge room door was closed. I pressed my ear to the keyhole. My face burnt with guilt, and I trembled in fear of detection — fear of what I might hear.

Mrs Bennett's voice was soft and muffled, but the man, when he spoke, was loud and forceful. I had an uneasy sense that the harsh voice was familiar.

"Mr and Mrs Wilson will not consent to either permanent fostering or adoption. I'm sorry, Mrs Bennett. There is nothing further I can do. Under law, they have the right to refuse."

There was a muffled reply, then the man's voice came again. "I can wait while you pack the children's things."

I stepped back behind the door of the adjacent room to avoid being caught eavesdropping. Mrs Bennett and the man stepped out and moved towards the front door. Mrs Bennett's eyes were red and she was dabbing at them with a lace–trimmed hanky. The man was fat, with ruddy cheeks and a thick neck. He wore a fancy suit and tie and he didn't seem at all distressed or sympathetic.

"Thank you, Mr Simms..."

Simms!

Fear and hatred hurtled down the hallway and enveloped me, binding my limbs and freezing my tongue and causing my heart to thunder. My legs threatened to give way.

I missed hearing the end of Mrs Bennett's softly spoken sentence, but I heard Simms say, "Very well then. Please ensure you return the children promptly". The door closed behind him and Mrs Bennett fell against it with a soft moan. Then she composed herself and marched resolutely to my bedroom. I followed her and dared to ask why that man had come, but the pain etched on my face told her I already knew.

11: A FARM HOLIDAY

MOREE, MAY, 1960

In May, 1960, school closed for a ten day break before the start of the mid school term. I was called to the Mother's office to be told I had again been selected to go on a holiday.

"A farmer from Moree has asked to take you," said the Mother. "He's taking John Sanders too. You are very lucky, you know? I hope you will behave yourself. You must be very polite and obedient."

"Yes, Mother," I replied dutifully, suppressing excitement at the prospect of a week on a farm, away from the boredom of the orphanage.

"You will be expected to help on the farm and around the house. You must do your share of the work willingly."

"Yes, Mother."

Farm chores will be a joy.

Church families regularly took home kids for holidays, and we looked forward to a break from the monotonous routine and the nuns' cruelty. Most of the families were kind, like the Bennetts. We were well fed during those breaks and enjoyed more freedom to run and play. Sometimes, they would take us swimming and to movies and on Sunday family picnics. We were often used as cheap labour, especially by farmers, but we never really minded that.

Jenny went often with the same childless couple. They spoilt and pampered her. They adored her and she them. I was always pleased to see them arrive to collect her and deeply saddened when they brought her back.

I didn't get to go often. Perhaps because of the privileges I enjoyed as a footie player, the Mother sought to deprive me of most other treats. She claimed I was defiant and she disliked me for it, claiming she could not send me to a decent family until I learnt respect for my elders. It would be unfair to kind people to leave them to cope with my disobedience and insolence. True, I lacked respect for the black–clad witches who prayed daily and claimed a love of God, yet treated little children so cruelly. I might have allowed that lack of respect to show, but Mr and Mrs Bennett would have said I was a good kid—polite, obedient, respectful, and always willing to help. Father

Joseph treated me with respect and I reciprocated. I was insolent and defiant only when abused. On a farm, I would work hard and try my hardest to earn a repeat invitation. I didn't show it, but I was wildly excited.

Mr Jackson arrived mid–morning on a Saturday, driving a dusty, white Holden ute. He tossed two battered suitcases into the back, ran a rope through the handles and tied it to the side rail to secure them. He greeted John and I with a grin and a slight tip of his battered broadbrim hat. He was stocky, rugged, fair-complexioned but well sun–tanned, with huge, expressive, green eyes.

John sat in the middle of the single–bench seat, so I had the benefit of a clear side view and a fresh autumn breeze when I chose to lower the window. Mr Jackson had little to say on the four–hour drive, except to occasionally point to a landmark, or to remark on the condition of grazing stock, grassed paddocks or shallow dams. He told us he ran a wheat farm and he would teach us to drive a tractor and milk cows. He asked how we liked school.

"I've heard you're pretty good at football, Paul. I wasn't too bad myself in my schooldays," he said.

He said Mrs Jackson was a very good cook and she was looking forward to having two strapping young lads to appreciate her talent.

"You'll need plenty of sustenance," he added, "because there are always plenty of heavy chores to be done on the farm and in the house. I hope you'll be willing to help out when needed."

We dutifully confirmed our intention to give our best efforts to whatever chore was allocated, and nodded solemnly when asked if the Mother had warned us to be obedient and polite.

"I can be a harsh disciplinarian when required," he cautioned. "I won't hesitate to punish you if you step out of line, but I do hope I won't need to."

We hoped he wouldn't need to also. I didn't plan on doing anything to anger him, but as yet his expectations were something of a mystery and there could be no certainty we would be able to live up to them. That was the trouble with going off with strangers. It was easy to displease when one didn't know what their rules were, no matter how hard one might try to be good.

It wasn't punishment I feared. I was quite accustomed to savage beatings and it was unlikely Mr Jackson would inflict more pain than the magpie with her scrubbing brush or the Mother with her wide belt, but I wanted to please; to be liked and admired. Again, briefly, I would lose the label 'filthy urchin' and be just an ordinary kid, helping out in the paddocks during the day and enjoying the warmth of a real family in the evening and a woman's tender 'goodnight' at bedtime.

The farm house was a rambling 50–year–old weatherboard structure. Wide verandas on three sides were covered with a slightly rusting bull–nose iron roof angling off a pyramid hip that rose to a sharp point in the centre. A weather vane decorated with a rooster rotated above the peak. Timber double–hung windows were pushed up high and here and there a pair of French doors was anchored fully open to catch the afternoon breezes. The timber floors were faded from frequent scrubbing and the walls were lined with wide boards that probably were once white, but had yellowed with age and were liberally littered with grubby stains, chips and scratches.

The homestead had a homey feel, and we were welcomed with a huge hug, a plate of hot scones with strawberry jam and two tall glasses of fresh milk. I liked Mrs Jackson, and was sure I was going to love it here. I promised myself I would try very hard to be good enough to be asked back again.

Mr Jackson brought the suitcases in and led the way to a sleep–out on the end of the back veranda. There were two steel–framed beds with green chenille spreads and a single small wardrobe opposite, with a small mirror set into the door and six drawers in the lower part of the left side. A shelf ran the full width of the room — above the bedheads — laden with books, matchbox cars and a little bag of marbles. A cricket bat leant against the side of the wardrobe. I couldn't see a ball anywhere, but surely there must be one. I imagined Mr Jackson bowling to us in the twilight, after tea, and urging me to aim carefully and strike it hard, then run fast.

Ordered to unpack, we dutifully arranged clothing in the drawers and pushed empty cases under beds. We washed carefully in the tiny bathroom at the other end of the veranda, after relieving ourselves in a smelly outhouse where a tin can rested under a broad wooden bench with a lift–up flap in the middle. A cold metal toilet seat partly covered a hole that exposed a swarm of blowflies feasting on big brown turds floating in thick, yellow–brown sludge. It reminded me of home. The flushing toilets at the orphanage were a luxury few country people were familiar with.

The Jacksons had a girl living with them — not their own child. Fostered, adopted, or perhaps a relative's child? She was about 14. It appeared she was expected to do a great deal of the housework. I didn't know if she went to school, but I never saw her read or write while I was there and she never joined in conversations. In fact, she rarely spoke, and always in monosyllables. When she was spoken to, it was always a barked order or a vicious criticism of her work. She was wan, emaciated, haunted, but promised prettiness if nourished.

Mrs Jackson served a delicious tea of hot corned beef slices with white onion sauce, mashed potato, boiled pumpkin and carrots and tender green beans. Afterward, there were juicy peach halves coated in thick, yellow, home–made custard.

"Be sure to drink all your milk, boys," Mrs Jackson said with a smile. "You'll need lots of energy tomorrow. Make sure you wash well and dress in your best clothes for church in the morning."

After dinner, we sprawled on a rug in her living room reading boys' adventure stories while Mr Jackson reclined in a leather armchair and snored and she sat on an upright dining chair with a canvas–covered box beside her, carefully working an embroidery sampler. It was the perfect happy family scene, except that I had no idea where the girl had gone and it seemed odd she was excluded.

At eight–thirty, Mrs Jackson lifted her eyes from her work, smiled gently and said, "Bedtime, boys. Put the books away now please." We obediently returned the books to the lower shelf of the bookcase in the far corner, chorused "Goodnight, Mrs Jackson. Goodnight, Mr Jackson," and walked sedately from the house, breaking into a run as we stepped off the veranda to race each other to the outhouse. Minutes later, freshly washed faces ruddy, we smiled up at Mrs Jackson as she tucked the bedding in around us, kissed her fingers, and pressed them gently on our foreheads, whispering a soft "Sweet dreams, boys. Sleep well". A warm glow enfolded me as I heard her tiptoe from the room. I had to remind myself firmly that this was only a short holiday. I had suffered one bitter disappointment, and I must never set myself up for another.

On Sunday we rose early and were greeted by the smell of salty bacon frying. We washed and dressed and slicked our hair in place, then made the beds up neatly, placed folded pyjamas under the pillow and pulled the bedspread up carefully to cover it all. I walked to the kitchen, greeting my hosts with a polite "Good morning, Mr and Mrs Jackson" before taking my place at the already laid–out table. We feasted on bacon, eggs, home–grown tomatoes, thick toast and fresh milk, before dutifully marching off to clean teeth and comb hair again and wait at the front door. A maroon FC Holden sedan, adorned with chrome strips and spats, and with four smocked white–satin cushions lining the back parcel shelf, pulled up near the door. We climbed into the back seat. The girl didn't join us for breakfast and didn't accompany us, but we noticed her working in the kitchen as we left the house.

Mrs Jackson took a few minutes to emerge, dressed in her floral Sunday dress, stockings, heels and a wide–brimmed pink hat with a bunch of roses on the left side. She eased herself into the front seat and the sedan cruised down the gravel driveway and out on to a dusty dirt road. Mile after mile of seemingly endless wheat paddocks flew by before the start of the tarred road. We turned left, then right, and pulled into a grassed parking area beside a quaint little weatherboard church, devoid of stained–glass windows and without any steeple, but with a small wooden cross fixed to the front of the gable peak, and a sign that read 'St Matthew's Catholic Church' fixed above the arched double front door.

Mrs Jackson proudly introduced 'her boys' to a dozen families whose names I had no hope of remembering, then instructed us to bow to the cross and take places in a pew beside her. The organist was playing "Nearer My God to Thee". As the congregation rose, gathered up their hymn books and began to sing, the priest and two robed altar boys appeared at the back door and began their short procession down the centre aisle.

Mrs Jackson had a sweet singing voice, but Mr Jackson only mouthed the words while staring silently at the hymn book. I tried hard to get the words of the hymns and prayers right, repeat the Creed correctly, and sit still and silent through the long sermon. I waited until most of the crowd had made their exit before genuflecting to the altar, tiptoeing down the aisle, shaking hands with the priest and mouthing a polite "Good morning, Father. Thank you for your sermon," then retreating to the scant shade of a gum tree to stand silently waiting for my hosts.

"You behaved very well in church, boys," Mr Jackson said. My cheeks glowed.

"Oh yes!" Mrs Jackson agreed. "I was proud to sit beside such well–behaved young lads."

When we returned to the homestead, she rewarded us with thickly sliced lamb roast coated with mint sauce and gravy, served with a generous assortment of baked vegetables and followed by stewed apple and creamy rice pudding. I was sure I'd died and gone to heaven. Nothing could be more perfect. I prayed silently that the Lord might somehow make this last for ever.

It lasted just another hour.

Mrs Jackson asked us to retire to our room and read quietly. Sunday afternoons were a time of rest and quiet. We were pleased of the opportunity and delighted to find some interesting boys' adventure stories on the shelf above my bed. I slipped out of my Sunday clothes and hung them carefully in the wardrobe. Leaving just my singlet to cover my chest, I pulled on a pair of shorts and lay on my belly on the bed, a book open on the pillow.

I hadn't finished the first chapter when the awful noises started in the room next–door. I felt the colour drain from my face. John was trembling. The Jacksons' room was at the other end of the house, but it was Mr Jackson's resonant voice we heard through the thin wall and the girl's pained whimpering and begging to please stop. We could only imagine what she was suffering and what Jackson might be doing to cause her distress.

I crawled up on to John's bed beside him. We huddled there for a seemingly interminable time, listening to the creaking of bed springs and Mr Jackson's pig–like grunts and deep, satisfied sighs. The occasional sharp slapping sound was followed by the girl's muffled scream and his coarse, sadistic chuckle.

The girl must have done something to greatly displease, because we heard a cat–like wail and Mr Jackson muttered some vile expletives. John gasped in horror at the language, bumping hard against the wall.

We froze.

The doorhandle turned and the door creaked. Mr Jackson entered the room. He was dressed only in a sweat–soaked singlet and boxer shorts, with a revealing wet patch on the front.

He found us, scarlet–faced, trying to clamber down from John's bed. The flame of rage rose in his bull neck and his lips tightened. His eyes glazed over. Fear followed him into the room and wrapped itself around us, paralysing our limbs and tightening our throats so that, even had we dared, we could not speak.

Jackson spoke savagely. "You filthy, perverted boys. How dare you eavesdrop on people's private conversations?" Flame shot from his mouth and swords from his eyes as we cowered and pressed against the side of the bed for protection.

"You will say nothing of this to anyone, you hear me?" he warned. "If you dare to speak of what you think you heard, I will beat you to within an inch of your life and you will be branded filthy, perverted liars and sent to an institution for bad boys. You will live in a tiny cell with bars on the window and door and you will be allowed out only to be beaten and worked half to death. Do you hear me now?"

I nodded silently.

"You would do well to remember you are guests in my house, and guests do not eavesdrop on their hosts' private conversations. They mind their own business. So, I will have to give you both a lesson in good manners. I warned you I could be a harsh disciplinarian, didn't I?"

I tried to say "Yes, sir," but my vocal chords refused co–operation. John just nodded and hugged his knees tighter.

"You do not ever speak to that girl. Do you understand me? Never!"

I managed a wimpish "Yes, sir," John nodded vigorously.

He left us to suffer the awful deep–in–the–pit–of–the–stomach gnawing produced by guilt, shame and anticipation of punishment, but in the evening he and his wife were again model hosts and the girl went about her work as if nothing untoward had happened. If Mrs Jackson was aware of her husband's transgressions — whatever, specifically, they may be — she gave no sign.

In the morning, we were wakened early to a hearty breakfast. We were each handed a lunch pack and ordered into Mr Jackson's utility. He drove to one of the lower paddocks.

I learnt to drive a tractor that holiday and spent endless hours driving around and around, eyes fixed on the edge of the last furrow, holding a perfectly straight path. Twelve hours a day John and I worked, for most of the day under a fierce, blazing sun — ploughing, chopping wood, digging, milking, and picking. Twenty minutes for a rest and a drink of water at 11 and three and 40 minutes for lunch of lukewarm, soggy sandwiches that would have been appetising if fresh. If Jackson caught one of us pausing to catch a breath, or if we made some inadvertent error in the performance of a task, he accused us of slacking off and declared a lesson in diligence was called for. Like the promised lesson in manners — which we eventually received early Monday morning — all our lessons were delivered with a stockwhip. And judging by the cuts and welts on her legs, we assumed the girl received plenty of similar instruction.

Sitting on a tractor with burning thighs and behind was an agony beyond description. It was a blessed relief to be assigned, for a short while; to a chore I could perform standing. In the evenings, I spent as much time as possible lying on my belly. I winced when I took my seat for evening meals and I felt Mrs Jackson watching me, but neither her words nor her expression exposed her thoughts. She went about her business quietly, never disagreeing with her husband or contradicting him, rarely daring to initiate a conversation.

The following Sunday, we heard the sounds again. We crept up on to John's bed to listen for a time, but long before the grunting and sighing ceased John took care to smooth his bed. When Mr Jackson entered, he found us crouched on the floor between the beds, deeply engrossed in a game of marbles. We were dressed for the trip home by then and our cases were packed and standing near the door. Within the hour we were on a train, rumbling and swaying past miles of amber wheat fields and grey–grassed grazing paddocks. For the one and only time in all the years I spent at St Patrick's, I was pleased to be going back.

Despite Jackson's warnings, I told the Mother of the man's brutality and was surprised that she responded with concern and kindness.

"I know that man," she said, her voice brittle and breath coming out in ragged little puffs. "The girl may well end up wearing nun's robes. I shall ask for intervention to save the poor child. And no St Patrick's child will ever be sent to that place again."

The mind is a powerful tool, and I learnt early in life how to use it as my primary defence. I deleted the horrors of that week from my memory. They never happened. I smiled over recollections of my first tractor ride, Mrs Jackson's kindness, and her melodic voice humming in the kitchen and singing hymns on Sunday. I salivated over memories of a roast lamb dinner and corned beef with tasty onion sauce and peaches and custard dessert. I told Ben and Jimmy I'd had a great time on a huge wheat farm owned by a wealthy cocky who taught me to ride horses and milk cows, and one day I hoped to own a farm of my own. And while creating this fantasy world, I secretly plotted my escape from St Patrick's and all the fear and misery that life as an urchin encompassed.[vii]

12: RUN–A–WAY REBEL

ARMIDALE, AUGUST, 1960

"Ever thought of running away, Jim?"

"Got no place to go."

"But I have. Why should a fella stay here? I got a home to go to and I sure as hell got no reason to stay in this hole."

"How do you expect to get there?"

"There's ways. Walk. Hitchhike. It's not all that far."

"What if you get caught?"

"Dopes get caught, but so what if I did? What can they do? Those penguins don't scare me. I'm not scared of anyone."

"Sister says kids who try to run away get sent someplace else. Reform school. It's a special jail for kids."

"This is a jail, so what's the difference? Anyway, I won't get caught. Why don't ya come with me? My dad'd look after you."

"Won't go without Ben."

"So? We'll take Ben too. We'll clear out tonight after lights out. Now, get lost and don't tell nobody. I gotta work out a plan."

It was in the late winter, a few months before my 12th birthday, that I decided the only way to achieve my dream of going home was to run away. I had waited for years and suffered horribly hoping someday government men would fulfil the idle promise they made when I was nearly eight. It was clear they never would, so it seemed the only solution was to take matters into my own hands.

In the end, there were four of us. At dinner, we wrapped bread in handkerchiefs and stashed it in our pockets. I stole fruit from a case in the pantry and stowed it under a bush, to be collected on the way out. At ten o'clock that night, four small boys slipped trousers and jumpers over their pyjamas, crept to the end of the dorm, climbed on the end bed, slid over the window sill and, one by one, slid down a drainpipe to the ground below. I retrieved my bag of fruit and we made ready to begin our trek.

Before we had taken half–a–dozen steps, a loud bang upstairs stopped us. Jim had forgotten to close the window — or maybe it wasn't possible to do so while clutching a slippery pipe. We stood frozen and silent for what seemed an eternity, wondering whether to go on, turn back, or just hide. Heavy tread on the balcony above. The crisp, commanding voice of Sister Agnes ordered us back upstairs.

In the morning, four boys trailed into the huge dining room and stood obediently in a row at the back, watching the others devouring porridge and stale bread, listening to the shrill screeching of Sister Agnes lecturing, scolding, warning. The other children finished their meal, but were ordered to stand in silence. An interminable wait. Heavy steps. The Mother Superior, carrying that inevitable strap, emerged through the side door.

As ringleader, I was last to be punished. I watched as, one by one, the others were commanded to make the walk of shame to the front of the hall, turn, bend over, and receive a sound thrashing. One might have expected the Mother's strength would wane a little, for she put all she had into the task, but she somehow managed to conserve sufficient energy to beat me harder than I remembered being beaten before. It was all I could do not to yield as she taunted me and commanded me to cry. When she was done, she turned to the group.

"Be warned," she barked. "You can expect much, much worse than these foolish boys received if you even think of running away. You cannot escape. You will be caught and brought back and you will suffer dreadfully."

Then she faced me and declared in a whipping voice, loud enough to ensure all the children could hear clearly: "Well, young man. You have been warned and you have chosen to ignore the warnings. As of right now, your football–playing days are over. You will never be allowed to go with Father Joseph to a Saturday match again, or to stay for after school training."

Bile rose in my throat. My neck and ears were on fire and my head throbbed. Bruised, burning legs threatened to give way under me. But I deliberately lifted my shoulders, straightened my back, puffed out my chest and glared at her.

"But I shan't be here much longer," I muttered stubbornly under my breath, "And when I leave here, I will play football and I'll be a sporting star and I'll show you, you devil–witch. I will have my revenge."

I silently counted the months until my 12th birthday.

My decision to run away might have had something to do with the fact that I would soon be transferred elsewhere — further from my family and far away from my little sister. If the nuns had their way, I would go to St Vincent's, a boys' home in Westmead, run by priests. All the St Patrick's boys went there when they turned 12 and stayed at least until their 15th birthday. It was reputed to be much worse than St Patrick's. Boys whose older brothers had gone there spoke of it as 'hell'. They talked of awful things that went on there. They said boys went there who had committed crimes. It was a training ground for criminals and most of the boys who went there graduated to juvenile hall. Some said boys were molested by the priests. I didn't want to go there. I wanted to go home.

Boys had to be confirmed Catholic to go to St Vincent's and I had already begun confirmation classes, but I told the nuns I didn't want to be a Catholic and I wouldn't be confirmed. At first, they pleaded with me. Hadn't I served as an altar boy? Hadn't I enjoyed helping Father Joseph serve Holy Communion? Surely I didn't want to disappoint Father Joseph?

I wanted nothing more than to please Father Joseph and of course I enjoyed donning robes on Sunday mornings and helping Father serve the bread and wine. I felt quite important, robed and carrying the big gold cross, walking up the aisle at the head of the holy procession. I basked in the Father's praise at the end of the ceremony. I loved Father Joseph, but I did not want to be a Catholic. I met the nuns' questions with a stony, defiant, unqualified 'No', and kept my thoughts about the Father to myself.

They banned me from serving at the altar, and they banned me from fetching fruit for the cook. They even made me stand in the corner of the playground and watch the other boys play. And one afternoon each week they made me board the bus and go with all the other boys to confirmation classes.

I knew Father Joseph was puzzled. In his company, I was obedient, respectful, and quick to offer help with any chore. I quoted the Bible accurately, recited the catechism correctly, knew the ceremonial procedures and performed them with reverence and grace. Yet I persisted in saying that I would not be confirmed Catholic.

The nuns beat me, of course. They told me I must be a good Catholic. They said I might be thrown on to the streets to starve if I didn't take confirmation, because I wouldn't be accepted at St Vincent's. They said I'd go to hell where the devil would torture me with fire for the rest of eternity, but I wouldn't be swayed. I had no idea what alternatives might be on offer, but I would not be confirmed a Catholic. No matter how they punished me, I kept refusing.

Finally, Confirmation Day. Along with 13 other eleven–year–old boys, I dressed in Sunday best and lined up to board the bus for church. I entered St Mary's Catholic Cathedral quietly, genuflected dutifully to the cross and walked slowly up the aisle with all the others to my assigned place.

I knew the nuns were watching me anxiously as the service progressed, eyes burning into my back. A bright red shaft of light from the stained–glass window over the altar seemed to pierce my heart, and I feared that God might strike me dead for what I was about to do.

St Mary's Catholic Cathedral

I recited the Creed, kneeled to pray and sang the hymns in a high–pitched boy–soprano voice, not yet broken. When the priest asked the boys questions, I answered in chorus.

By now, the nuns will be convincing themselves I've conceded.

Fourteen boys moved forward to kneel in a line at the altar rail. I silently took my place near the far end of the line. Father Joseph moved to the top of the line and began to question each boy in turn, blessing them and asking them to confirm their faith. Each boy responded dutifully, in a hushed voice, reciting in Latin and obediently confirming his faith. Twelve times, Father took a small step sideways and repeated the blessing and questions. The 13th move placed him squarely before me, only the black of his long robes visible as I knelt before him. I felt a desperate urge to please as the Father's gentle hand descended to rest on my head. Father recited the blessing. Then the question.

"No." The sound bounced off walls and echoed through the cathedral. It was followed by an echoing chorus of long oohs and short, sharp gasps. The boy beside me poked my side. Trying to appear unruffled, the Father repeated the question.

"No, I do not," I said, in a clear firm voice, and the 'oohs' and sighs were repeated.

Father Joseph asked the question a third time.

"No," I repeated, loudly enough to be certain the entire congregation would hear.

94

A fourth time, the anxious Father asked the question. His hand pressed harder on my head. I shrugged it off and looked up to see his eyes pleading with me to reply in the affirmative. The Mother's threats echoed in my brain and my head pounded as that fellow, Determination, shouted her down and begged me to hold firm in my choice of the unknown over the hell of Westmead.

The Father was frowning now, and I quailed beneath his disapproving look and gulped hard. An icy fear snaked through my veins, but I stared resolutely at him, commanded my throat muscles to unlock and repeated in a firm, clear voice, "No". Then I rose from the kneeling cushion, nodded to the Father, genuflected to the altar, and marched down the aisle, head held high.

Predictably, the Mother called me to her office that afternoon.

"Filthy heathen," she screamed. "Evil little beggar! You have inherited the bad blood of your parents and despite our best attempts to cleanse you and teach you God's ways, you have chosen to follow them to Hell. You will burn there for all eternity and I will praise God for exacting His revenge for the pain you have caused us. But first, you shall suffer in Purgatory. You will be sent to a dreadful place where you will learn the meaning of cruelty and pain. There will be none of the privileges and pleasures you have enjoyed here. Your life there will be hell and you will reflect every day on the foolishness of your behaviour today."

I glared at her, determined to show no fear, but my blood had turned to ice and I struggled to swallow the boulder in my throat.

"Perhaps three years of suffering in Purgatory will serve to cleanse you and you will beg to be allowed to accept the Faith? Before I condemn you to an awful fate, I have a duty to try one last time to teach you God's ways."

She unbuckled her belt. I felt her iron grip on my upper arm. Then I felt the first stinging blow. My blood thawed, then boiled. I welded my teeth together and commanded my vocal chords to be still. I ordered the little voice in my head to repeat over and over, "You can't hurt me, you stupid, evil bitch. Enjoy this, because you will never beat me again".

She beat me more savagely than I had ever been beaten before. She commenced the beating in her office, but I tried to run and she followed me and beat me in the hallway. I ran to the asphalt quadrangle between the kitchen and the playground. She followed me there and made a ceremony of beating me in front of 58 pairs of watching eyes, stopping all pretence of play.

She beat me with the buckle end of her belt, and it cut my skin. She beat me until I fell to the ground, then she paused and ordered me to rise and beat me until I fell again. When, finally, I could not rise again, she thrashed and flogged, and when I curled up in a little ball to try to protect my tenderest parts from the blows, she kicked me again and again with that heavy black boot. All the while she shouted at me that I would take the Catholic faith, if she had to beat me to within an inch of my life to make me.

I would not yield.

When she was done with me, a herculean six–foot–one–inch 177 pounds of black–robed, leather–booted crone collapsed against the kitchen door huffing and snorting, her face ashen, her wimple sweat–soaked and her lips and chin sagging. The strap fell from her grip. While I lay consumed with an agony more terrible than I could ever have imagined suffering, and with a murderous rage more intense than I could ever have conceived it possible to feel, the Mother raised her hands to clutch her chest and closed her eyes.

The next day I was called to the Mother Superior's office to be advised I would be sent to an Anglican Boys' Home in a small town about an hour away.

"It is run by a man — a former army officer," the Mother said in a warning tone, "and I'm advised he does not tolerate disrespect or disobedience. He will straighten you out, young man. You'll not get away with the kind of disobedience we've had to suffer from you here. Within a day or two, you will be wishing you had taken confirmation as you were instructed, and gone to Westmead with the other boys. It was a bad choice you made and you will pay for it now and for many years to come." She clicked her tongue in disgust.

"Such a wonderful opportunity. To be taught God's ways and how to be a man by good God–fearing Brothers. To be cared for by men like Father Joseph. You loved him, didn't you? And you let him down so badly, you ungrateful little beggar. You could have been among men like him, but no, you chose to live life as a heathen. Now you will experience hell, and may it be every bit as dreadful as we have taught you to expect. You deserve to rot in hell for the rest of your days, and so you shall. I shall praise the good Lord for exacting the appropriate revenge on you for your ingratitude to those who have shown you such kindness."

For just a moment, I felt a pang of remorse. Perhaps, after all, I ought to have taken confirmation and gone away with my 'brothers'. The Mother's words sent a shiver through me, but I forced myself to remember the awful things I'd been told about St Vincent's and I reminded myself of my father's advice. "Treat everything as an adventure, son."

I was about to embark on another adventure. Whatever lay ahead, I would find a way to make it bearable. I had survived St Patricks , so I would survive this new home too. I would befriend the cook or the handyman, volunteer for kitchen chores, quiz the other boys about the best ways to win favours.

I would make it bearable, and in three more years, I would be free.

13: A NEW HOME

DECEMBER, 1960

The black car came again in the early summer of 1960, just after my 12th birthday. I was to travel alone this time. No farewells were allowed. My sister knew boys didn't stay, but she was not told where I was to go. Children in the playground stopped their games to stare and wave, but were not permitted past the fence line. Had they asked, they would not have been told where I was being sent, nor permitted to maintain any contact with me. But we had all been so thoroughly conditioned that none would dare to ask, and so thoroughly desensitised that none of us knew how to care.

The black sedan rolled down the long drive, through the huge iron gate, round to the right, on to the highway, past the high school, and out of the town. Leafy liquid amber soldiers formed a guard of honour, standing smartly to attention, one every 20 feet, motionless, silent, bidding me a solemn goodbye. I shivered in the back seat, but not from cold, for the sun poured through the windows of the big sedan making it quite hot inside. A massive hand squeezed my chest until I struggled to breathe. My gut churned and my heart pounded and thumped and occasionally gave a little flutter like a moth caught in a web.

Perhaps I made the wrong decision? I might have been travelling with a group of boys my age to a Catholic boys' home far away. The nuns said it was a nice place.

But I didn't trust the nuns and I didn't want to be a Catholic.

I focused on the grassy brown paddocks littered with sheep. The occasional clump of trees stretched as far as the eye could see. Here and there, a homestead chimney peeped from behind a cluster of trees. Occasionally, I caught a glimpse of a horseman and his dog, urging sheep across a paddock, and I was reminded of my father.

Ducks danced over a large expanse of water in one paddock quite close to the road. Here and there a muddy little creek, edged in green, sliced pastures. The scenery reminded me of home and I longed to run on the sand and swing on willows and lie in the grass with Rusty licking me all over. For a little while I pretended I was going home. Fear was replaced by excitement, but I couldn't keep the fear at bay for long.

The paddocks were greener now. The trees were mostly gums, but here and there a cluster of stately green pines reached for the clouds or willows wept into a muddy dam. The black sedan crossed a grid on to a narrow dirt road, and I read the sign "Ohio Station".

A sheep station! Am I going to live here? Don't get your hopes up.

I caught sight of a big mud–brick rendered homestead, with several smaller timber outbuildings scattered around it. It was a sort of mucky yellow colour and it looked much more cheerful than the dark brick of the orphanage.

The sedan drew to a halt between the homestead and a small timber cottage with a long veranda. A woman emerged from the homestead wearing a garish floral dress. A colourful apron was tied approximately where her waist ought to have been. She wore flat, lace–up shoes and thick stockings. Her eyes sparkled and her cheeks shone and there was a welcoming warmth about her that probably ought to have eased my fears, but I had learnt to distrust even the most pleasant–looking stranger. I'd been cautioned to fear this place and those who ran it.

"Welcome to Ohio," she called. "I'm Mrs Tuck, Matron, Mum — whichever you feel comfortable calling me. My husband and I take care of all the boys here. You'll make 22 now, counting our son, Peter, who lives here with us. You'll meet him soon — when they finish their game."

She nodded towards a group of boys kicking a soccer ball about in a nearby paddock. The driver opened the rear door and summoned me. I stood there shivering, despite the summer heat. The driver set my little suitcase down beside us and handed the woman a large brown envelope. She wrote something on a page attached to a clipboard. Then the driver walked slowly around the sedan. The door slammed and the motor whirred. Gravel crunched under spinning tyres as the now dusty brown sedan slid down the long driveway and out of sight.

Still trembling, I followed the woman through a large institutional–style dining room furnished with several long tables, through into a dim hallway and up a narrow flight of stairs to another hallway that led to a large room with two neat rows of metal–framed beds.

Oh God! Those all too familiar tightly pulled covers and sharp mitred corners. Small metal cabinets separating the beds. Tiny spaces between the beds, barely wide enough to provide space to dress. Polished linoleum floors. The air rank with that acidic disinfectant odour. The smell of fear!

I was surprised to notice books resting on top of several of the personal tables. There was even a little bag of marbles on one. A single dormer window looked down over a vast green lawn that rolled past a post–and–wire fence to a tree–lined creek. Boys sat on the banks holding fishing rods, or waded in the shallows. Cows and their calves grazed serenely under smiling little summer clouds. The sun polished tree leaves and the water surface and trickled through the dormer glass to toast my chill limbs. Mrs Tuck was still smiling.

For the next three years, this will be home.

Ohio Boys' Home, Walcha NSW

Creek at Ohio Boys' Home

On my first afternoon at Ohio, Matron discarded the clothes I'd brought and issued replacements. They were hand–me–downs, but they were in fair condition and I noticed all the boys were much better dressed than the St Patrick's children. I was assigned chores and instructed when and how they must be performed. Older boys the Boss had appointed as 'corporals' took pains to ensure I understood the penalties for not completing them properly. I was pleased to be able to help. Onerous chores were part of life in an institution, but I was surprised to find the Boss and Matron thanked boys for their help and coached them gently if they struggled to do something the right way.

The corporals carefully explained the house rules to me, and the consequences of breaking them. They warned me against being late for meals and cautioned me to never think of relaxation until my chores were properly completed.

"Always speak respectfully to Boss and Matron and obey their instructions, stay out of trouble at school, and treat the other boys courteously," one of the seniors advised, adding "Clean your teeth morning and night, polish your shoes every morning and keep yourself and your section of the dorm clean and tidy." The latter caution wasn't needed. I'd had adequate training in personal hygiene and neatness.

The Matron led me to the kitchen and I sat and watched the kitchen boys prepare vegetables and the Matron cook dinner. She sang as she worked, beautiful Welsh folk songs and hymns and ballads, sung in the sweetest resonant voice. She wore a warm smile, and if any little mishap occurred she laughed a deep belly laugh that sent little waves of flesh rippling from shoulder to elbow. She talked to the boys as they worked—about school, friends, sport and the books they were reading. It surprised me that she seemed genuinely interested in whatever interested them. She invited me to tell her how I was feeling or what interested me or what food I liked, but not with direct questions that demanded response. When I didn't answer, she just smiled and said perhaps I'd feel more like talking later.

She made a tasty beef stew for dinner, with creamy bread and butter pudding to follow. I'd suffered my last cold, unappetising meal. She was an excellent cook and she relished watching the boys enjoy the food she prepared for them.

There was no 'silence at meal time' rule here, but talk was ordered. The Boss and Matron asked the boys about their day. Between courses, there were organised mind games, devised by the Boss to develop thinking skills and memory and sharpen wits. After dinner, the kitchen boys cleared the dishes and washed up, and the rest of the boys retired to the library to read or do homework or play quiet indoor games. There was a warmth about the place that contrasted sharply with the austerity of St Patrick's. The boys all seemed remarkably happy. I noticed that Boss and Matron often tousled hair or patted a shoulder affectionately and paid compliments. They said 'please' when they asked a boy to do something and thanked the boys for good behaviour. When they spoke to me, their tone was friendly.

I undressed that first evening in the boys' shower block, feeling deeply self–conscious comparing my skinny, bruised body with the solid muscled forms and clean skins of the others. I was smaller than several of the younger boys. I had a bald patch on the side of my head where I constantly pulled my hair out by the roots. My ribs stuck out. None of the others wore dark blue–black or yellowing bruises on their backs and behinds or sharp red welts edged with broken skin across their upper arms and legs.

I stepped across a long drain and on to cold, wet concrete and turned on a tap below one in an unseparated row of spraying mouths dropping from a single horizontal pipe above. After soaping myself, I turned to let a warm spray hose my back.

Mr Tuck, the man the boys referred to variously as 'the Boss' or 'Dad', ducked to enter the shower block. He towered over even the tallest of the boys and he had a certain presence, a don't–mess–with–me sternness in the set of his jaw and his steely expression. His eyes warned you he was keeping a close eye on your every move. I remembered the Mother Superior's warnings about him and cringed a little.

I started to tremble, realising the Boss was watching me closely. I was conscious of him staring at my bare backside as I turned to rinse my chest and belly. He drew breath sharply, and when I turned again the colour had drained from his face and his shoulders were slumped. He raised his hands to cover his face, and then he turned away. When he turned back, his eyes were watery and there was a wet patch on his sleeve where he had wiped his face. He struggled for a minute to compose himself, then he marched up to his own son and hugged him hard.

"Look after him like a brother," he said softly. It took a moment to realise he was referring to me.

14: WE WERE BROTHERS

WALCHA, DECEMBER, 1960

In the morning, we were wakened early. The familiar institutional routine of washing, dressing, bed making and dormitory inspections preceded an orderly march to the dining room. But the porridge was served creamy and hot and the bread toasted and served with a selection of spreads. There was no bed–wetter parade of shame either. Wet linen was quietly removed to the laundry and replaced, with neither comment nor retribution.

The homestead was set on a generous acreage donated by a wealthy grazing family and the Home was largely self–sufficient. Before school, boys milked cows, fed chickens and collected eggs, chopped and carried wood. The kitchen boys washed the dishes and packed school lunches with fresh bread, while other boys swept and mopped floors.

We lined up before school for an inspection by the 'corporals', who checked to ensure everyone was clean and presentable and had completed their chores, then we ran three miles to school. The run home was a race, because first back got the biggest slice of cake. The Matron baked fresh every day and the cakes were rich, with real cream filling and thick icing.

Even on my first day, I streaked ahead of the others. I could run! I was often first home, and the only time I wasn't among the first to the door was when a teacher kept me late in class or when there was a sporting event on after school. I'd sacrifice cake for soccer any day!

There were more chores to do after school — tending vegetable gardens, cleaning bathrooms, fetching washing off the line and folding linen — before we were allowed to play. An hour or two of play or sports practice preceded dinner, and then we were ordered to the library to do homework or read until bedtime.

On Saturdays, the boys played cricket or soccer. They had their own soccer team. They told me the Boss coached them, drove them to matches — no matter how far away — and barracked enthusiastically for them, delighting in seeing 'his boys' win. I arrived there in the summer and the soccer season didn't start 'til May. There was no cricket match that Saturday either, so the Boss passed out pocket money and drove those who wanted to go into town to the pictures. Others roamed the hills and played. It seemed the boys were allowed quite a bit of freedom.

Sunday began with a church service in the library, conducted by a visiting minister. The service was in English and I was surprised that it was fun. Afterward, the minister talked and played and I saw that all the boys loved him.

"Right, boys. Boxing shed!" the Boss called after lunch. I followed the others to a shed where a little platform was surrounded by a rope at waist height. A variety of punching bags hung from the rafters. In one corner, there was a box of gloves. Some boys donned gloves and several started pummelling the bags, while the Boss pointed to two who jumped into the ring and commenced a sparring match. The Boss called instructions, stepping up into the ring at one point to clasp a boy's wrist and guide it, advising him where to aim. I watched intently, but in silence.

Old boxing shed, as revisited in 2010

Those first weeks there, waves of panic swept over me whenever I was spoken to, when I caught someone watching me, or when there was something I was required to do. I did everything I was told. When I wasn't sure what to do, I studied the older boys and copied them. I was anal about hygiene, neatness, punctuality and chores, but during inspections, a fist tightened around my heart and threatened to rip it from me. As far as I was able, I kept well out of the Boss's way. And I never uttered a single word.

The Matron called us for afternoon tea, after which came band rehearsals. They were practising carols when I arrived. The Boss had rallied the townsfolk to help with fundraising activities and bought a supply of instruments — cornets, horns, euphoniums, trombones, tubas, cymbals, drums — and smart band uniforms. He taught all the fellas to play and they performed at Anzac Day parades, fetes and festivals. He even hired the band out sometimes and set the money paid aside to pay for special treats, like camping holidays.

The Matron gave me a cornet mouthpiece and showed me how to practise blowing into it. Another challenge! Excitement and terror battled for supremacy. I knew which I wanted to feel, but electric jolts of adrenalin shook me and then cold waves of terror froze my gut. I ripped at my hair and sought out quiet, lonely places. The other boys seemed so at ease. Perhaps that should have reassured me, but it somehow made me more afraid.

I had been there three weeks when the Matron and Boss finally called me aside and pleaded with me to talk to them.

"We're worried about you, Paul," the Matron said. "We can see you're afraid of something, but there's nothing here to be scared of. Honestly. We want you to be happy here."

The Boss called to Peter. "Take him to your room, Son," he said. "Show him your things. Make friends with him."

"Get him to speak!" the Matron said, her voice sharp and tense and her face wringing.

Pete took me into his room and showed me his stamp collection, coins and books. I was fascinated. I relaxed after a while, and eventually Pete was even able to tease me a little and I took it in good humour. He told me how things worked around the Home, which boys were good at sport and which of the boys he disliked.

"I don't dare show dislike, though," he said, "and you should be careful not to also. We have to get along with everyone here."

I told him about the cruelty at St Patrick's and the Mother's grave warnings about the Boss. It shocked him and he was quick to assure me the Mother had it all wrong.

"The Boss doesn't thrash boys for misbehaving?" I asked, incredulous.

"He'll clip your ear," Pete said, "but he'll certainly never beat you."

We were in that room for hours. The Boss and Matron listened at the door for a time, but long before I finally spoke, I heard them steal away.

You couldn't have found two more opposite kids. Peter was a burly, confident, devil–may–care teenager, afraid of nothing. I was a skinny, malnourished, frightened little boy. On that day, we became brothers.

15: A BOY FROM OHIO

DECEMBER, 1960

Christmas festivities began just days after I first spoke. The Christmas tree went up in the corner of the library, and we all helped the Boss decorate it. We hung streamers about the walls and blew up balloons and pegged dozens of Christmas cards to strings hung across the windows.

The boys staged a Christmas concert and a huge party followed to which each boy was allowed to invite one or two guests. The Matron and Boss invited lots of friends and of course the town and church dignitaries were there as guests of honor. The Ohio band played carols, and boys sang and staged little plays. Smithie, who had amazing recall, played memory games. The audience clapped, cheered and praised the boys for their talent and dedication to rehearsing. I resolved to practise really hard so I could play superbly next Christmas and hopefully they might compliment me.

The Matron baked and iced a huge Christmas cake and made a rich plum pudding with sixpences scattered through it. Each of us was allowed a small glass of sherry. Most of the boys had considerably more than their allotted rations. I felt certain Matron knew, but she just smiled at them indulgently.

I was a little embarrassed when all the boys except me presented the Matron and Boss with little gifts. Everyone received a gift from Matron. They were tokens, I guess; nothing of any value, but I was thrilled beyond words at having something to unwrap. It made me feel wanted… cared for. Loved I guess, although I wasn't confident that anyone could actually love me. The nuns had taken pains to ensure I had no illusions about being worthy of affection. After all, I had bad blood. Only grudging Christian charity had kept me from being left to starve to death.

Determined to show my appreciation for their kindness, I resolved to make sure I had money to buy gifts for the Matron and Boss next Christmas. I wanted to buy gifts for some of my 'brothers' too. I noticed that many of them exchanged presents and they bought presents for their party guests and for their teachers. They seemed to have ample funds to cover the costs of a dozen or so small items. That surprised me, for I knew the 20 cents the Boss gave each of us on Saturdays was always quickly spent.

The mystery of where funds for gift purchases came from was solved some months later, when Peter took me on my first wool hunt. The boys went out regularly on weekends with large hessian bags that they filled with dead wool and sold for almost as much as a poorly paid family man earned for a week of laboring. It was hard–earned money, but not so tough when we could find slippery, grease–caked wool fallen from the sheep's back. Mostly it had to be plucked from the rotting hides of stinking, maggot–ridden carcasses by those of us with stomachs strong enough to stand the over–ripe stench and the view of bloody half–eaten innards spilling out. Huge blowflies buzzed about our ears and lips and I had to spit and blow to stop them entering my mouth and nostrils.

Simmo earned his pay easily for a time. He snuck into the wool sheds and stole the fresh–shorn fleece from the sorting bins. It puzzled us how he was always first back home, yet had the largest hoard. We would struggle in exhausted, often burnt and blistered from too much exposure to a savage sun, but he looked as fresh as when he climbed out of bed in the mornings.

He was caught out, of course. The buyer noticed that the wool in his sack was always clean and of a high grade. A cranky cocky visited the Home one Saturday evening and asked to speak to the Boss in his office. Simmo was called in shortly after and given a right earbashing. He was banned from joining wool–hunting expeditions for a month. The cocky wanted us all banned permanently, but the Boss argued our case. He was hard on us when we erred, but he always stuck up for us with outsiders. No–one else was permitted to speak against 'his boys'.

#

"Monkey, Monkey."

I was returning from a Friday afternoon wool hunt, tired and irritated, when I heard the familiar name called with an unfamiliar accent. The tone was unmistakably one of ridicule.

Pete always called me "Monkey", but it was a term of endearment. No–one else was permitted to call me that. He would have decked anyone who dared to tease me.

Pete had gone out somewhere and he wasn't yet back. I was alone with my tormentor, so I swung around and thumped Smithie hard in the stomach. He hit back, and I struck again, this time on the side of the head.

"Break it up, fellas," a corporal shouted from across the paddock, and in minutes the Boss was striding towards us, glaring. For the first time, after a full five months at Ohio, I was in trouble.

"Boxing shed. Right now!" the Boss shouted. Contrite, but secretly a little excited, I ran to the shed and bounced up into the ring. I spent many happy hours in the shed, thumping the heavy leather punching bag and punching the speed bag and mounting the ring for friendly — and sometimes not so friendly — sparring matches.

"Gloves on," the Boss said sternly. "Give it your best, but stick to the rules and may the best man win."

Smithie was bigger than me and an experienced boxer. I fought valiantly, but I took a towelling that day and I breathed an audible sigh of relief when the Boss finally called time and pronounced Smithie the victor.

"Shake hands," the Boss ordered. I stepped forward, a little reluctantly, hand extended. My opponent shook it warmly, whispering, "Sorry, mate. Can we be friends?" I nodded. Inevitably, whoever won and however hard the punches, we always left that boxing ring good mates. After that day, Pete, Smithie and I became an inseparable trio.

It was my first serious fight and one of very few I lost. After suffering a humiliating defeat, I made a firm resolve to become expert at the sport. I practised at every opportunity and begged the Boss and the older boys to teach me every winning technique.

The Boss wasn't quite satisfied with seeing me whopped in the ring. "Starting a fight demands punishment," he declared sternly as I prepared to leave the shed, nursing a mildly bruised body and a badly bruised ego. "You'll both spend tomorrow afternoon in bed."

I stifled an urge to smile. While missing out on the pictures was mildly disappointing, bed was not an unpleasant place to be on a cold Saturday afternoon — especially as we were allowed to take a book. The Matron even brought a sweet snack up at afternoon–tea time.

#

I'd been at Ohio almost nine months before I experienced a harsh punishment, and I berated myself, afterward, for my foolishness. It was Pete's fault. I rarely got into trouble at Ohio, but when I did, it was nearly always his fault.

Pete was sent to bed early one evening as punishment for some minor misdeed. He was hungry, so he opened the door a crack and beckoned to me.

"Sneak into the kitchen and make me a sandwich," he whispered.

Stealing food was a serious offence, but I figured I owed Pete. He was my big brother and he took care of me. I crept out of the library and around the back way to the kitchen, and made a cheese and tomato sandwich, taking care to clean up thoroughly and put everything back in its place. I crept to the door of Pete's room and tapped lightly. He opened the door a crack, reached out, and I placed the sandwich in his hand. Begging my heart to stop thumping so loudly, I drew a deep breath and darted back into a corner of the library, where I grabbed a book and held it over my face, pretending to be engrossed. I'd been swift and silent, so I was quite sure I'd escaped detection, but when the Boss called my name at breakfast next morning, I knew I was gone.

"Woodheap duty. Two weeks," he said sternly. I gulped hard and stifled the urge to wail a protest. A few of the boys whispered "Ouch," and sympathetic looks assured me — in case there was any doubt — that the next 14 mornings would be extremely unpleasant.

There was no room for negotiation over retribution. Neither was there any tolerance for complaint or displays of emotion. We were expected to take punishment like men. As much as I wanted to blame Pete, I had to admit that I'd knowingly broken a significant rule. The punishment was deserved and fair, but woodheap duty was a dreaded chore. I was unfortunate to earn this penalty in the dead of winter, when the night and early morning temperatures were well below freezing, sunrise came late and slow, and frost inches thick blanketed everything.

The next morning, I rose at 4:30 — well before even the first hint of pearly dawn — and dressed quickly and as warmly as practical. I tried to run down to the woodheap, but the frost was so heavy that just walking without slipping was a challenge. I exhaled fine white jets of smoke and the cold burnt through the soles of my shoes. It reminded me a bit of washing pissy sheets at St Patrick's, where I'd slithered and slid about the paddock struggling to reach the clothes lines. It was even colder at Ohio, but chopping wood was not nearly as unpleasant as washing pissy sheets in freezing water.

I wiped the frost off the axe with a rag, set a large block on the chopping block and commenced chopping. At least the physical exertion warmed me a little, although the frosty wood burnt my fingers.

Fetch a block. Position it. Raise the axe. Take aim. Bring it down with all your strength.

Crack! The block split.

Lift the axe. Strike again.

Sometimes a weakened section would split apart and bits would fly everywhere. Occasionally, one struck my leg.

Handle the split pieces carefully. Watch out for splinters. Work faster. You have to finish this job before breakfast or you'll be in more trouble.

As the pile of chopped logs grew, I drove the axe into the chopping block, piled my arms high with wood, then walked as fast as I could without slipping into the kitchen to fill the woodbox near the stove. Then back to the woodheap to repeat the sequence.

Position the block. Raise the axe. Aim. Bring it down with all your strength. Dodge the flying timber. Fetch another block. Position, raise, aim, strike. Fetch, position, raise, aim, strike. Fetch, position, raise, aim, strike.

Gather the pieces. This time to the library to fill the box near the fireplace. And there were boxes near the lounge–room fireplace, the Boss's office, the laundry copper...

The morning wore on and the sun began its slow climb, painting the sky a soft pink, but hardly raising the temperature. My arms ached. Despite the cold, I dripped perspiration.

Finally, I was done. I would have liked to collapse into bed, but now there was bed making and morning chores to attend to. The last thing I needed was to fail morning inspection or be late for breakfast. Two weeks might quickly become four, or who knows what other awful penalty I might incur? I washed carefully, climbed the stairs hastily and set about ensuring the bed cover was perfectly straight and the corner mitres were perfect.

The Boss ruffled my hair affectionately as I entered the dining room. "Good job this morning, Paul. Thank you. Keep it up."

As if I have a choice!

"Only 13 mornings to go, eh! Bet it will be a while before you invite that punishment again?" the Boss said, chuckling. I nodded silently, telling myself firmly I had no right to feel resentful. It was harsh punishment — a far more effective deterrent to future disobedience than the most savage beating. By the time I'd completed my two–week sentence I was convinced there was some validity to the nuns' warnings about the Boss. He wasn't cruel, but he certainly commanded respect and obedience. He was also a kind and patient teacher, and fiercely protective of 'his boys'. He taught us survival skills and self–defence and cultivated a sense of pride in our abilities and achievements. I was still an orphan, living in an institution, but there were no cruel reminders. Survival was no longer a daily challenge.

But in two years' time, I have to leave the safety of Ohio. What happens to me then?

The rules of the system dictated that, while still a State ward and subject to the whims of bureaucrats, I would have no home and no–one to care.

16: BOOT BOY

NOVEMBER, 1961

"Happy Birthday to you. Happy Birthday to you. Happy Birthday, dear Paul…" The Matron emerged from the kitchen at dinnertime on my birthday wearing a radiant smile and carrying a huge chocolate cake bearing 13 brightly burning candles.

"I think the Boss has a surprise for you, Paul," Matron said, when the singing and cheering subsided. I looked questioningly at Mr Tuck.

"I've decided to make you a corporal," he said, smiling. The boys clapped and I glowed.

"And," he continued, rapping the table for silence, "I'm going to appoint you apprentice boot boy. You are going to learn to mend shoes."

I could hardly contain my joy. I was six years old again, watching Dad make whips, feeling the warm, soft leather between my fingers and asking Dad to teach me to work it, dreaming of becoming a leatherworker one day.

I'll be a bootmaker when I leave here. I'll work hard and learn well and I'll get an apprenticeship. One day, when I'm older, I'll own my own shop.

I followed the Boss to the boot shed the next afternoon, bubbling over with anticipation. My fingers itched and my nostrils were filled with that pervasive warm, raw odour of cowhide mixed with the addictive acrid smell of Cargrip glue. I remembered that smell from my toddler days.

The boot shed had been a wool–sorting shed in years gone by and the building was well–worn. The oily lanolin smell of raw wool still hung about the rafters. It was dusty, draughty and unpainted, but it had the special warmth old sheds have, or maybe it just reminded me of home. It quickly became a sanctuary — my personal cubbyhouse — a place of respite when the constant noise of more than a score of rowdy boys tired me.

Every afternoon I went down to the shed and waited patiently for the Boss to inspect the boys' shoes and send all those with holes in the soles or toes or broken heels down to me to fix. While I waited, I caressed the lasts and the big old sanding and polishing machines. I held the leather, stretched it to test its strength and moulded it over the polishing wheel to test its malleability. I stroked it to feel the slight roughness and contrast it with the plastic smoothness of the rubber used for patching. Running my hand over the huge old rustic bench, smoothed by years of wear, I admired the way the tools were all laid out in perfect order: skiving knives, hammers, stitcher, pullers, and tubes of glue. Everything at the ready for a quick, efficient repair job.

I learnt quickly how to cut rubber pieces from old car tyres to repair soles and how to tack loose heels firmly in place. A warm, satisfied glow crept up from deep inside me when I applied the final polish to a now–strong new shoe.

"Show me the join line," I challenged the owner of a shoe after applying a new half–sole. Often even I could scarcely tell that a mended boot was not brand new.

I loved the feel of the leather. Like my dad, I had a talent for working it.

"My dad was good at leatherwork," I told the Boss. "He made whips."

The Boss smiled and patted my shoulder.

"I'm going to be a bootmaker when I grow up, and make shoes and whips and fancy belts and wallets. I might even own my own shop."

"You could do all right, too," the Boss replied, "There's never any shortage of work for a good leatherworker."

My father was an innovator too. A Mr Fixit. Like most battlers in the bush, he could improvise to manufacture all kinds of tools and devices, mend mechanical instruments, fix cars and tractors and construct kitchen and cleaning aids. I guess I'd learnt a bit from watching him. I'd always enjoyed fixing things. I'd been given a broken toy boat once that I took carefully apart and examined, then fixed with a spring removed from a biro. I was ecstatic when the fix worked.

While working in the boot shed, I realised I, too, had a talent for inventing. After repairing only a dozen or so boots, I started to envisage ways to modify the tools to make the work easier. Over the years I was there, I crafted several new tools of my own design and made modifications to the equipment. The shed became a place to unleash my creativity and I delighted in the feeling of achievement when I left each day after working with the tools I'd created to proudly rebuild, repaint and repolish to make old boots new.

I had been boot boy for seven months when the winter sport season began. I was finding it hard to focus on my afternoon chore, because sport was still my first love. We played soccer at Ohio, not the Rugby League I had played while at St Patrick's . Our team was the only one in the district to go through a season undefeated. I played inside right.

Skive… glue… tack… shape… buff. As I worked, one wintery afternoon, my mind wandered to replay the moves that had won us last Saturday's game. I had missed a kick. It didn't happen often, and I was furious with myself. It was the boot, though. So awkward and unresponsive. So uncomfortable. If only…

The next afternoon, I took a soccer boot to the shed. I examined its shape and felt the leather, comparing its feel with the different types of rubber and leather scattered on the benches. I pondered the merit of various changes in the shape. That night, I dreamt of crafting a new style of boot — one that was more flexible and comfortable, more responsive to kick with. In the morning, I confirmed my ambition. I would be an inventor. I would design a new kind of soccer boot.

Every day, as I hammered, pulled, polished and buffed, I imagined myself crafting that new–style boot. I heard the expressions of gratitude of the players as they marched triumphantly from the field after winning their first match wearing it. I dreamed about it constantly when training or playing, and when working in the boot shop. I sketched designs. I tested the malleability of leathers. It became almost an obsession, and for the first time since Simms destroyed my world, I felt confident of my future. I had ambition. I had plans and a way forward — a life to look forward to.

I had a way to leave my miserable past behind and be someone. An entrepreneur. An inventor. A craftsman. Independent and free.

Working in Ohio Bootshop, circa 1962

17: NOWHERE TO RUN

SEPTEMBER, 1962

In the spring of my second year at Ohio I befriended a newcomer who talked constantly about home and family. I began, again, to think about my parents and brothers. I wanted to see them again and to know why they had never come for me — to be part of a normal family and not a 'home boy'. They were kind to me at Ohio. I loved the Matron and Boss. I called the Matron 'Mum', but she wasn't really. I wanted my own mum and to live in a normal family home and not an institution. I decided to run away with Bluey Jackson and go home.

Bluey claimed to plan and map our escape carefully. We set out very early one Saturday morning, two fit, eager lads who feared almost nothing, but poorly equipped. We had scrounged only a few pieces of fruit and packed a jumper and a single change of underclothing.

With the September sun high in a clear sky, broken only by the occasional filmy streak of white cloud, we climbed grassy hills and crossed cool, trickling creeks. Over one fence, squeeze between the wires of another to avoid snagging on the barb on top. A huge black bull appeared from behind a clump of trees and thundered towards us, head down, menacing horns aimed directly at our chests. We ran to the fence, scrambled over, and fell panting on the grass on the other side. Rolling, laughing, making faces at the bull restrained by the tight wire, bellowing to announce our presence. There was nobody to hear.

We gathered up our scant belongings and walked on. Miles of grassy hills. Miles of sameness.

"Are we going in the right direction? How many days will it take? How far is it, exactly?"

Bluey Jackson had no idea, but he was getting very tired. "Perhaps we should rest a while?" he suggested tentatively.

We shared an apple and sipped from a water flask. We sat a while, resting our backs against a tall tree, enjoying its shade. The sun was rising higher. Mid–morning? Eleven, perhaps?

Bluey took off a shoe and sock to examine an angry blister on his heel. His feet were hurting real bad.

"How far do you think we've walked?"

"No idea," I replied. "Maybe five miles? How far is it?"

"Not sure. Maybe 10 miles? Maybe 20? Maybe 50? I know it took a couple of hours to drive from there."

"Do you even know where 'there' is?"

"I know it's north. It was afternoon when I came and the sun was on our right."

"But you don't really know the way," I said, my tone mildly accusing.

"Well… not exactly, but… you know… enough. I can find it. I know I can find it."

"If your blistered feet will carry you far enough."

"Do you want to go back?" A hint of hopefulness, relief at my seeming reluctance to go on. Neither of us wanted to be the first to admit defeat.

"Maybe," I replied. "Do you? I'm not sure this was such a good idea."

"We haven't exactly given it much of a shot, you know. It's still early. We haven't even spent a night out in the open yet.

"It will be very cold out here tonight."

"Yeah, but we'll get in awful trouble."

Just then, a car came into view on the lonely dirt road. It announced itself with a huge cloud of dust and the faint roar of an engine, and as it came closer, with the crunching sound of gravel under its wheels. Bluey jumped up immediately, ran to the edge of the road and held up his thumb.

"Come on, Paul. Quickly!" he yelled. "We'll get a lift." The farmer pulled over obligingly and leant across to ask where we were headed.

"Guyra," Bluey replied without hesitation, and to my surprise the farmer nodded and invited us to jump in.

"Lucky coincidence," the driver said. "Just exactly where I'm going."

He drove on while Bluey and I grinned at each other in silent delight. We couldn't believe our luck, but a few miles down the road, without uttering a word, the farmer turned a corner. The engine hummed and the gravel crackled. The trees and cottages I saw through the rear window became increasingly familiar. I bit my lip, recognising the direction we were headed. My gaze shifted from the scenery to focus hard on the farmer's hairy tanned arms, firmly set shoulders and the oversized work–hardened hands that gripped the wheel. They looked just like my dad's.

Recalling the savage beating and the punishing deprivation following my last run–away attempt, I ventured a peek at Bluey.

What's he thinking?

He had turned pale and was gnawing at his fingernails.

The farmer skirted around the back of the Ohio property and came down through a rear paddock to stop about 50 yards from the homestead. My stomach was mincing and churning that apple now, hurling its scant contents about, forcing burning bile up my throat. The other boys were all lined up in front of the old homestead, waiting. It was Saturday afternoon. At about this time, they usually piled into the Boss's beat–up Kombi and bumped down the gravel drive and into town to the pictures — cowboy shoot 'em ups; Smiley and Davey Crockett movies. The Boss gave us all two bob to buy ice creams or chocolate bars or Caramel Columbines at interval. Columbines were my favourite. I would suck them very slowly, making them last and last so that my pockets were still full when the movie was over and I had plenty to suck on through the week.

Movie afternoons were the highlight of the week, except in soccer season.

I wonder how long it will be before I'm allowed to go to a Saturday movie again? Or to play soccer.

"There you go, fellas. Home safely," the farmer said, turning to smile knowingly at us as he stopped a few yards from where the Boss stood. "Out you hop now."

Bluey and I shot nervous glances at each other. The Boss was standing in front of the Kombi, glaring in our direction. The other boys stood to attention, deathly silent, solemn faced, waiting to watch an execution.

"So, the runaways return, eh?" The Boss waved his thanks to the farmer and the car drove off. Bluey and I stood a few feet from the executioner now, heads bowed, silent.

"Get up to your rooms, both of you. I'll deal with you two later." His ominous tone raised a lump in my throat. My belly was somersaulting.

"The rest of you, in the van. Let's get you to the pictures before you miss any more of the action."

A dozen lads relaxed and scrambled for positions in the old Kombi. The Boss climbed into the driver seat, as Bluey and I marched into the homestead and up the stairs, solemn–faced and silent.

I sat on my bed, staring at the floor, listening to the silence of the huge empty homestead. No rowdy boys jostling and fighting. No singing or music practice. I wished I was at the pictures eating Columbines or in the boxing shed, pummelling. I wished I was playing soccer or in the boot shop, working.

I wished I was anywhere but here.

My stomach rumbled. I'd only had one apple since breakfast, and I was thirsty. My mouth was dry with fear.

How much longer before the Boss will return? What will he do to me? Woodheap duty?

Once was quite enough.

Will he beat me?

I remembered, again, the beating the Mother Superior had handed out when I tried to run away from the orphanage. I remembered the Mother Superior warning me her beatings would seem like a gentle pat compared to what the man at this Boys' Home would deal out. That man would pull me into line. That man would make me behave. I shivered a little, and tried to think happier thoughts. I'd been here quite a while, and so far I had never known the Boss to beat anyone.

There was one time Matron wanted him to give little Snowy Weston a hiding. Snowy had been giving her cheek and, after several warnings, she lost her temper. It shocked all the boys. The Matron wasn't known to lose patience often. She stormed into the library and informed the Boss Snowy Weston needed a lesson in manners and asked would he please take him to the office and administer a thrashing. The Boss put down his newspaper, commanded Snowy to follow him, and strode off to the office.

Five of us followed, keeping a safe distance behind and glancing about nervously to be sure we weren't seen. We huddled in the hallway, just out of sight of the Matron, who stood by the closed office door with her arms folded, frowning. Muffled voices, then a sharp slapping sound. Once, twice, three, four, five, six times. After each came a shrill cry. Then there was the sound of sobbing. We stared at each other, shocked, disbelieving. The Matron gave a satisfied 'Hrrrrmmmph', unfolded her arms, and strode off to the kitchen. Snowy emerged, red–eyed, and I scrambled back to the library before the Boss came striding back to his chair to resume his reading, looking quite pleased with himself.

Later that night, Snowy Weston confided that the Boss had instructed him to cry out loudly and to rub his eyes to make them water and turn red. Then he had proceeded to take off his belt and hit the floor at Snowy's feet six times. He warned him that next time he might not get off so lightly, but he ruffled his hair affectionately as he sent him off to apologise to Matron.

The Boss clipped my ear once. That was an incident I would never forget. I'd never forgiven Thommo, who ought really to have been the one to be chastised.

The kitchen boys packed the school lunches in a big Arnott's biscuit tin—one of those lovely old tins with big colourful parrots on the sides and lid. I wished desperately they would pack our lunches in individual packs. We had to line up at lunch and one boy would hold the open tin out and we would reach in and take out two sandwiches each. It marked us as home kids.

Thommo was holding the biscuit tin one day and he was being a smart arse. He kept pulling the tin away when anyone tried to put their hand in. I saw him doing it, so when it came to my turn, I grabbed the side of the tin and pulled it. Thommo lost his balance and rocked a little, struggling to keep a grip on the tin. It wobbled, and a couple of sandwiches spilled out on the ground.

That afternoon, he squealed to the Boss. We had just come in from school and were in the kitchen, panting after our usual three–mile run home. Matron was handing out fresh scones. Thommo put the empty biscuit tin on the sideboard and turned to the Boss and said, "Some of the boys missed out on lunch today. Wilso' was stuffin' about an' grabbed the tin and some of the sangas fell on the ground".

The Boss strode across to where I stood, raised his arm, and swiped hard across the back of my left ear. It stung like hell, but it wasn't the pain that upset me. The Boss was angry with me. I didn't deserve it, but there was no point in trying to tell the Boss. I would deal with Thommo later. I just stood there smarting and glaring at Thommo, wishing Matron wasn't there to hear and see, wondering how long it would be before I could redeem myself and how I might do it.

I hadn't felt like that since the last time Dad punished me. I ached, burnt and seethed with rage when the nuns belted me, but I never once felt remorse for anything I'd done, nor distress that one of them was angry with me. I hated them with every fibre of my body. I didn't want them to like me. I didn't want their approval.

This was different. It upset me to think the Boss might disapprove of my behaviour. The thought of disappointing the Matron disturbed me deeply. Their opinion of me mattered, although it surprised me a little to have to acknowledge that. I hated to have the Matron and Boss angry with me. As much as I feared punishment, I would rather suffer a thousand beatings or a year of woodheap duty than suffer the Matron's disapproval. I sat on the bed, deeply regretting my foolishness, asking myself how I could have let myself be influenced by Bluey.

Bluey was a new kid. He knew nothing about this place. Sure, the chores were onerous, and the rules were strict, but the food was really good. The Boss was never cruel, and we had plenty of time to play.

The Boss taught me to box and to play the cornet. Once, he piled us and all our gear into the Kombi and took us to Pottsville Beach for a camping holiday. There was a festival on in the next town. Smithie and I stood on lifeguard towers and played "Blue Bells of Scotland" in rounds. The Boss and Matron said we were really talented and boasted to everyone how proud they were of us.

In the evenings, I sometimes stood for hours in the pottery shed watching the Matron's big, strong hands caressing lumps of clay to craft beautiful pots that she sold to buy us Christmas gifts. The big wheel hummed and her fingers pulled and pinched and grooved. Muddy water spewed out to spatter my arms and legs and the shed floor. The rich, earthy, mineral smell filling my nostrils warmed and comforted. Blobs slowly took shape as bowls, plates, urns, vases. As her loving hands shaped the clay, her questions and stories, gentle voice and caring glances shaped my personality, my view of myself and the world. She made me feel loved and worthy.

She would talk to me for hours about my schoolwork and sport and the books I was reading. She told me fascinating stories about her youth in London during the war, working as a cryptographer for the army, decoding secret messages, and about the bombings and the air raids. She told me of the horrors the Boss witnessed on the battlefields, watching whole families mowed down by bombs in the streets of London. She talked of how — although that hardened him — it did not prepare him adequately for the shock of seeing an abused, terrified child present with the bruises and welts and broken skin I displayed on my arrival at Ohio. She said the day of my first shower there was the only time she ever saw him cry.

She told me about the day she first visited Ohio and saw how cruelly the boys there were treated, and decided, then and there, the Lord had called her to come and show these boys love and kindness.

Her title was Matron, but the boys mostly called her Mum. I resisted for a time and she never pressured. She was happy to be called 'Matron' or 'Mrs Tuck' if it was more comfortable. She understood most of us had mums, and she could never replace our mothers in our hearts. But somehow, after a while, it just felt right to call her Mum. She was everything I expected a mother should be.

Bluey didn't appreciate this place yet. Maybe he never would. He hadn't experienced the horror of St Patrick's. He didn't know what this place was like before the Matron and Boss came here either. Some of the other boys had told me about the minister who ran the place before. They said he connected wires to the penises of bed–wetters and gave them mild electric shocks. They said he forced boys to rake the long gravel driveway with shackles on their wrists and ankles. Some said he forced boys to climb the windmill tower and then he shot at the windmill blades while the boys stood rigid in fear, desperately hoping his aim was good. Those boys had good reason to run away.

Footsteps on the stairs. Not the boss's heavy tread. Softer. Matron?

She opened the door. She was carrying a tray. A glass of milk, a sandwich, a thick slice of chocolate cake.

No. I'm seeing things. Or is this just to torment me? Perhaps she plans to eat in front of me. Maybe she'll just set it down and make me look at it. Think about what I missed out on by running away. Maybe...

She set the tray down on the personal table beside my bed and sat down beside me. She touched my shoulder gently.

"Are you all right?"

"Yes."

Anything but all right, but I'm not going to admit it.

"You must be hungry."

"A little." I'm starving. *But you know that, don't you. You are enjoying tormenting me. You are punishing me for running away. I don't blame you. I deserve it!*

"Why did you try to run away?"

"I don't know."

"Don't you like it here?"

"Yes, but..."

"But? But what, Paul? Talk to me, please. No. Here, eat first. Have some milk. Talk can wait."

What is this? A trick?

"Come on, Son. Eat up. Don't tell me you don't want that cake."

I reached nervously for the sandwich. She sat silently, watching. First the sandwich, then the milk, then cake. What a treat! The matron was an excellent cook. This was infinitely better than Caramel Columbines. It was fresh baked, still warm, rich and dark, with thick chocolate icing and cream in the middle.

Why would she give me a treat? What comes next?

"Now tell me, please. Why did you want to leave us? Has something happened here? At school maybe?"

"No." Guilt weighed heavy on my shoulders. I wished I hadn't gone. Why had I? They were good to me here. She seemed hurt that I had wanted to go, as though it implied she had failed me somehow.

Why should she care? Twenty–two boys. What does one more or less matter?

She was studying my expression, trying to read my thoughts, searching for answers.

"Then why?"

"No reason. Not really. It's just that, well..."

"Well?" Her voice was still soft and gentle. No threatening undertone. No warnings of punishment.

"I wanted to see my mum and dad and brothers. That's all. I miss them. I wanted to go home. It's been such a long time, and when the man came and took me away he told me it would be only for a few weeks, and... I just wanted to go home."

123

Despite my best efforts to hide emotion, my voice rose and cracked. I struggled to hide the moist drop that threatened to trickle from the corner of my eye.

Seemingly endless silence while she considered my words. I wished I hadn't blurted it out now. It sounded dumb. It was dumb to think I could just walk out of here and go home.

I don't even know where home is.

I stared at the floor. She didn't seem to be angry with me.

She should be angry — or maybe she's leaving it to the Boss to punish me.

It seemed odd that she should give me chocolate cake though. Or maybe not! I heard somewhere they gave prisoners on death row the meal of their choice before they took them off to be hanged.

"What will the Boss do to me?" I couldn't contain it any longer.

"What? Oh!" She laughed softly. "So you're afraid he'll punish you, are you?"

"Well, he said—"

"Paul, no–one here is going to punish you." She spoke slowly… lovingly. "We want you to be happy here, but you must understand. I know it's hard, but you have to stay here. You can't go home. I know you want to see your family. I would too, after not seeing them for so long. The man who took you away shouldn't have told you it was only for a while, because it wasn't. He was cruel to lie to you. It was for ever, Paul, or at least until you are all grown up."

I wiped my eyes on my sleeve and turned my head away from her.

"You are a ward of the State — a child in care, so you have to stay here until the Government says you must go somewhere else, or until you are old enough to live alone. It's a terrible thing and it shouldn't be this way. No child deserves this, and you are a good boy. You deserve better, but we care about you and we are doing everything we can to give you a good home and make you happy. And if there is anything wrong — anything making you unhappy — you must come and tell us, and we'll try to help. We'll try to make things better, if we can. Do you understand?"

"Yes. Thank you."

"Good. Now rest while I take a tray to Bluey, then come downstairs and help me make dinner. I'm cooking roast lamb. With all the other boys at the pictures, there's just you and Bluey to help." A mischievous twinkle lit her eye, huge bosoms heaved with that deep, resonant laugh. She lifted herself off the bed and collected the tray. I swung my feet up and leant my head back, hugging my knees to my chin. I watched her as she carried the now empty tray downstairs. Then I lay back and gazed at a blistered ceiling.

It's good here. The food is good. We win most of our Saturday soccer matches. I like working in the boot shed and I like helping Matron make clay pots.

Sometimes I would go with her to the creek banks to dig for clay and then help her wash and sieve it ready for the pottery wheel. She would let me help her fire up the big kiln and load it, and two days later I would help her unload all her beautiful works.

There were books to read in the evenings and a warm fire. No pissy sheets to wash in icy water, no whining charges to pick up after, no squawking penguins lashing me with a leather strap or scrubbing brush.

It's not a place one should want to run away from. But what happens to me when it's time to leave here? Where do I go then?

I answered myself with the resolution I had made the day I first entered that boot shed.

I'll be a bootmaker. I'll do well. And when I finally go home, Mum and Dad will burst with pride at what I've achieved, and I'll help them to not be poor anymore.

18: FIFTEEN — BUT NOT FREE

NOVEMBER, 1963

Fifteen! Freedom!

Birthdays were never that special. They were marked at St Patrick's only by the singing of the traditional birthday song. At Ohio, there were cakes and singing and good wishes. A birthday often elevated me to a position of greater responsibility and a heavier workload. Otherwise, the only real significance was that it brought me closer to that magical birthday that would finally set me free.

After our 15th birthday, the Government would not provide funds for our keep. We would be sent out to find work or sign on as trade apprentices, hopefully to be offered board and lodgings with a decent family.

I was going to be an apprentice bootmaker. I asked my teachers and the town bootmaker how to go about getting an apprenticeship. I found out where to go to apply, how long the training took and even how much I would be paid in my first year of training. I dreamt, planned and celebrated; my fingers itched in anticipation.

A government worker driving a sleek black sedan came to interview me a few months before my birthday.

"Mr Tuck tells me you are keen to join the army, to go to the Apprentice School like so many of your mates," he said, making marks on the pages on his clipboard.

I stared at him nervously.

Who told him that? Why? The Boss knew I didn't want to go in the army. Don't argue with your elders! You'll get a clip in the ear and the Boss will tell you to do as you are told.

"That's very good, Paul. I'm sure you will do very well in the army."

Do very well? Is that all that matters? Does it matter if I'm happy?

I bit my lip and took a deep breath.

"Actually, sir," I said, trying hard to sound very respectful, "I want to be a bootmaker." The man kept writing, seeming not to have heard.

"I repair shoes for the boys here, and I'm very good at it. I like the work."

"That's very good, Paul. I'm glad you are making yourself useful here and learning some good skills." He said it with disinterest, still writing.

"I'd really like to take on an apprenticeship in leatherwork. I've found out all about it. I told the Boss that's what I'd like to do."

"I'm sure Mr Tuck will do whatever is necessary to ensure your future, Paul. You should take his advice. He is a wise man, and he is genuinely concerned for your welfare. Now, I think I'm finished here. I will submit my report. The army will send your school reports to our office in Sydney, so we'll be able to keep an eye on your progress. I wish you all the very best."

Did this fool not hear a word I said? Of course he heard. He just doesn't care. None of these government workers do. They don't care that my mother kept our house clean and my mum and dad loved me and looked after me. They don't care that the nuns beat children mercilessly and called them 'filthy urchins' and 'trash' and deprived them of decent food. They don't care about kids. All they care about is pushing pencils to write stupid reports.

The officer extended his hand, and I shook it reluctantly. I was seething, but I didn't believe what he'd said about the Boss. I was quite confident there had been a simple misunderstanding.

The Boss will put things right. I'll tell the Boss again that I don't want to go in the army. That I want to be a bootmaker. I'll ask the Boss to put in the application for me.

It turned out the Boss had already set the wheels in motion for me to join the army. When I approached him about the bootmaking apprenticeship, he said it was too late.

"Applications have closed, Paul," he said, "but I'm sure you'll like the army. You'll be with Peter and some of your older brothers. Surely that pleases you?

"I know that you don't really want to join the army, Paul," he continued, "but I hope someday you'll understand why it's the best thing for you. I know you think you are all grown up now, but suddenly let loose at 15, headstrong, excitable young lads who have been subjected to years of rigid discipline so often go looking for adventure and get themselves into trouble. Once you leave here, there is no–one to watch out for you. I want to be sure you'll be kept safe until you are thoroughly mature. I want you to have the chance of a good career. There is no opportunity for State wards to finish school, but the army will give you two more years of education. You will learn valuable skills, be well paid and have a lot of fun. Balcombe turns boys into fine young men."

I wanted to protest over having to sign away eight years of my life to be admitted to the Army Apprentice School at Balcombe. I wanted to complain that the discipline there was prison–like — so much so that judges often gave young offenders the choice of Balcombe or jail. I wanted to tell the Boss I'd had enough of institutions. I wanted my freedom, to follow the career path of my choice, but I knew better than to argue with the Boss. In any case, the Boss made it clear that the decision was made and there was no way it could be changed.

"Most of you will probably sign on again," the Matron had remarked enthusiastically when the Boss talked of the opportunity he had arranged for the boys and the potential benefits. "After 20 years' service, you can retire on a pension for life, still young enough to build careers in civvy street with a secure income to back you. Or, if you choose to stay longer, you can rise through the ranks and eventually retire on a generous military pension."

Their talk tempted some. Several of the boys wanted to be soldiers and musicians, so looked forward eagerly to being old enough to join up. At least that's the impression they conveyed, although perhaps only to please, or maybe because it seemed a fait accompli. We had been taught that real men wear masks and must never show hurt or disappointment. I didn't share my distress with my Ohio 'brothers'.

The Boss's own son had been keen to join. Peter went off happily to Balcombe a year before I turned 15, following in his father's footsteps. I liked playing music for a hobby, but I had no desire to do it every day for the rest of my life. There was an opportunity to take on a bootmaking apprenticeship and earn an adequate wage. When I had learnt my trade, I could own my own shop and make lots of money and maybe even employ apprentices. I would invent a new kind of soccer boot. I had an ambition, and joining the army did not fit with my plans, but it was clear, now, that turning 15 didn't mean freedom after all. I was still legally a minor and a ward of the State until age 18.

The irony of the situation was that despite being still a child in care for another three years, I had to be financially self–sufficient. I was expected to survive the last three years of childhood without guidance or security — without a soul in the world to care what became of me or to offer me comfort. Had I not been sent off to join the army, I would not have even been offered a place to sleep. I had all the responsibilities of an adult, but none of the privileges.

I struggled to go to sleep that night. In my dreams, I was chased up the riverbank by a fat, ruddy–faced man with pointy ears sticking out and beady little eyes, pouched cheeks and a twisted, sneering smile. He spoke to my father in a whining bleat. He said, "Paul and Jenny are going for a little holiday, but they'll be coming back home soon".

The fat man watched, a cruel smirk twisting his lips, as I stood in a barren playground pining for home and asking the older boys what 'soon' meant. I kicked the dust and counted off the days, then the weeks, then the months.

Finally, I gave up counting and just accepted that Simms had lied. I was never going home.

Now, it seemed I was destined to remain incarcerated through adulthood. I was doomed to forfeit every hope and dream and aspiration I had ever dared to nurture.

I dreamt about Geoffrey Simms often and blamed him entirely, up until that time, for my unhappiness. I swore I'd kill the bastard one day.

Now a man I had dared to love and trust—a man I sometimes called Dad—appeared in my dream as a jailer, pushing me into a cell and slamming the door firmly behind me. A soccer boot and a last drifted past my cell. I stretched my arms through the bars, but the Boss appeared, grasped them, and thrust them away beyond my reach. Then he reached up and pulled down a sign that read "P.F. Wilson. Bootmaker", threw it on the floor, and stamped on it until it splintered and turned to sawdust.

I woke, cold and trembling, in the earliest hours of the morning. The dorm was dark and still. Beyond the dormer window, old man moon was still playing with the stars. A vow replayed in my mind: a vow made as a little boy not yet eight years old. "No matter how they hurt me, I will never, ever cry."

I had honoured that vow, suffering their beatings and enduring incarceration, torment and deprivation. I had never allowed a tear to fall. But that morning, all the accumulated pain and suffering and fear and frustration of seven long, painful years of imprisonment and separation from family formed itself into a huge ball, capped with the hard ice of betrayal by one I had foolishly allowed myself to trust. And then that ball came thundering down to roll over me and crush me.

I turned on my side, pulled my knees into my belly, buried my face in my pillow and cried.

19: AN URCHIN NO MORE

JANUARY, 1964

The wheels seemed to sing, "Go to jail. Go to jail," as the train rattled and swayed towards Sydney for my enlistment interview.

I'd yearned to board the train that would finally take me away from the home and the surrogate parents I'd come to love. I'd counted months and then weeks until I could join men in heavy aprons cutting, stitching, carving and buffing to make boots, belts, handbags, wallets and whips. Again and again, I dreamt of long days at the buffing wheel. And the soccer boot! I saw it, felt it, smelt it, shaped, sanded, buffed and polished it, then set it on a little stand for a champion team to examine and admire.

One day, I would have my own little boot shop. Maybe I would start a chain of stores, selling bridles, saddles and jodhpurs and riding caps. The sign out front would read P.F. Wilson, Esq., and one day, two decades or so from now, it might read P.F. Wilson and Son. I might put a skiving knife in my son's hand and teach him to slice and bevel.

The train wasn't taking me to a place where I would spend my days caressing and shaping warm sheets of leather. There would be no skiving knives and stitchers, and no raw acrid smell of leather and Cargrip in my nostrils in the evenings. In their place, army–issue khakis and the famed blue 'poofy suits' that 'Appys' — as the Balcombe apprentices were referred to — wore on dress occasions. Spit–polished boots. Rifles, bayonets, a silver cornet and a music stand. Five o'clock reveille and five–mile runs to the beach and back before breakfast. Inspections. Barked orders and sharp salutes.

As the train neared its destination, the tiniest ray of hope fought like a weak torchlight to penetrate the darkness that engulfed me.

Perhaps they won't accept me?

I tried to fail the entrance test. I sat when commanded to stand and stood when commanded to sit and knowingly gave wrong answers. I returned home to Ohio with a heart filled with hope that I struggled valiantly to hold on to, and yet I knew it was hopeless.

"Congratulations, Paul!" the Boss called, waving the expected letter, and beaming. The other boys cheered, but I grieved.

Two weeks later, carrying a tiny battered suitcase filled with the last home–boy clothes I would ever wear and with no personal belongings — not a single relic to remind me of my childhood — I climbed into the Boss's old Kombi for the 12 mile drive to the station. With £5 in my pocket to tide me over 'til my first payday, I boarded the train to my future. I thrust my suitcase on to the luggage rack and stared stubbornly ahead, hands clasping the arm–rest, ignoring the Boss on the platform waving an enthusiastic goodbye.

I love train rides. There's a certain inevitability about them, with nothing to do but relax and enjoy the steady rhythmical rocking and the clickety–clack of the wheels on the track, watching the fields, cottages, rivers, bridges and skies flying by. You have no control over the whistles and toots, the stations sliding into view and out, the bustle of passengers boarding and demounting, the tears of friends waving farewell and the hugs and smiles of greeting. Passengers lug suitcases on board and shove them up on to brass luggage racks and, with little more than a nod to fellow travellers, settle back with newspapers or books, or close their eyes to try to sleep. Everyone knows how long it will take to reach their destination and there is absolutely nothing anyone can do to speed the journey or to alter its course.

There was nothing I could do to change the course of the train that carried me far away from the familiar rolling hills of Ohio Station, the rustic warmth and raw odour of the boot shed, the stench of sweat in the boxing shed, the soothing warmth of the sun streaming through the library windows on an autumn afternoon, and the cosiness of gatherings around a crackling open fire on a cold winter night.

It's a wonder my love of trains survived that awful journey. Had I been inclined to keep a journal, the entry for that day would have recorded anxiety that few teenagers would ever know, and the pain of a betrayal so hurtful that even on the day they laid him in the ground I would curse the Boss and refuse to mourn his passing.

Inevitability? My life was an inevitability. Like passengers boarding a train, I forfeited every right of choice or decision until I would reach my destination eight years from now. The 'powers that be' would map my itinerary from departure at 15 to disembarkation after my 23rd birthday, and I would have no option but to grit my teeth, clench my fists and endure the ride.

I slept, read and watched the fields, towns and stations pass until I reached the point at which I had to change trains for Melbourne. Sitting there, on that hard timber bench with its elaborate wrought–iron lace ends, under the giant clocks at Sydney Central Station, suitcase between my knees, I watched the crowd jostling and shoving. Arriving passengers stretched their necks to peer anxiously about, searching, and then drop their cases, spread their arms and break into broad smiles as loved ones pushed through the crowd to embrace them.

If only there was someone here to embrace me. If only I had someplace to go, some alternative to boarding the Melbourne train.

There was no–one and nowhere. At the end of this journey, two huge metal gates would open to a world of desolation and despair.

If I could have written to my dad, I would, of course, have described this journey quite differently. I might have written, "With £5 in my pocket and just the barest of necessities — a few clothes that would be soon discarded in favour of better — I boarded the train, filled with anticipation, and set out to begin another adventure".

I tried, for most of the awful journey, to view it that way. Peter had talked enthusiastically of running on the beach and playing sport and working out in the gymnasium. He excited me with talks of bush camp–outs. Shooting was something I enjoyed immensely as a young child, dreamt about and yearned to do as I grew. Now I would be handed a rifle and paid to practise. Peter assured me that the meals were superb and food was always in abundance. I was to receive a regular salary to spend as I pleased.

Dad had always told me to make the best of every situation. I really was determined to try, but I yearned so desperately for freedom. The pain of deprivation of it coloured every expectation, and for the rest of my days would colour every recollection.

#

My hand shook and the gorge rose in my throat. My head spun like a whirlwind and threatened to depart my body, but I dutifully signed the contract consenting to spend the next eight years of my life incarcerated. I entered a fenced compound dotted with rows of unlined tin Romni huts and was escorted to one marked Ypres and commanded to enter.

Fourteen steel–framed beds were set equally spaced, in lines of seven against each of the two longer walls. Beside each, a bare–topped personal table provided drawers for singlets, socks and underwear, and a narrow locker gave space to hang uniform shirts and jackets. The arrangement of the furniture created neatly measured tiny squares of territory for each occupant — barely large enough to turn around in and providing storage space for nothing but uniforms and the absolute essentials for personal hygiene. On the foot of every bed, linen and blankets were folded precisely in half, a pillow and perfectly folded pillowcase positioned meticulously on top. Nothing else in sight. Not a speck of dust visible. Cold. Sterile. Familiar. And the smell of fear!

I inhaled deeply. Terror wrapped itself about me, blinding me and constricting my chest so I struggled to breathe. It burnt my throat and nostrils, screamed in my ear and pressed like a massive weight on my shoulders, and tried to pull my legs from under me.

So this is to be my life for the next eight years, defined to the smallest detail, confined and regimented. Every action, every thought, in response to rules and command. Every day lived in fear of the consequences of falling short of expectations, or somehow angering a superior.

I chose the bed closest to the door. It was an unpopular position, because wind whipped in whenever someone entered or left. But it was closest to the outside, giving me regular glimpses of a small open space.

Medical tests and immunisations preceded the issue of uniforms. I stood silently in a long line, shuffling forward every few minutes, edging closer to the uniformed medic jabbing a long needle into one arm after another, extracting cylinders of blood. Ahead but one stood a taller boy wearing tight–fitting jeans and shirt with sleeves rolled high above the elbows, a cigarette packet protruding from the sleeve roll on one side. He slouched a little, hands thrust deep into his pockets, placing most of his weight on one leg. He wore a slightly sneering half–grin. Mr Cool! He strode up to the medic's table and presented his arm as though in expectation of receiving a stamp of honour or a pass to freedom.

The medic raised that huge needle. Mr Cool faltered. The colour drained from his face and he collapsed, unconscious, in a crumpled heap at my feet. Those in line smothered giggles. I felt a brief surge of relief that at least some of the boys were less confident than they appeared. From then on, Mr Cool and I were firm friends.

Medical procedures completed, we marched to the uniform store. I surveyed the rows of clothing with mixed emotions. The garments promised significant discomfort and the uniform, more than anything else, signified total loss of freedom. Yet in army uniform I would not feel conspicuously shabby, identified as a 'home kid'. Here, I could be one of the group. No–one need ever know my embarrassing secret, and I resolved to never tell it.

Whatever pretence is necessary — whatever insignificant little untruths must be told — when I shed my home–boy clothes today, I'll cease to be an urchin.

20: LIFE AS A ''APPY"

BALCOMBE, JANUARY 1964

The mind–deadening routine began with five a.m. reveille and a five–mile–run to the beach and back. I used to enjoy long distance running, but at daybreak, in a chanting pack with barking sergeants forcing the pace and screaming threats at anyone who slowed or faltered, the sport gave no pleasure.

Back to the barracks to shower and change. Make the bed with perfect mitred corners and cover tight.

Inspection. Stand in frozen anticipation while a 'stripe'—as non–commissioned officers are called—searches for a microscopic speck of dust or an item of clothing not perfectly folded or resting a fraction of an inch from its allotted place. Hair length is measured. The army barbers gave new meaning to 'short back and sides'. Chins of those old enough to sport facial hair are inspected for the correct use of the razor. I silently pray that the uniform I ironed last night is perfect and the boots I so painstakingly spit–polished shine enough to please.

A 'stripe' drops a coin on each bed and watches how high it bounces. Luckily, I'm well practised at making beds to institutional standards, but the unfortunate lad in the bed next to me suffers bellowed abuse, while the corporal rips off all the covers.

"Do it again, and do it right this time," he screams.

Despite being well–practiced at hospital corners, I formed the habit of making a tiny opening through which to sliver into bed at night, and I lay like a statue so I could be certain that in the morning I could make the bed to the expected standard in the time allotted.

Breakfast in a cold, crowded institutional dining hall, rank with the smell of boys' sweat. At least the food is good.

Locked away, alone, in a tiny soundproof cubicle, I practised music for endless hours. Scales. Exercises. Lip trills. My fingers ached, my jaw throbbed and my head pounded. The cell walls closed in on me, crushing me.

After lunch, I joined group rehearsals at which I suffered ridicule or a stern reprimand for every trivial mistake. Cold and tense, I peered at black dots until the staves warped and the notes blurred and danced from line to line. My ears buzzed and my fingers stiffened. My heartbeat was louder than the drums, but out of time… so fearfully, mockingly out of time.

In the late afternoon, I changed into shorts and shirt and reported to the gym. The workouts were demanding. Thankfully, I was fit and agile.

After dinner, on my second night there, a senior thrust a pair of boots in front of a roommate and commanded him to polish them. He dared to refuse and was promptly dragged off to the ablutions block where a mob of seniors beat him.

The request was repeated the following night, targeting a different roommate. Forewarned, he consented to perform the task, but apparently didn't shine the shoes well enough to please, so was forced to 'run the gauntlet'. Seniors lined up in two long lines, armed with boots, brooms and belts. The unfortunate junior was compelled to run between the lines, while seniors mocked and jeered and flailed the errant youth. The attackers showed no mercy, and when the run was done, none either offered sympathy or treated wounds. There were stern warnings of much worse to follow if the wounded youth dared to give any sign of suffering or anger, implying that he might seek revenge.

I realised that it was only a matter of time before I was targeted for torment, but when my turn came I was ready with a strong left hook. A corporal quickly stopped the fight and rearranged some furniture to make a boxing ring.

They'll be confident I'll be taught a lesson I won't forget in a hurry. But they don't know I was trained to box. Thank you, Boss.

I knocked my opponent down, and urged him to stay down and save himself. He ignored the warning and came back for more. Over and over, I put him down and urged him to quit. Over and over he rose and begged to be hurt again. Eventually, they called the winner, and I was rarely subjected to bullying from the other boys again.

I wasn't spared the regular demands to hand over any sweets or trinkets a senior saw me with and desired, though. They unwittingly did me a favour. I bought a packet of cigarettes once, but after realising I'd unwillingly gifted all but one, I never bought another.

At the end of the first week, we made the first long, forced march with full pack and rifle. Nine–mile marches became a regular event, and 20 mile marches at least once each year. The combination of heat, uncomfortable uniforms and the weight of a pack and seven–pound rifle made summer marches almost unbearable.

At the end of the second week I was assigned my first night of guard duty. Every two hours I had to wake and march around the perimeter of the camp. Savvy soldiers 'sold' their guard duties. They called it selling, but in fact it was more a case of buying a substitute. Some blokes accumulated a nice little savings nest egg doing extra guard duties. I quickly decided it was worth the cost of a substitute to avoid the pain.

We were rostered to perform kitchen and cleaning chores regularly, but before the end of my first month I had done more than a dozen extra hours of mess and toilet–cleaning duties as punishment for minor transgressions. In the second month I suffered the more severe punishment of being forced to run a dozen laps of the oval in full battle dress with pack and rifle. Painful at any time, it was murder on a hot summer afternoon.

Polishing the brass

I was conditioned to constant ridicule and verbal abuse. I'd had five years of cruel taunts and vile put–downs from sour, bilious bitches who hated men, despised little boys, and whose inability to cope with life in the real world led them to retreat to an artificial universe. The nuns saw children from underprivileged families as contaminants to be cleansed by beating the spirit out of them. Those whose spirits would not be broken were bullied and tormented until they grew old enough to move on, at which time nuns pronounced them lost and predicted a sorry end. But although still painfully aware of my inferior status in society, and often ridiculed by peers when the Boss and Matron were out of hearing range, I had enjoyed blessed relief for the past three years. Even during those years at St Patrick's, brothers and priests and Sister Anne occasionally showered me with praise and compliments, and I won respect from peers with my sporting prowess.

Here, I found little opportunity to build confidence or self–respect. Seniors, tutors and some of the officers regarded ridicule as an art form, competing constantly for the title of 'most hated bully'. We were forced, mostly, to endure the torment in silence, standing rigidly to attention and replying "Yes sir" and "No sir," on cue, giving snappy salutes and even thanking them for subjecting us to public humiliation. Then we were ordered to march off to the kitchen, latrines or parade ground to suffer cruel, undeserved punishments. Or we were forced to run the gauntlet for mildly airing a gripe, resisting unfairness or exposing any sign of feeling resentment, fear or pain.

#

"I copped a weekend of CB," Bruce said, dropping on to his bed and covering his face with his hands. My roommate had been charged with disobeying some command, and marched in full uniform up to the C.O.'s office to stand to attention while formal charges were read. He was asked to explain himself, and then the sentence was read out. Confined to barracks. Poor fellow was beside himself.

His sentence commenced the following morning. Every half–hour he had to run to the guard room, present for inspection, then run back to the barracks and change into a different uniform. The frantic three–quarter mile run from guard room to barracks soaked clothing with sweat, especially when wearing heavy winter uniforms. I joined his other mates to help him remedy the damage ready for the next change, but even with help it was all but impossible to make it back in 15 minutes immaculately presented in different attire. The smallest flaw in appearance resulted in a savage dressing down and threats of further penalty. The routine continued all day, with only a half–hour break for lunch. The embarrassment of knowing that everyone saw him leaving the barracks every 15 minutes in different attire, and knew why, added to his pain.

"It was hell, Paul. You can't begin to imagine."

"I can. I saw what you went through, mate," I said, wishing I could have helped more.

"Part of it," Bruce said. "Not the dressing down–in the office every half–hour, the terror of that jerk sergeant finding an imperfection and adding another day to the sentence, or the fear of what uniform he'd order me to appear in next. I just kept praying it wouldn't be formal dress or battle dress. I sweated so bad in battle dress, and formal dress takes so much work to get perfect. Fifteen minutes wasn't nearly enough, no matter how fast I moved.

"Thanks for your help, mate," he added. "I wouldn't have got through without it."

"Wish I could have done more," I said, aware that for the rest of my time in the army I would live in constant dread of similar punishment.

21: A PLACE TO CALL HOME

APRIL, 1964

Easter! A brief period of respite. No morning runs; no inspections, shouted reprimands or taunts. No confinement in tiny cubicles practising scales and exercises hour after hour.

Dozens of excited youths crowded around phone booths, queuing for their turn to call and advise families of what time to meet their train or bus. Tickets were purchased; travel schedules were checked. The huts hummed and buzzed with chatter about plans for fishing trips, beach picnics and special family dinners.

I sat silently on my bed, wrapped in an all too familiar cold sensation of emptiness. I made no calls. I bought no tickets. I had no place to go.

By mid–morning, only I and one or two others remained. I rejoiced at seeing the last of the loved and wanted depart, thankful for solitude — an end to the painful reminders that I had no–one to visit and no–one to care.

The gates and fences still confined me, but for one glorious week I rose when I pleased, ate when I pleased, and spent long leisurely days wrapped in a blanket in the TV room watching Bonanza and Rifleman and other cowboy series. When the hunger bug bit, I ran to Burger Bill's canteen caravan to pay 20 cents for a hamburger, then ran, shivering, back to the TV room to snuggle back into a blanket and feast. Somehow I still managed to pay a fair compliment to the chefs who prepared the usual portions, despite reduced numbers of diners, so that I had a veritable feast to enjoy at meal times. For one glorious week I didn't have to spit polish boots and iron uniforms. I didn't have to fear being made to run the gauntlet, or being ridiculed in group rehearsals.

And then the awful routine began again. The days stretched out before me like stepping stones on a path into a deep, grey fog.

#

I never received letters. I wrote to no–one. I knew letters to my sister would never be delivered. I could have written to the Matron, or some of my Ohio brothers, but years of institutional living conditioned me to see people come and go from my life with neither emotion nor sentimental reflection. The people from my past ceased to exist the day I stepped forward into the next phase of my existence. So I was astonished, towards the end of my first year at Balcombe, to hear my name called at mail call. The letter was neatly hand addressed — not official. I turned it over and was surprised to see the name "W. Wilson" above the address. The initial perplexed me. I opened the letter carefully, prepared to discover it had been sent to me in error and must be re–sealed and returned to sender.

"Dear Paul,

No doubt it will surprise you to receive a letter from me, your father's youngest brother. I learnt where you were from Mr and Mrs Tuck, to whom I was referred by the nuns at St Patrick's.

I am writing to ask if you would care to spend your Christmas holidays with my wife and I, our two small sons, and your sister, Jennifer, whom we have brought from St Patrick's to live with us."

The letter continued to list Bill's address and telephone number, and invited me to call or write, or just show up if it suited me. It was signed "With love, Uncle Bill".

I was overcome. My hand shook, my belly turned somersaults and the blood rushed to my feet, so that I feared I might faint. After three long, lonely holidays, suffering the awful emptiness, isolation and humiliation of being unwanted, I would be among those excitedly checking travel schedules and buying tickets.

Three weeks later I boarded a train, filled with an excitement and anticipation I had never known before. This time the train wheels sang "Wanted. Wanted. Wanted".

Bill Wilson was waiting at the station, hat in hand, wearing a laconic half grin. My heart lurched when I saw him. He looked just like my dad. He seemed surprised that I remembered.

My beloved Jennifer stood beside Bill. Prettier than ever and now shaped like a young woman, she stood trembling with excitement. It was four years since she had seen or heard from her big brother. I was a soldier now. She wasn't sure how she should greet me, and I made no move to hug her. We stood staring at each other, silent, afraid of neither knew what.

I shook hands very formally with my uncle, and then followed him to his utility, thrust my suitcase in the back, and climbed in beside my sister. Her little body felt warm and soft against mine and her sweet perfume filled my nostrils. After a few minutes, I dared to place my arm around her. She smiled up at me and snuggled against me. A voice in my head said "At last, one thing has been put right in this rotten world".

I seldom spoke of my life to anyone. I'd learnt long ago never to reveal my feelings or show emotion. Allowing folk to get to know you empowered them to hurt you—to take away from you the things that gave you pleasure and to deny you access to the things you craved. I made small talk with my aunt and uncle and played games with their little boys. I helped my uncle in the garden and my aunt in the kitchen. Their home was filled with warmth and love. They were kind and generous to me, but they didn't pressure me to talk.

For the first time since Christmas at the Bennetts, I went Christmas shopping with a family. I enjoyed choosing gifts for my aunt, uncle, sister and the boys. I happily spent more than I could reasonably afford, overwhelmed by their generosity in return.

As the days wore on, I found myself talking to my sister about my life; asking her how it was for her while we were apart. The picture I painted was of a joyous life, filled with adventure. I never once complained.

We never spoke of our parents and relatives never raised the subject. By then, they were part of a long–forgotten past. They had ceased to exist.

I was overjoyed to see that my sister was blissfully happy. For the first time since she was five, she was safe and loved. I could go back to Balcombe with one less concern. Not that I'd worried constantly about her, but I thought of her often and reproached myself for not fulfilling my promise to my father to take care of her. I wasn't to blame, but yet I felt I ought to have somehow found a way.

It was my aunt who first broke through the wall I had erected. She reminded me of the Ohio matron, Mrs Tuck. She was warm and gentle and she laughed a lot. She had a happy knack of inviting me to open up, without me ever feeling pressured.

"So what do you do for leisure during term time," she asked one day.

I shrugged. "Not much. We weren't allowed outside the gates for the first six months. After that, I stayed in most of the time anyway. We are forced to wear those dreadful poofy suits and I hate being seen in that uniform. In any case, there's nowhere much I have any inclination to go."

I hadn't meant to go on. I hadn't meant to say that much, in fact, but somehow her sympathetic look made me want to confide in her.

"All the uniforms are ugly and uncomfortable and I have to wear them every waking hour. Our hair is cut to regulations. Our bodies are shaped to regulation by rigorous exercise routines. Sometimes I'm tempted to believe that, if they could, they would surgically alter our faces to conform to a model."

"You hate it, don't you Paul? You pretend well, but you're miserable," she said sadly.

I shrugged again and pushed my chair back from the table.

"It's not so bad. I like playing music. I'm well fed and well paid. And it's not for ever."

Bill sat down beside me that evening, placed a hand on my shoulder, and coughed self–consciously. There was an awkward silence for a moment. I looked at him questioningly.

"You're unhappy in the army, I hear," Bill said at last.

"It's OK."

Kiss arses. Lick boots! They humiliate me on the rifle range, calling me out and declaring that no–one would ever want to go to war with me beside them because I'm the worst shot in the battalion. Yet when I hit the target perfectly with every shot that afternoon, not a word of acknowledgement is spoken. They call me derogatory names and taunt me. They make me salute at least a dozen times a day and subject me to a bellowed rebuke if the hand movement isn't perfect, or if the officer I'm saluting finds the tiniest imperfection in my appearance, step or attitude.

I sleep in a tiny square of a sterile hut with 13 blokes, half of whom I dislike. I jump to barked commands every waking minute and live every day in terror of displeasing a stripe or a senior and suffering unspeakable punishments. It's not OK, but I can't tell him that.

"Paul, we could give you a permanent home here. I could speak to the powers that be about you getting out, living here with us, and pursuing a career of your own choosing."

The room seemed to tilt irrationally. It began to spin. I was on a roller coaster, soaring at breakneck speed. A surge of terror gripped me as I imagined reaching the peak and pelting down the other side. How fast would I fall? How hard would I crash? Every promise of something good was inevitably followed by disaster. Any gift I dared to enjoy was quickly removed to a place beyond my reach.

I leant back in the chair and put my hand to my forehead. My head thundered. My uncle's words echoed over and over, taunting me, testing me. I wanted to trust Bill. I wanted to believe his offer was sincere. I wanted to scream "Yes. Yes. Please, please yes!", but instead I said in a quiet, sad voice, "I signed on for eight years. There is no way the brass would let me out of that contract."

"Perhaps if we legally adopted you..." Bill said. "Joan and I... we'd be delighted to call you our son."

I struggled with that offer for a very long time, for the only thing I wanted more than freedom was to belong to a real family.

"You are too kind," I said at last, "and nothing would give me more pleasure than to be part of your family, but you have enough on your plate with Jen and your boys. In any case, there is no way the army would ever release me."

"If you're sure," Bill said, his eyes probing, pleading, willing me to stop the masquerade. "At least promise me that you will treat this house as home whenever you have leave, and you'll write to us."

I would write. I would cherish every letter and delight in the obligation to reply. And when I had leave, I would board a train, revelling in the knowledge that, at last, I somewhere to go and someone to care — a place to call home.

22 GRADUATION

DECEMBER, 1965

"I can play a cornet without a mouthpiece, sir. I can't play one without valves."

As soon as the words were out, I wanted to swallow them. The examiner's lips tightened and the colour rose in his neck. His eyebrows lifted, his shoulders tensed and flames shot from the pupils of his eyes. With one foolish retort, I had just sealed my fate.

"I can tell a good musician from hearing 'Abide with Me'," my erstwhile mentor had said, advising me in preparation for my final exams. So while others practised "Carnival de Venice" and other equally challenging pieces, calling for lip trills and triple tonguing, I heeded the advice of a tutor to choose something simple and play it well. I rehearsed "Santa Lucia" until confident I could play it note perfect, with all the feeling and expression the piece deserved.

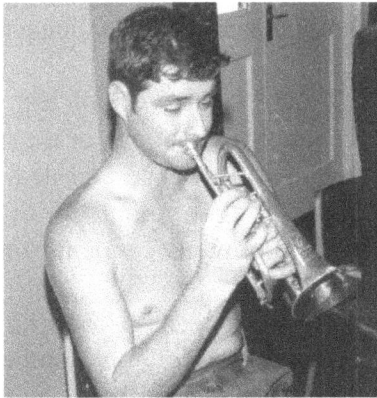

Practising

When the day of the exam came, I played superbly. I felt, when that last note rang out, lifted, lightened and drifting on air, intoxicated by the ecstasy of knowing that my rendition was better than faultless. It was evocative. In my mind, it transported the listener to Naples and entranced him with the magnificence of the waterfront and excited him with the boatman's invitation. The cornet laughed and cried and painted magical scenes as it told its story.

I embraced the challenge of verbal questions on theory with a feeling of exuberance. My knowledge was sound and I responded quickly and accurately until the final question. And then I made that fatal mistake.

"What is the most important part of your instrument," the examiner asked.

"The valves, sir," I replied without hesitation.

The examiner frowned. "Surely it's the mouthpiece?"

I dared to argue. A good teacher or a fair man would consider his student's response and acknowledge the validity of the argument, but there were many here who did not impress me as either good teachers or fair men, and this examiner was one of these. He was here, teaching boys, because he had an inflated ego, but limited ability. At least that was my opinion of him, and I convinced myself it was also the opinion of those who signed the posting order that sent him here. Having formed that opinion some time ago, it was difficult to understand what on earth possessed me to argue at such a critical time, but there it was again: the defiance that seemed to always bring me undone.

Those of breeding seemed to get away with it, or perhaps to know intuitively when it was safe. I was, after all, an orphan — a nobody. I had no influential family ties or friends. There was no proud family tradition of military service or musical accomplishment for me to boast of. I had no uncles or father who had served with my tutors and become mates, or were known to be mates of their mates or bosses. No amount of diligence or skill could compensate for that lack of breeding that showed far too often in arrogant retorts when I knew I was right, and in a stubborn stance when challenged in a way I considered unfair.

It was apparent to most that I saluted out of fear of the consequences of refusing, not out of respect for either the man or the office. My hatred of the army was as obvious as my love of music and dedication to excellence in my trade. I was learning, slowly, that no amount of dedication to my craft would ever compensate for my obvious contempt for the system and those who served it.

When the marking was done, I read '64%' with anger and resentment, mixed with a sense of inevitability. The only compensation was that I had passed. After two long years of soul–destroying rigor, my time at Balcombe was coming to an end. I was about to graduate to the adult army. It promised a little less rigor, considerably more freedom, and a higher rate of pay. It also promised six more years of uniforms and regimentation and shared, depressing barracks with rows of beds that must be made daily with perfect corners and tight covers. It meant six more years of ablution blocks that offered no privacy; regular long runs in full battle dress with heavy back–packs and rifles; barked orders; and threats of dreadful punishment for minor infractions. Yet there were those who chose this way of life, and who, given the chance to live their lives over, would happily make the same choice again.

We marched out in November. I had just turned 17, with six more years of my long sentence still to serve, and I was about to take yet another terrifying step into the unknown. National Service had just been introduced, presumably to boost the numbers of soldiers available to fight in Vietnam. Australia was steadily increasing its involvement in the war and army musicians were being sent over to assist the medical corps. There was a strong possibility I might see action. As an adventurous young man who considered himself bullet–proof, I regarded the prospect as exciting.

Before the march out, young soldiers diligently spit–polished boots to a mirror sheen. Uniforms were starched and ironed with creases so sharp they would cut cold butter. Hair was trimmed. Chins and cheeks were close–shaved. In excited anticipation, boys counted off the family members who would beam proudly from the grandstand benches, and promised to introduce mates to pretty sisters after. I dressed in silence. No–one would watch me. My aunt and uncle lived too far away and could not afford the trip.

I welcomed the order to assemble and the discipline of the ceremony. It silenced my chatty mates and distracted me from my loneliness. To the beat of the drums and the stately tempo of "Colonel Bogey", we marched on to the parade ground and around the oval. In fancy formations we led the parade, snapping responses in perfect unison to every shouted command, every signal of the hand or staff. For 40 minutes the battalion performed to ordered applause. No shouting. No cheers. I blew into the mouthpiece of the flugelhorn and fingered its valves, focusing intently on ensuring the correctness of every note and step.

Then it was over. The sergeant major dismissed us to join our families. The parade ground converted quickly to a picnic ground. Around each smartly uniformed boy a cluster of parents, grandparents and siblings formed to spread rugs, unload lunch packs and indulge in feasts carefully prepared by the catering corps, complete with celebratory wines in which even those too young to drink were permitted to indulge in strict moderation on this very special day. I stood alone and stared.

Finally, one of the officers approached.

Where should I be? What transgression had I committed by not knowing where to go or what to do when I had no family group to join?

The officer's voice, when he spoke, was surprisingly gentle. "Family couldn't make it today, son?"

"I don't have any family, sir." I shuddered in anticipation of the inevitable question, but the officer was sufficiently tactful to respond without even raising an eyebrow.

"Then best you join mine, young man. We'd be honoured to share our lunch with such a fine young soldier."

I followed him across the lawn to where his wife was unpacking sandwiches and cake. I sat in silence on the edge of a large chequered rug, grateful for the wonderful food, but decidedly uncomfortable with the ill–fitting company. I was no officer's son. Even their manner of speech was foreign—that ever–so–perfect plum–in–the–mouth diction, devoid of even the mildest slang or vulgarity and with never an 'h' dropped anywhere. It was sometimes difficult to understand and never even the slightest bit interesting.

At the graduation ball that night, I stood and watched in wistful silence through the Mother and Son dance. I leant against the wall, not in a mood to hum or beat time. Around and around they twirled, handsome young soldiers in full regalia and mothers in long, figure–hugging gowns, their hair coiffured and faces painted, looking sexy and stunning. Fathers watched from the sidelines. I squirmed uncomfortably as I realised I stood as the only boy among them.

A friend's mother's shot me a concerned glance as she spun past the first time. On the third whirl around the floor, she broke loose from Phil's arms. Her lips moved and her eyes questioned. Phil nodded. He stepped quietly aside. She approached me, smiling.

"Would you partner me for the rest of the Mother/Son dance?"

I took her arm gratefully and stepped out on to the floor. "I'm not much of a dancer, I'm afraid."

"I'll teach you. Just follow my lead."

"It's a Mother/Son dance. You really should—"

"Shhh. I saw you standing there alone. You looked so sad. Your parents couldn't make it?"

"I don't have any," I mumbled, flushing slightly. It was only a partial lie.

"Oh, I am so sorry, Paul. I had no idea. Have they been dead long?"

"Since I was eight years old. I barely even remember them."

I remembered them well. I turned away to ensure that she couldn't read my thoughts.

I remember where I came from and who I was and how my mother and father loved me, and what they taught me. And I remember the heartless lying bastard who took all that away from me and sent me to spend my youth in prison. The nuns taught me to hate. Now I have been trained to kill, and I will come for you, Geoffrey Simms. Someday... someday, I will have my revenge.

PART II

23: I FALL IN LOVE

TAMWORTH, JANUARY, 1971

"I should have been out next month," I said without emotion, "but I signed on again when they offered me an overseas tour." I lifted my upper body off the beach towel and propped on my elbow, resting my head on my left hand to gaze into her eyes. I'd known Frances just three weeks and I'd already decided that this was the girl I would marry. Impulsive? Perhaps, but it was love at first sight. I hoped desperately that she felt the same way.

Fran was the daughter of someone my aunt and uncle had recently made friends with. She was slim and pretty, with medium–length light–brown hair, and milky complexion— inherited, I presumed, from her English father. I saw from the first conversation that she was intelligent.

"It's three years." I said. "Two in Singapore, and the money's really good over there."

"So, you really do like the army then?" It was more a statement than a question.

"I hate it."

"Yet after eight years' service, you signed on again?"

I shrugged. "What else was there to do? I'm 23. It's all I've known since I was 15. I have no money, no education, no skills. No experience except as an army musician. There's not a lot of call for former army musicians in civvy street."

"So what will you do in three years' time?"

"I'm entitled to government–funded retraining when I get out. I'll have some money by then. I'll have choices. I'll go into business for myself, or buy a farm. I intend to be rich one day. This next three years is just a stepping stone towards that goal."

She was silent for a while and I wished I could read her mind. I propped there on a soft green lawn, gazing over her head at the divers bouncing on the board. Some sliced the air and neatly cut the water's surface, their pointed hands making the smallest, controlled splash. Others flopped clumsily in a thundering crash of dancing froth. In the wading pool at the end, toddlers splashed and kicked and gurgled. One or two migrated to the far end and waved chubby little arms in a valiant attempt to mimic the swimmers in the larger pool.

"I was supposed to go to Vietnam," I said, trying to suppress resentment. "I had a plan — me and two other guys. They both went. You come back from there with a bundle of money. We were gunna throw in and buy a dairy farm together. I love life on farms, and dairy farms make good money. I was bloody angry when they canned the posting. And the worst part was they gave my posting to another bloke because he went crying to the brass about needing to get away from a woman who was giving him trouble. Then he went on pre–embarkation leave and married her. Bastard!"

I rolled on to my back to stare at the sky, folding my hands behind my head. It was a deep, clear blue up there, but someone had taken a white pencil and here and there made just the faintest little scribble.

"That's why I hate the army," I said. "You're just a pawn on a chess board getting shoved about by a player who doesn't know you, doesn't know what he's doing and doesn't give a rats about you."

"Well, at least you didn't have to go to war. I should think you would be pleased about that."

"No. I wanted to go."

She sat up abruptly, and I followed and turned to face her. Her eyes were the deepest violet and so expressive you could often read her thoughts. I saw, now, that she was alarmed.

"Wanted to go?" she said. "To war?"

"For a bloke, it's the ultimate adventure."

She frowned, and considered my answer for a while.

Did I say too much — put her off me. What does it matter? I've got to go back tomorrow, and in a few weeks I've got to leave for two years abroad. We'll most likely never see each other again.

I'd had girlfriends before. I liked stroking their hair and fondling their breasts, but they were mates — good company and fun to be with, but nothing more. I was in love with Fran, but since when did I get to have anything I wanted?

"You could come with me," I said, then wondered what on earth possessed me to speak that thought out loud. Her mouth dropped open and her eyes popped. Well, I'd said it now. Might as well complete the thought, whatever risk that entailed.

"To Singapore," I explained. "We could get married and you could come with me. The army will provide a house for us, fully furnished, with everything we need in it. Linen, blankets, crockery, cookware. They supply the lot. They

150

pay wives an allowance, too, and pay for an amah to clean the house and do the washing, so you don't have to work in the heat. There's even a fan over the double bed, so you can stay cool when you're sleeping and..." I let my words trail off, thinking it unwise to say what I'd originally intended.

She opened her mouth several times and closed it again. She squeezed her eyes shut, and was silent for a long time. Her forehead creased and uncreased as the thoughts tumbled about in her head trying to form themselves into an acceptable reply. At last, she opened her eyes and gazed at me thoughtfully, summoning courage. "I hardly know you, Paul. We only just met."

"And I knew the moment I laid eyes on you that I wanted to spend the rest of my life with you."

"I just think we need to get to know each other better before we make such a monumental decision."

"Yeah, we should," I said, shrugging. "And I wish there was time. In a few weeks, I'll be thousands of miles away and I can't come back for two years."

She continued to stare at me silently for a time, a hint of tears forming in her eyes.

"Paul, I like you a lot. I do, really. I think you are a very special person, but marriage is for ever. At least it will be for me. I don't know you well enough to make that commitment. I'm sorry."

So that's that then. What did I expect her to say? If only there was more time. If only I could choose to delay my departure. But when did Paul Wilson ever have choices?

"Let's swim," I said, leaping to my feet and grabbing her hand to pull her along after me.

#

"My orders came through. I'm leaving in nine weeks."

We'd talked on the phone almost every night since I returned from Christmas leave and I'd written her long letters. I carried her replies in my pocket and I read and reread them. Love letters, but never any hint of long–term commitment. Although I'd asked her again, several times, her answer was the same.

Maybe I should ask for my posting to be cancelled? But for what? She mightn't ever agree to marry me anyway. And I wanted to go. I signed on again to go. Besides, the brass changed postings for blokes who had connections and for blokes with hooks; not for blokes like me. Blokes like me get barked at and told to obey orders, so it's easier just to stay stumm and do whatever is expected. I learnt that lesson a long time ago.

"If you want to change your mind about coming with me, you have until the first of April to put my ring on your finger," I said somewhat flippantly.

There was a long silence. I stood there, in that little red glass cell, gripping the receiver and picturing her in the musty board–lined office of that big, old boarding house. She would be perched on the edge of the worn pine table, among its clutter of papers and pens, with that thick, black, leather–bound Bible in the centre and the collection of prayer plaques behind. I wondered if the other girls were huddled at the closed door, taking turns putting ears to the keyhole and relaying her words in whispers down the line, waiting for a phrase to fuel the gossip fires and start them all giggling so that their presence was exposed.

"Fran? Are you still there?"

More silence.

"I'm sorry, Fran. I didn't mean to pressure you. I was teasing."

"Really? That's disappointing."

"What?"

"I was hoping you were serious."

"I... um... I mean—"

"I'm looking at the calendar, Paul. The last Saturday before—"

"Are you saying—"

"I think I'm saying that I want to go with you. I think I'm saying I will marry you."

24: A FAMILY OF MY OWN

ARMIDALE, MARCH, 1971

It was a small, informal wedding. We said our vows before a handful of her mother's friends and family. Afterward, 30 or so guests gathered in the garage behind her uncle's house. Neighbours brought flowers from their gardens to decorate the humble setting and aunts brought cold chicken and salad, bowls of homemade trifle and sponge cakes with jelly. With great tact and diplomacy, her mum ensured that the tradition of my guests on one side and hers on the other was not observed. I'd invited only my aunt, uncle, cousins and sister. One of my army mates stood beside me as best man.

Fran's mum had asked me nervously was there anyone I wanted to invite. "Your parents, perhaps? Where do they live?"

I shrugged. "There's no–one," I said quietly and as calmly I could manage. Then I walked away quickly so she wouldn't ask more questions, or see the sadness in my eyes — a sadness I was practised at masking well, although I'd never learnt to control the gnawing hollow feeling in my gut, or the dull ache in my heart whenever I was reminded of family or home.

How I yearned to invite my family. How desperately I wanted my mother and father to sit beside me on that special day.

How often have I thought of going home? What stopped me?

I didn't know where home was. If Uncle Bill knew, he was not inclined to tell me. I could find it, but it would take time. I had so little freedom. When I had days to myself, I sought the security and comfort of familiar people and places, or adventures with army mates. I went where I could be sure I'd be made welcome... where there were no haunting memories building walls of guilt and fear... no trepidation, no risks.

A sliver of sunlight peeped through the pine trees and a soft, cold grey mist obscured the clouds when — still in her bridal finery — my new wife took her place beside me in the garden to bid a smiling farewell. Her mother, aunts, uncles and cousins and a withered old grandmother in her best grey taffeta suit and feathered pink hat crowded in the doorway to wave. I wrapped my arm around Fran and brushed my lips against her cheek and breathed a deep sigh. I wanted only to be alone with her. My woman. My family. Fifteen years alone with my nose pressed against a window pane, watching others live life. At last, I had someone to belong to.

#

The motel rooms formed a line that climbed a little hill and descended down the other side. Numbered doors opened from a narrow veranda with bull–nose iron roof resting on white–painted colonial columns. At the rear, each room opened through French doors to a slate–tiled porch and a peaceful, sweet–scented garden beyond. Wooden love seats with white–painted cast– lace ends perched at the garden edge, then the garden fell away to a bubbling creek edged with weeping willows. Little green frogs hopped between flat, wet stones; their soft croaking barely audible over the cricket's mating calls.

I opened the French doors and stood in the doorway watching the willows swaying while Fran washed and changed and brushed her hair. When she stepped timidly towards me, nightie clinging to the soft curves of her breasts and pink nipples showing faintly through the thin cotton, I stepped back into the room and pulled the doors tightly closed. I turned and walked slowly towards her, placed my hands under her arms, lifted her gently and thrust her on to the bed. Then I dropped on top of her, stroking her hair and caressing her cheeks with my lips.

"Have you been told today?" I had formed the habit of asking her the question at least once a day. As usual, I answered for her. "You're beautiful."

She laughed, hugged me and whispered that she hoped I would still be telling her that daily when she was 80. I promised her I would.

"My family," I mumbled.

"A rather small family! We are only a couple," she corrected, wrapping her arms about my neck and pulling me close.

"My family. Someone I belong to. I never have to be alone again."

I let her undress me and she told me over and over that she loved me.

"I love you," I whispered back. Her words echoed through my head again and again and again. I said, "We will have babies. We will be a family. I will belong to a real family".

"Hey, slow down," she laughed. "It's our wedding night. I'm not sure I want to think about having babies just yet."

"I do," I said firmly. "I want to be part of a real family. My family."

Again and again, we made love. Over and over I told her she was beautiful, and I marvelled that someone so lovely could love me. In the early hours of the morning, she drifted into a peaceful, dreamy sleep.

When she woke, I was already shaved and dressed. I looked at her thoughtfully for a moment. An unexplainable fear wrapped itself about me and took possession of me.

"I hope you had the sense to use protection," I snapped, aware that I should have and regretting that I hadn't.

"What are you talking about? What's wrong?" she replied. She looked hurt and confused, and I felt a pang of guilt and adjusted my tone.

"Birth control. You did use something, didn't you?"

"Yes? Why?"

"So you don't get pregnant, of course. What else would you use birth control for? "

She stared at me, perplexed.

"I don't want a baby," I said. "I know what I said last night, but I let myself get carried away. I'd had too much to drink maybe."

"I don't think either of us want a baby immediately. I did suggest you slow down."

"I don't want a baby at all, ever. I need you to understand."

"I don't understand. Not at all."

"I don't want commitments," I said. Actually, I didn't understand either. On the one hand, I did want a family, desperately. On the other, I was terrified of the risk that implied of yet another devastating loss.

"Commitments? What do you mean you don't want commitments? You made commitments yesterday? Remember? Commitments to love me and care for me, in sickness and in health, 'til — "

"Until death do us part. But it never happens, does it? We want it to and we mean it to, but it never does. Life gets too hard. Couples break up. That's just the way it is. And when it happens, I don't want a tug–of–war–baby getting in our way. That's all."

"My grandparents didn't break up. My aunts and uncles didn't break up. None of my friends' parents broke up."

"But the statistics — "

"Statistics, Paul. Is that what we are? A statistic? You said you loved me? I meant it when I said I loved you. I meant to go on loving you for life and I believed you meant that too."

"I did. I do. It's just that..." I was confused now — disturbed and regretful.

How to fix this? What should I say? What should I do? Touch her? Would she push me away?

"I do love you," I said. "I'm sorry. I didn't mean it to come out like that. It's just that..."

"Just that what?"

"It's just that everyone I've ever loved has let me down. It's not safe for me to let myself commit to anyone."

She lifted herself off the bed then, wrapped her arms about my neck, stroked my cheek softly and buried her tear–streaked face in my shoulder. "I won't leave you, Paul. I will never let you down."

"Never is a very long time. Things change. I know you don't mean them to... don't want them to... but they do."

"Trust me. Please."

"I do. It's society I don't trust... bureaucracy... mad with authority arseholes who get off on making other people's lives a misery."

But every dog has his day, and someday Geoffrey Simms! Someday soon. And however much I want her, I cannot let commitment to Fran stand in my way.

25: TICKY–TACKY HOME

SINGAPORE, APRIL, 1971

Stepping into the street from the cool lobby of the elegant old Tudor–style Queens Hotel, that same sensation I felt when dismounting the aircraft — of stepping into a gas oven — came again. Spit–polished, olde–English elegance and plush comfort inside contrasted sharply with the crowded streets, lined on both sides by stinking open drains and rows of grubby little market stalls comprising heavily laden, rough wooden benches under coarse hessian canopies.

The Singapore air was thick and heavy with heat and humidity. A faint sewer smell mixed with sickly-sweet smells of Asian cooking and the powerful odour of chicken blood from a nearby market, where a native slammed a heavy cleaver rhythmically against a stained counter, severing heads, wings and legs from freshly plucked pink bodies. As we slid into the back seat of a battered Mercedes, the stench of Malay sweat added to the mélange.

Horns blasted and brakes squealed as the taxi weaved perilously from lane to lane. Occasionally, it veered to miss a panicked pedestrian dashing for the safety of an opposite crowded sidewalk or a panting runner or cyclist pulling a tourist–laden rickshaw. The cab rattled to a halt in the courtyard of an austere U–shaped building. The front blue–painted concrete walls wore four neat lines of evenly distributed apertures. Next to every fourth one, little half–walls marked a tiny front balcony.

"We're moving into the proverbial little box made of ticky–tacky," I said, washed by a sudden wave of depression.

From dormitories to ticky–tacky boxes furnished with army–issue linen and crockery. Well, at least I can go home at night to a meal of my own choosing and the privacy of my own bedroom and bathroom.

Our flat was on the top floor. There was no lift, so I was relieved to be met by two housing corps clerks who gallantly offered to carry some of Fran's luggage up four steep flights of polished concrete stairs. The stairwell was narrow and dark, fully enclosed by green–painted walls and opening at each floor to two facing blue–painted doors. At the top, the housing clerk produced a large ring of keys and opened the door on the left side. Inside, a long, narrow room stretched from the front door to a rear balcony accessed through heavy wooden concertina doors. On one side, near the centre, two more blue doors opened to tiny, dark bedrooms. On the other, a short hallway led off to the kitchen, and an open door revealed a much larger, lighter bedroom dominated by a double bed covered with a faded blue and white printed linen spread.

I guessed the closed door near the kitchen entry must hide the bathroom facilities. I took care, glancing into the master bedroom, to point out to Fran that there was, indeed, a fan over the bed. That had been the carrot I offered Fran when I proposed and she teased me about it for ever.

At the front–door end of the narrow living room, a metal–edged laminex table with four steel V–legs perched between two pairs of vinyl–covered kitchen chairs. At the other end, a cane lounge covered in electric–blue cotton and two matching armchairs were arranged around a chunky coffee table on a faded square of red, blue and white patterned carpet. Apart from the carpet square, the blue and white mosaic–tiled floors were all bare. The mid–green painted walls were bare. There were no curtains in the main room — only heavy, folding shutter doors. The bedroom windows were covered with what looked like the sides of hessian flourbags.

I wandered into the kitchen. It was a long, narrow room with a raw wooden table on one side, a raw wooden bench and sink with two open shelves above and a freestanding gas cooker on the other, and a tiny louvered window beside a door at the far end. The door opened to a long side balcony from which you could have reached across through the neighbour's kitchen window to steal scones from cooling trays resting on their sideboard — except I later discovered the only thing they cooked in there was fried rice and pork and soy dishes, creating nauseating smells that were later to seriously aggravate Fran's frequent bouts of morning sickness. At the end of the balcony, a cluster of cleaning equipment included an old–style cotton mop, gal squeeze–bucket, broad broom, straw broom, dustpan and brush, gal wash tub, and an ancient wooden washboard.

I returned to the living room to find that Housing Division Clerk Number One, a Lance Corporal, had flicked the switches to start two heavy overhead fans whirring. Clerk Number Two, a private, had seated himself near the now open folding doors and was fumbling with his papers. I glanced across the rear balcony — equally reach–out–and–touch–me close to the adjacent flat — and noted the neighbour's large collection of erotic underwear and negligees pegged to two wooden clothes horses. Two scantily clad, silken–haired Chinese girls were lounging on canvas chairs with open newspapers spread face down across their bellies.

"You're in a prime position here, mate," the Lance Corporal declared with an evil grin.

"What, four floors up without a lift, other flats on two sides and walls as thin as paper? Christ, I'd hate to see a crook place! You guys have got some weird ideas!"

"I didn't mean that. The missus'll hate it, but hell, you gotta see the bright side of life. Look out there. " He pointed to the balcony opposite.

"It's worse than I thought. Either we open everything to public view, or suffocate in this hellhole. Next you'll tell me the neighbour's got a peephole to the bedroom."

"Come off it. That lot out there aren't going to bother you, but you'll get a free floor show now and then."

"Meaning?"

Just then, a Malay girl emerged from another room and wandered out on to the balcony. She was wearing a semi–sheer housecoat and she carefully laid out several pair of skimpy panties and bras on the railing to dry. Then she flopped on to a banana lounge and began brushing her long hair.

"It's a den, junior. A whorehouse. Massage parlour as the nice folks say. Christ, this place is wasted on you. It ought'a be reserved for randy guys with frigid wives. Next you'll tell me you're a newlywed."

"I am."

"Oh God! Talk about takin' coal to Newcastle. Well, what the hell? Honeymoons don't last long. You'll learn to appreciate the place before your time here's up and meanwhile you can gain a lot of handy information watching who comes and goes. They turn a red light on in the window when they're open for business. Oh, and if you've got a thing about chinks, there's a damn good white whore in flat nine, but the price is high."

I was careful to keep my back turned to him. "Can you get your paper–work done and get outa here? I told you. We're on a honeymoon."

"Sure thing, Junior. Whatever you say."

When darkness fell that night, Fran glanced across to see the washing gone, men smoking on the balcony, a dozen or more girls prancing about half–naked in a dimly lit lounge room, and, outside, on the front corner of the flat, a single red lamp burning.

"Wonderful," she exclaimed. "A thousand miles from home and family, a uniformed husband who will be away from home half the year, and I'm to live in a little box sandwiched between an endless traffic jam, a Chinese kitchen and a brothel! There's only a portable galvanised tub and wooden washboard for a laundry and four steep flights of stairs to climb to see the outside world, whatever it might comprise, apart from rickshaws, men in colourful dragon costumes, insane Chinese taxi drivers, and stinking markets selling freshly butchered dogs and cats."

"Welcome home," I said, thinking that this was infinitely better than dormitories or barracks. At last, I had a home.

#

I came home the next day from my first day at work in a new unit angry and humiliated. I was welcomed with the usual initiation trick. It was standard in most institutions and I should have expected it, but it was six years since I'd stepped — as the new boy — into the unknown. I let my guard down.

I didn't tell Fran, because I was embarrassed to have fallen for their silly pretence. I wanted to fall into her arms and be comforted. I wanted to enjoy at last being in my own home with my woman.

For 15 long years I had retired at the end of the day to a tiny cubicle in a crowded dormitory — rank with the smell of fear — and struggled to sleep amid the tossing and turning, farting, and snoring of blokes I'd never choose for roommates. For 15 long years I'd risen every morning on command, to barked orders and inspections and breakfast in cold, institutional dining halls. At last I could look forward to freedom and privacy at the beginning and end of my workdays.

Fran was in the kitchen, cooking dinner. I wrapped my arms around her and began to caress her, but she pushed me gently away and protested that the oil would burn if I distracted her. A comforting warmth wrapped itself about me.

"Have you been told today?" I asked, and answered for her, "You're beautiful."

She turned and smiled at me.

"Do you know how good this feels?" I knew there was no way she could.

"Get changed, Paul, and let me finish making dinner, and then I can make you feel very much better." A mischievous glint flickered in her eyes, seductive, inviting. Ecstatic, I started for the bedroom.

The mood changed. Tight bedcovers, hospital corners, my boxer shorts folded and stowed neatly under the pillow. My drawers were rearranged, with all the civvy clothes I'd pulled from my suitcase and shoved in carelessly now folded in perfect neat piles. The assortment of coins and cufflinks I'd dumped carelessly on the dresser now neatly arranged in a small dish. Everything orderly. Everything neat. The faint odour of detergent rising from a freshly washed floor. The smell of fear!

A wave of panic gripped me. All the accumulated suffering of 15 years of discomfort and pent–up frustration at the sterility and coldness of my world — 15 years of suffering torment and abuse for the tiniest wrinkle or the smallest flaw in the shape of a mitre; 15 years of "Yes, sir. Sorry, sir," when

I wanted to spit and swear and throw things — shaped itself into a simmering ball of rage and wrapped me in sheets of fire.

I reefed at the bedcovers. I tugged at the sheet corners until they loosened and then gathered the sheet up in a ball and thrust it on the bed. I pulled drawers from the dresser and emptied them on to the floor, throwing the drawers down on top.

"Damn you!" I screamed. "What do you think this is? An army barracks? A bloody orphanage dormitory? Don't you think I've had enough of bloody mitred corners and disinfected floors and clothes folded with military precision?" I swiped my arm across the dresser, sweeping coins and jewellery and her hairbrush and comb on to the floor in a clatter.

She was in the doorway now, white–faced and trembling.

"I'm going to the pub," I shouted.

"But dinner is ready," she protested in a whisper.

"Fuck your dinner. And fuck you." I stormed out and bounded down three steps at a time. I was striding up Katong Road, searching for somewhere to buy beer, before I realised I was still in uniform, with my shirt buttons undone.

The fifth vile, warm Tiger beer finally quenched the fire in my belly. Stiff limbs relaxed. A misty image of her appeared before me and I was a frightened little boy again. I reached out, but my arms were too short. I tried to call to her, but the words stuck in my throat and choked me. I squeezed my eyes tightly shut to stop them watering. I forced myself to take deep, slow breaths.

I finished my beer and drank several more. I lost count after about the eighth. I stumbled back to the flat and climbed the stairs slowly, reluctantly.

She was asleep when I entered. She had replaced the dresser drawers and the piles of clothing were gone. There was an untidy pile on the dresser. She had made the bed up after a fashion. No tightly pulled covers. No hospital corners. Just a lower sheet tucked rather carelessly under the mattress and a top sheet draped casually over her. Her pillow was wet. A pile of screwed–up tissues littered the bedside table.

I pulled off my clothes and thrust them in a pile on the floor, climbed in bedside her, and fell instantly into a deep sleep.

In the morning, I found my clothing folded somewhat casually and dropped in not–too–precise piles in drawers. Neat, but not to military standards. I stepped from the shower to the smell of toast and bacon. She took care to keep her back to me and said nothing. Remorse weighed on me. My stomach churned and my head ached. I tried desperately to do justice to the breakfast she served, but after the fourth mouthful I charged from the room with a mouthful of vomit.

I went to the bedroom for my socks and boots. The bed was made. Neat. No tight covers. No mitred hospital corners.

I went to Fran and put my arms around her and kissed her tenderly. "Have you been told today?" I whispered, hoping she wouldn't push me away. "I'm so sorry, Fran. I don't know what came over me."

She kissed me, but it was reluctant, grudging. "I'm trying to understand, Paul," she whispered. "But I need you to help me. Talk to me, please!"

I shook my head. "I don't want you to be part of that world, Fran," I said. "I don't want to live in that world when I'm with you."

#

The days passed in a haze of happiness. I woke in the morning to stroke Fran's hair and ask her when she was last told. She decorated the little flat with wall hangings and ornaments and pretty bedcovers, and dainty antimacassars on the backs of the lounge chairs. She cooked me wonderful dinners, and when I was home in the evenings she snuggled against me to watch movies. When I had time off before an evening concert, we lay on the floor listening to symphonies together.

She had taken piano lessons for a couple of years and sang. She said she never understood music though. She told me I opened a new world. I told her the stories the music told and how to understand the tale. I talked about the composer's life and the society he lived in, how different styles of music evolved through the ages, and which parts of a piece were difficult to play and challenged me.

At the end of our third month there, I took her to a ball. Dances were regular events and army wives delighted in the chance to don their finest gowns, coiffure their hair and 'strut their stuff'. Fran bought a new dress for the occasion. She looked radiant and stunning when I opened the taxi door for her. She beamed when I asked her had she been told today, and reminded me I had asked her several times that day already.

I wasn't much of a dancer and disliked the sport. I planned to spend the evening sitting in a quiet corner, sipping beer and watching. I guess I just assumed Fran would sit beside me, quite content with a glass of wine and some nibblies and my lewd comments on the officers' harlots and the sergeants' dragons.

We enjoyed a pre–dinner drink. I introduced her to mates' wives. We chatted easily for a time, and then we dined — a sumptuous feast of prime steak.

I walked to the bar for another beer, and I brought her back another glass of wine. We sat for a while to let the dinner settle. We chatted to friends and watched the dancers. It was perfect. My friends admired my gorgeous woman and I basked in their compliments to her.

"Are you going to ask me to dance, Paul?" she asked when the Master of Ceremonies announced a slow waltz.

"I don't dance."

"I can teach you. The waltz is easy."

"I don't want to learn."

"Come on, Paul. I love to dance. You'll enjoy it."

"What are you now? A bloody drum major?"

"What? What are you talking about?" How could she know that the drum major had announced the event with the barked order, "You will all go and you will enjoy it"?

"OK. One dance," I said, washed by a wave of remorse and desperate to make amends. We took half–a–dozen turns around the dance floor. I hated every minute of it.

"It's an obscene sport," I said, returning to my seat. "It's for cheap women and men on the prowl."

"What are you talking about? That's nonsense, Paul. Honestly! It's ridiculous!"

"Women come to dances to tease men and flaunt their curves," I said, "and men come to dances to rub up against women. When the women get a few drinks in them they want more than rubbing and they take off with any bloke who's handy. They get it off on the back seat of his car or in a dark corner of the yard behind the dance hall. Half the time they are so bloody drunk they don't even remember in the morning."

She stared at me, astonished. "That's insane, Paul. You're being ridiculous. Cheap women and unfaithful men will get together one way or another, but most people just enjoy dancing as a sport. A dance is a great social event. Everyone enjoys dressing up. People enjoy the company. It's good exercise and it's fun."

"That's your take on it. Fine," I said, and strode off to the bar for another beer.

When I returned, she was gone. I searched for her. She was on the dance floor. A warrant officer's arm rested across her back and he held one hand in the air. She rested her other hand on his shoulder. Their bodies weren't touching.

I felt the heat rise into my neck and my lips tighten and my head start to throb. I strode across the floor, gripped her upper arm and pulled her savagely. "We are leaving," I said harshly. "Say goodnight to your boyfriend."

She stumbled, tripping on the hem of her dress, but I dragged her behind me down the stairs and across the parking lot, pushed her into the back of a waiting taxi, slammed the door, and climbed in the front. "Katong, driver," I snapped. "Step on it."

We rode in stony silence. She climbed the stairs without a word and went straight to the bedroom to change. She washed her makeup off. I stood in the doorway watching her.

"You see what I mean about dancing," I said. "I leave you alone for half a minute and you're off flirting with another bloke."

"I wasn't flirting, Paul. He asked me to dance. There was nothing in it. It was just a friendly whirl around the floor. Totally innocent."

"Is that what you thought? Stupid, naïve girl! There is no such thing as an innocent whirl around the floor with a bloody uniform. Every bloke in this army is out to get it from every bitch he can con into taking her clothes off. And every bitch in the world will have it from any man who offers it if she thinks she can get it without her husband knowing. I know what women are."

"I'm not like that."

"No? Of course you're not! You're miss little sweet and innocent who closes her eyes and thinks of England when her husband wants it. You don't even enjoy it and you would never do it with anyone you weren't married to."

"The last bit is absolutely true. I wouldn't."

"You're just like the rest of them. They all say the same thing. And they all do the same thing. Even your straight–laced prim and proper lady aunts. I'll bet half the men in town know what they look like with their clothes off and what their grunts sound like when they are into it."

"That's a disgusting thing to say, Paul. How dare you?"

"Your mother couldn't hold a marriage together. Which bloke did her husband catch her with?"

She slapped me then and I hit her back. I punched her in the eye and in the stomach and I swore at her. Then I pushed her down on the bed and ripped her panties off and held her savagely while I forced myself into her.

"Is that what you were after?" I spat. "Think a fancy pants warrant officer would have a bigger one than me? Give you more pleasure?"

She lay like a statue under me, silent tears streaking her face, lips tightly set. When I was done, she turned her back to me and I heard her sobbing softly. I hated myself. I hated her. I hated the world. I swore I would murder that bastard warrant officer.

Everything I wanted — everything that gave me pleasure — someone snatched away.

26: MURDER ON BUGIS STREET

JUNE, 1971

I went down Bugis Street the next evening. I left Fran at home angry and brooding and threatening to leave me. That was no surprise. It was rather surprising she had stayed this long. It was hard for her living in a foreign land and trying to mix with a social group to which she would never belong. I wasn't a soldier by choice. I hated the army, and she would never be a soldier's wife.

I carried my guilt over last night like two monstrous suitcases, weighing me down and causing my shoulders to sag. I pictured her at home, miserable.

It would serve me right if she sought male company. I don't deserve a faithful wife. It's probably best she leave. I love her, but I'm no good for her. She deserves better — someone who isn't haunted by demons and driven to crazy fits of jealousy and rage. Someone who can be gentle and tender with her, the way I am when the demons leave me alone. Someone with ambition and a career path, who can offer her a future.

Bugis Street was dirty and dangerous and corrupt. I went out of curiosity, because it was famous everywhere for its gaiety, evil and iniquity. I wandered alone through the pasar malam in Chinatown, with its colourful hangings and its quaint discordant music. The cymbals clanged, the hawkers shouted, and weird and fascinating wares were displayed for sale. The air was thick and heavy. The sweet smell of sweat mixed with scents of perfumes, sticky sweet rice cakes, chow mein, and the stink of raw fish, dog, cat and rat.

Along Queen Street, I stopped now and again at a boozer for a long, tall glass of Tiger, sitting to rest and drink at one of the dozens of little round tables that crammed footpath and roadway. I paused, when I thought a shadow or a gawking crowd obscured me, to stare at the flashy cross–dressers strutting awkwardly in their high heels and pulling back their shoulders to project their artificial breasts. It was easy to tell the beanie boys from real women. They were drop–dead gorgeous and I marvelled that a man could make himself up to look so feminine and lovely.

Lingering at one table, obscured by a group of boozing G.I.s, I watched the famous 'Dance of the Flaming Arseholes' performed on the flat toilet roof and listened to the Aussie sailors' foul–mouthed chant. Occasionally, a tartily attired young Chinese or Malay accosted me to offer entertainment, quoting prices ranging from extortionate to almost free. When I shook my head, they squawked insults in their native language and pushed past me to the next prospect. There were plenty. The streets were packed with tourists, American G.I.s and ANZUK servicemen — many seeking sex with either prostitutes or homos, and there were plenty of both to choose from.

I was fascinated, but uncomfortable, so I pushed on to Tanjong Pagar where the dock workers drank at night. I was ill at ease among the gangs of ruffians shouting swear words at transsexuals and puckering lips at the pretty pros gyrating sensuously among them. I considered seeking a rickshaw to go back, but my search took me closer to the docks. I was near the water now. Here and there, between reflections of the brightly coloured lights, were shadowy corners and dark niches.

When I first saw him, I was uncertain. Then I looked more closely and recognised him. Jungle! The bullying Balcombe senior I had outwitted for a prime camp spot some six or more years before. He had nicknamed me "Jungle", calling out "Hey you, Jungle" and prompting the whole platoon to laugh as he explained his jibe. "Green and dense," he had said mockingly.

I had exacted my revenge on a bush training exercise. Jungle laid claim to the prize campsite — sheltered, shady, and well grassed. He invested a full 20 minutes pitching his tent and meticulously preparing his camp site. He was just preparing for a welcome rest when I approached him, sniffing.

"I smell snake," I said, my nose wrinkling. Jungle frowned and glanced nervously about him at the long grass.

"Yep. Definitely snakes here. I'm from the bush, you know. I know when there are snakes about."

Jungle pulled down his tent and gathered his belongings and made a hasty retreat. I made little attempt to hide my mirth as I pitched my tent and unpacked my belongings right on the spot he had vacated. "Who's green and dense?" I muttered to myself with a chuckle.

Jungle wore three stripes now and the badge of the Infantry Corp.

Huh. So Mr Big Time is a footslogger? The thought pleased me. The stripes made no impression.

He was arguing with a feisty little Malay. The words were inaudible, but the waving arms, Jungle's threatening fist and the Malay's fierce spit spoke of the intensity of their dispute. The Malay pulled a knife. Jungle pulled a pistol.

It was over in an instant. The shot wasn't loud, only a swift, sharp crack. The Malay fell. The soldier calmly wiped the sweat from his face with his handkerchief and tossed the pistol into the dark river. It hardly made a splash. He turned and walked in my direction.

Nervousness turned to fear. I recognised him. It was likely he'd remember me. Even if Jungle's memory was short, bandsmen are generally well–recognised, if not well–known, for we are so often out on public display. The focal point at military ceremonies, we were noticed, in civvys, for our less–than–optimum physique. We were frequently observed making rowdy returns, at two or three a.m., from a late–night gig. The engineers, clerks and infantry men would emerge bleary–eyed on balconies, whining that we woke them and disturbed their infants, shouting abuse and ordering silence.

I shrank back, eased stealthily towards a pylon and crouched behind it, panting, squeezing my lips to silence my breathing and holding my chest as though trying to quieten a thumping heart. I waited and listened. How long? No sounds. The dull thud, thud and the occasional clink, as the metal caps of Jungle's boot kicked a bottle or can, had faded and stopped.

I dared to rise now, sliding to the side of the pylon and leaning forward to peer into the blackness. Empty. He was gone, or hiding, waiting? The pier stretched ominously into the blackness, lapping water caressing its legs. There were hiding places under it and in boats anchored alongside, and up among the stacked containers, and in the warehouse doorways, set back, as they were, to form little sheltered porches.

I sought out the shadowy corners I'd earlier taken such care to avoid, creeping along, close to the walls, or darting from one doorway to the next, clinging to the darkness.

What if a harlot invites me inside? Would I welcome the promise of safety, or run from the risks of her ire when, having given her the nod, I rejected her favours? Do I fear the soldier more, or the prostitute and her pimp?

I dripped sweat and was conscious of my body odour, despite the heavy, sweet smells of the sticky tropical night. My breathing was loud and desperate over the clanging, singing and shouting. I felt the eyes of a hundred transvestites and a thousand warfies watching me intently as I scanned the crowds to see if the footslogger's eyes were among those fixed on me, monitoring my every move.

Which way did the soldier go? Did he see me? Does he know what I witnessed? Will he come after me to silence me?

I inched along a darkened stretch of wall, then tried to blend with a mob of raucous sailors, although my attire was different and my face was pale with fear where theirs were ruddy from the grog and gaiety. It seemed that every finger pointed at me and every eye stared. I feared any moment now they would cry in unison, "He's here". Over and over, I imagined the lunk bearing down on me. I felt his iron fist smash my jaw and tasted blood. My head swam and my legs gave way.

I pulled myself upright and swallowed hard. There was no blood. There was no wound. I clenched my fists and primed myself to choose my mark, duck the soldier's blow, and reply quickly with one fast, deadly swing.

What's wrong with me? I'm a boxer, and all but unbeaten. That arsehole, Jungle, is no match for my speed and skill. I could kill the bastard with one punch.

My self–assurances were unconvincing. I ducked back into the shadow and slid along another wall section. I found the middle of a large group of European tourists and ambled casually, listening for the soldier's heavy tread, but taking care not to look behind.

Finally, I was back in Chinatown among the hawkers, men–women and crowds of Europeans swilling beer, flirting with the trans', and occasionally allowing themselves to be led off with a gleam in their eye by a pretty Oriental to a grubby overdressed parlour and a semen–stained bed.

I hailed a black cab and called "Katong, Johnny", using the name soldiers used for all Asian cabbies. The taxi rattled and shuddered up a back lane and on to the main road. Entering the courtyard, I urged the cabbie close to the left entrance. I paid the John his double fare without complaint, then ducked out and ran up four flights of stairs, shaking out my keys in readiness before I reached the first landing.

In the morning, I flicked the pages of the paper without comment and feigned disinterest when the murder was reported on the TV news. I told Frances nothing, but for weeks I nurtured a deep fear. I rehearsed my reaction if I saw Jungle.

Stay calm. Be normal. Nod, smile, keep walking.

Should I go to the MPs? The local police, perhaps? Would an Aussie soldier get a fair trial here? Would the brass allow a trial at all, or would they simply drag the soldier off to Holsworthy after a perfunctory court–martial held only to appease those who demanded a semblance of justice? Perhaps, anyway, Holsworthy would be a picnic compared to an Asian jail?

Perhaps I was mistaken? Perhaps I hadn't recognised the murderer correctly? Maybe it was self–defence? The locals could be aggressive sometimes.

I remembered the night I argued with the cabbie over a fare. I was terrified that night. I might easily have ended in a ditch with a knife in my chest if I hadn't thrown a handful of bills at the man and run.

And what about Simms, the man I swore to find and murder for sentencing me unjustly to spend my youth incarcerated? I'm planning a murder and perhaps Jungle had equally good cause.

Fascinated by the antics of the Kai Tais, my mates went often to enjoy the vibrant nightlife. I never went down Bugis Street again. Over breakfast,

I began the first of many agonising debates with my conscience. Annoying pangs would invade my thoughts at the most inconvenient moments: while performing, just at the climax of that solo when the notes rang out in perfect sequence and the tone was sweet and clear, and only the music should occupy my thoughts. They would come while I tried to sleep, my wife curled in a foetal ball beside me, pressing her tight buttocks against my thighs.

When reading, I often had to go back and read the chapter over again, and still an annoying twinge of guilt tainted the author's message. When I watched a movie, I was sometimes so distracted that I missed a key part of the plot. I dared not ask Fran what I missed for fear of her interrogation. She must not know of my dilemma. Then I would have to tell her what I planned to do to Simms.

I ought to have reported the incident. Evil should be punished. An eye for an eye; a life for a life. That's what they taught me. They, who brutally beat little children for the most minor transgressions. They, who cursed me with the belief that I was so worthless that I had no right to life. They, who told me I was the scum of the earth, born of no–goods and destined to be a no–good. Who were they to tell me what was good and what was evil?

I was taught it was wrong to kill and then I was handed a gun and trained to be a killer. And I planned to kill a man one day. Simms deserved to be killed. He killed me, in a manner of speaking. He killed my spirit. He only left an empty, hurting body to stumble and struggle through life cursed.

I planned to become a killer and the killing I planned was justice. The community wouldn't see it that way. Society would condemn me. The community only understood about killing bodies. No–one in the justice system understood the murder of a soul.

27: THREE STEPS TO RECOVERY

JULY, 1971

I was drowning in an ocean of remorse and fear. Fear of Jungle. Fear of losing Fran.

I'd said "sorry" a thousand times. I'd begged her forgiveness. Then I'd told her she should not forgive me, for I knew what I had done was unforgiveable. I said I knew I didn't deserve her and I wouldn't blame her if she left. I expected she should, for her own sake.

People came and people went in my life. I had been determined to be prepared for her to go, but I could no more reconcile myself to the idea of life without her than to losing my right arm. Then she spoke two words that turned my whole world upside down.

"I'm pregnant."

Panic gripped me, but it was mixed with an ecstasy I could never have imagined. I stared at her blankly for a moment, trying to take it in.

"I can't leave, Paul. I can't deprive my child of its father. But you have to find a way to control your irrational outbursts. Something has hurt you very deeply — broken a part of you. Tell me about it, Paul, and maybe I can find a way to help you mend."

I shrugged. "I don't want to talk about it, Fran, and you don't want to know. It was all a very long time ago and it's over. Forgotten."

I caught her in my arms then and lifted her off the floor and twirled about singing, "I'm going to be a daddy. I'm going to be a daddy". I kissed her tenderly and said "I'm so sorry I hurt you, Fran. Forgive me, please. I promise it will never happen again. I love you. God, how I love you!"

If only it could end. If only I could forget.

#

Murdering Simms was one of three steps I planned to remedy what I perceived was wrong with my world. My second step, vital now that I was to be a father, was to acquire wealth. The wealthy dictated to and suppressed the masses. They created and manipulated the system that enslaved the less advantaged. I wanted to be rich enough to give my child everything I never had, powerful enough to effect changes that would ensure no kid ever suffered as I had. I wanted to find a special place to build my version of Ohio — a place for homeless boys to call home, to be safe, to learn how to live and to find their place in the world.

I never respected the rich. In my opinion, most were deserving of loathing and scorn for the way they acquired and used their money. I was convinced all wealth was acquired through inheritance, crime or amazing luck. Hard work could only ever keep the wolf from the door, but I'd fluked a big win on a racehorse once and I'd become obsessed with the idea that if I could find a way to pick winners, I could achieve my dream. I began an intensive study of form, the configuration of racetracks, and the different results achieved by selected horses running different distances, in different conditions, and with different jockeys on their backs. I hardly ever wagered money, but I was convinced there had to be a statistical formula that would provide the key to consistent winning. I was determined to find it and then to use my winnings to achieve my dream.

The prospect of fatherhood, combined with observations of life in Singapore, revived another obsession. I wanted to find my family. The nuns had indoctrinated me with the belief that my parents had abandoned me. The fact that they had never sought me out tempted me to believe. My own lifestyle caused me to fear what I might return to if I could ever find them. After years of seeing families living in neat little houses with running water and electricity and plenty to eat, the memory of a rough, poverty–stricken lifestyle disturbed and embarrassed me.

Witnessing the lifestyle of poor Singaporeans changed that. The cheerful little paupers slept rough and scrounged food, or slaved all day for less money than I'd had in pocket money as a teenager. They walked littered streets with stinking open drains alongside carrying filthy water richly polluted with food scraps, urine and faeces. Yet the bent–up old rickshaw driver laughed and joked as he ran along pulling his cart full of tourists. The young boy who worked his way up rows of army houses polishing lines of shoes and boots left at the front door each morning, earned barely enough to buy a cup of rice a week, but he sang happily as he went about his work.

We hired an amah to clean and do the laundry. Eng talked happily of the rough hut she had shared with her seaman husband, nine children, chooks and a few pigs, before the Government forced them to move to a single sterile room in a high–rise, with a washbasin and single kerosene burner at one end and a shared latrine down the hall.

I watched with amazement as that cheerful little woman shuffled about our apartment scrubbing floors, beating mats and scrubbing jungle–green uniforms on a washboard before dumping them into boiling starch and ironing them until shirts and shorts stood stiff and erect. The nuns would have called her a heathen when she declared that the pictures decorating our walls must always hang on a slight angle so that any evil spirits would slide off the top. They would have recoiled in horror when she banged, clanged, clapped and shouted as colourfully dressed natives joined funeral parades waving pointed sticks at the air to frighten the spirits away from their dead. But she was a good, kind, honest woman. She would never beat a small child until his skin was broken, nor brand him 'filth' or 'trash' and threaten him with hell and damnation for no greater crime than being born poor.

Listening to her, I remembered how unattractive the civilised lifestyle had seemed after living feral and free in the bush. The memory of poverty and rough living no longer overwhelmed me. I began to again think and feel as I had as a child, before brainwashing and indoctrination tempted me to believe a life of rigid discipline, cruelty presented as training and existence in sterile dormitories and austere eating and recreation halls, was healthier than living as I believed nature had intended.

Hawkers weren't permitted into the army camp, but a wizened old Chinese woman came into the camp each Wednesday peddling children's clothing. I wondered how this woman gained admission. A neighbour was taking lessons in Chinese and, one Wednesday morning, she brought her tutor to translate for her so she could quiz the woman.

"They've given her a lifetime pass to peddle her wares to soldiers," the translator said, "as a thank you for her service to Australian and British soldiers imprisoned here during the war. She was a servant in the prison camp, employed by the Japanese apparently. She used to smuggle mail in and out, and bring in medicines for sick prisoners."

The woman became agitated then, rattling on in her own tongue for an extended time. The translator listened intently. Finally, she paused.

"That's quite a story," he said. She seemed to understand his exclamation, and she muttered some instruction and pointed at our little group. The translator began his tale.

"Seems a prisoner came in with shrapnel wounds in both legs, all infected. Showed no sign of healing. She brought a little box of maggots and introduced them to the wound to eat away at the infection. Later, when he began to mend, she helped him escape to the beach to bathe his legs in the healing saltwater. She took him food and water every evening, but after several days of hiding on the beach, he walked back into the prison and turned himself in. It was an island. There was no place else to go." [viii]

I studied the hawker for a moment, remembering my mother talking of Dad's awful war experiences. Then I pulled out my wallet and extracted a $50 bill. The hawker's eyes popped and her face split into a huge gummy smile. I chose some pretty little dresses and cute little baby boy suits from her basket and pressed the bill into her hand.

Over breakfast the next morning, without a word of explanation and in a tone that defied her to question me, I told Fran, "I've made a decision. When we go back to Australia, I want to find my family. I want to go home".

28: BLOKES LIKE ME

WAGGA WAGGA, JUNE 2010

"How things change," Paul mused, slowing the Roller as he approached the "Welcome to Wagga Wagga" sign with its caution about driving speeds in city streets printed neatly below. "We arrived and left here in a reconstructed Morris 1100, bought from a wrecking yard for a few hundred bucks, and so loaded its chassis almost scraped the ground. Nearly 40 years now, Ern, and we've never been back. Driven all over New South Wales, but always bypassed."

"Were you particularly unhappy here?" Ern asked. His creased brow suggested his memory bank was shuffling snippets, searching for references to events in Paul's life that might have happened in this town.

Paul shrugged. "Not particularly. It was just another miserable chapter. The last months of my incarceration." A hesitant half–smile played at the corners of his lips, but didn't reach his eyes. They remained glazed and cold.

Paul and Ern focused on road signs for a time. When Paul next spoke, it seemed more to himself than his companion. "Professional musician to labourer, on a third the pay," he mused. "The price of freedom!"

They turned into the airport parking lot just as the plane from Sydney dipped, bounced and taxied. Paul strode across to the arrival gate, hands in his pockets, expression bland. But when he saw Fran — dressed in fitted linen slacks and a tailored Fletcher Jones woollen blazer and smiling radiantly — his eyes lit and his cheeks dimpled. He kissed her cheek, took her bag, and slipped an arm casually around her waist to guide her to the parking lot.

"Have you been told today?" he asked. She laughed in reply — a high, tinkling, self–conscious little giggle.

"Our mission today, darling," Paul said, "is to tell Ern about the months we spent here and the beginning of my life as a free man."

She frowned. "You still think of it that way, don't you? It was the army, Paul, not prison. You had a lot of fun."

"Andy Dufresne had fun at times during his incarceration too," he replied flippantly. "But he was a hell of a lot happier when he got out." In response to her puzzled look, he added <u>Shawshank Redemption</u>. Ern remarked that the analogy was rather extreme.

"Being in jail means having food, shelter and leisure time provided for you," Paul said, now very serious. "Therefore, it appears to be a desirable state. The difference between being in jail and being a king in a castle is that the king is causative — his thinking affects others. The prisoner is the subject of someone else's causativeness — the thinking of others controls him. To me, the army was jail, because I continued to be the effect of the thinking of others. I had no control over my life."

"And when you got out, I remember you being in a state of absolute exhilaration for a day or two, and then crashing so badly it terrified me," Fran said, her face contorting with the pain of recollection.

Paul's face paled to the shade of old parchment. He looked dazed and hurt. "I realised I was still imprisoned. Sterile cubicles, barked orders and rigid routine were my world for so long, I didn't know how to function outside that environment. Ultimately, I guess my own thinking imprisoned me — my inability, due to training, to believe in my ability to be causative in my own world."

WAGGA WAGGA, JUNE 1973

"It was my bloody stripe, Fran. Bastards! I was transferred back to this shit hole instead of the city because there was a promotion waiting for me here. Col told me that before we left. He set it up."

I waited for the noise of a passing train to stop. We had been back from Singapore two months now. I was posted to Wagga Wagga and after shuffling us from one temporary residence to another, claiming a housing shortage, the army had eventually moved us into a tiny cottage right next to the rail line. Every time a train went past, the whole house shook.

"They gave me a fucking consolation prize," I said. "They're introducing French horns into the band, and they let me transfer from cornet and play horn for a change. In different circumstances, I'd be rapt. I love the horn, but it's pretty crappy compensation."

Fran put her hand on my shoulder, but I pushed it away.

"You didn't help! The dickhead couldn't pass a simple maths test, but he drives the band sergeant to work every day. And with you helping him pass the exam, well, that's it, isn't it? He gets my promotion and I get a fucking French horn."

She ignored the accusation and went back to peeling vegetables. We both knew I had asked her to help Joe with his maths. She didn't know it would affect my chances of promotion.

"Don't know what I expected. Not as if it's a first."

She spun around then, and stared at me. I never talked to her about my past.

"Second year at Balcombe, they put me in charge of a minor work operation. All except one of the team worked willingly. I asked the slacker politely to help, but he ignored me. I said, 'Mate, I don't have any stripes, but I was put in charge of this operation. Everyone else is doing their bit. Come on. Have a go. Do your bit'. He sneered and said, 'Get fucked!'

"I glared at him for a minute. He raised his fists. I hesitated for a sec, then answered with one swift punch to his upper chest. He reeled a bit and his thick–rimmed glasses began to slip."

I paused for a swig of beer.

"I was focused on the damn glasses, watching them slide — like in slow motion. I let my eyes follow them, praying they wouldn't break. The hook came as I watched, totally distracted. Slacker's fist came down on my top lip and a moment later blood was streaming down my chin. I groped for my handkerchief, pressed it to the wound, staggered backwards, and slumped to the ground. Slacker just shrugged and went back to sit under his tree, leaning back on its trunk. He stuck another cigarette in his gob, flicked the lighter and inhaled. He just sat there puffing and looking smug."

"An hour later, a Corp doctor was examining the holes my teeth had made in my top lip. I said I tripped and fell against a tree trunk, but of course he knew better. I had five stitches. I had to continue playing my instrument normally all the time that wound was healing. The pain was excruciating. It taught me two lessons. I never lost concentration in a fight again, and I gave up any fantasies about rising through the ranks. I obviously wasn't cut out for a position of authority."

"That's hardly a fair assessment, Paul. You were a kid and a bully took advantage of a situation."

I shrugged. "That's what Gordon McLaren said when he tried to get me promoted. He turned up in Pucka as band sergeant when I was 21. Says to me one night 'How come you don't have hooks, Paul. You're good at your job. You should have been promoted before now. I'm going to make sure you get the next promotion'. A month later this arsehole comes back from Vietnam and says to the boss 'I want to be a corporal' and guess what? They promote him over me. Bum licker, of course. Always running around making a big show of asking what he can do to help. That's what you have to be to get pro-moted in the army — a bum licker!"

"And you, Paul, are definitely not that," Fran said quietly.

"Won't become one either. They make me sick."

"But you could be a little less antagonistic, couldn't you?"

"I stand up for myself, that's all. I don't take shit."

"You go around whistling 'Waterloo' every time you pass a warrant officer who rubs you the wrong way. You don't think that gets up his nose?"

"I like the tune, and I like whistling."

"That's what you say to anyone who objects to your behaviour, but I know better and so do they. And what about taping a sergeant's ranting and playing it back to a group of mates and their wives?"

"You rolled around the floor laughing. He carried on like a loony. It was bloody funny! Anyway, I said it was a Bill Cosby tape we were laughing at and no–one said different except a sergeant who was eavesdropping and imagined he heard something he didn't."

I stood up to drop an empty beer can in the bin and pull another from the fridge. I pulled at the tab angrily and took a deep swig. "That stuff happened in Singapore. Nobody here knows about it."

"But maybe they see signs of that rebellious attitude."

"Whose side are you on, anyway?" I was snapping at her now, annoyed by her seeming disloyalty. But she was right, and I knew it. I undermined myself when it came to career advancement. Perhaps I didn't want to advance. I wanted freedom, and deep down in my subconscious, I knew advancement would only get in the way.

"I'm on your side, Paul," she replied emphatically. "I feel for you. It's deeply disappointing, for both of us, and it's unfair. I just think you could give yourself a better chance for next time."

"Next time. Yeah. Right. There's always a bloody next time. That's what they said. And next time there will be another arse–licking jerk sucking up to the boss. Don't know what I was thinking anyway. Blokes like me don't get promotions."

Blokes like me. Fran had been married to me for over two years now, and recently delivered our second child, yet she didn't know me. She had no idea who I was before we met. It was as if my life began when we got together. I knew it bothered her that I seemed to have no past.

I told her I had done some scuba diving before we met and loved it, but all my gear was stolen. Having had one terrifying encounter with a shark, I'd lost interest in the sport. She knew I joined the army at 15 and she knew I hated it. I'd never told her why I joined. My life was strictly compartmentalised. I'd sworn to keep my early years a secret, and I'd honoured that promise to myself.

She knew I'd spent time in an orphanage. I'd gone to school with her cousins in those early years. She knew I called my aunt and uncle's house 'home'. Beyond that, there was nothing. No photographs of me as a boy or youth, nor of family, friends or special places. There were no school report cards, award certificates, sporting trophies or personal mementos, nor books with inscriptions inside exposing them as Sunday School prizes, school awards or gifts from a loved one on some special occasion. I claimed no friends, just workmates and past acquaintances in whom, regardless of their past role in my life, I had little interest except as drinking partners, and for whom I held no affection.

There was no talk of past dreams or future aspirations, except to get out of the army and win a fortune on racehorses, both of which I knew she considered unachievable. Well, perhaps I could get out of the army, but to do what? I signed on again because I had no other options. I was a single man then. Now I had a family to support.

"He's diligent and dedicated to practice to the point that the other men often ridicule and torment him," a sergeant's wife had told my surprised wife once. "He spends every spare minute at work practising." But I never brought musical scores into the house and never played at home. My diligence at work was to compensate for having no natural talent. I was entirely unsuited for my profession. It was my job and I did it conscientiously during working hours.

I knew Fran often wondered why I entered a profession for which I claimed to be so unsuited; why I signed on to a life I claimed to hate so much. When she asked, I replied simply that I'd had no choice and refused to explain.

I drank heavily, rebelled against authority often, and was occasionally violent. But I was secretly fiercely proud of my good conduct record and my reputation for diligence at work. I was all bravado and bluster when faced with threat or warning or claiming to be planning evil deeds, but harsh treatment had taught me to fear punishment. It was the values my parents taught me in those early years, though, that kept me honest.

Fran was the only woman I'd ever been with, and that astonished her.

"Young musicians in uniform," she had commented once, "I would think you would have girls everywhere swooning over you."

I shrugged. "Guess I was never very interested. I could get a date whenever I wanted one. Had a steady girlfriend for a while. Strictly platonic. Mostly I was more interested in dart and snooker competitions in the local pub… and boxing, 'til I got busted fighting in uniform."

"Oh?"

"We were in Melbourne, playing at the show. After the diagram march, a group of us went for a drink. When we passed the Jimmy Sharman Boxing Stadium, I told another bloke I'd won a few quid against their troupe boxers when I was a teenager. Dave suggested we volunteer to accept a challenge. We were in ceremonials, so I resisted, but he said we could take our white coats off. He promptly offered to enter the ring.

"He won his rounds, and then it was my turn. There was five quid on offer for surviving three rounds. I'd never been beaten in the Sharman tent — and rarely outside of it. Besides, I wasn't about to appear chicken after my mate walked off with a prize.

"I stripped down to my trousers, but with an audience watching I could hardly fight in my underwear. Partway through the last round, I looked up to see the band sergeant scowling at me from the back of the crowd. Don't know how I managed to win that round, with one nervous eye on the sergeant all through the last half. Thankfully, he wasn't a bad bloke. I escaped with a severe but unofficial reprimand and a caution that if anyone else had caught me I'd have been skinned alive." I laughed at the recollection.

"But yeah," I continued, "young soldiers usually have no trouble picking up willing bed-mates and most of them have no scruples when it comes to sleeping with any girl or woman—married or otherwise. I never considered it worth the risks, emotional or physical. Anyway, I like to do it between sheets I know are clean and with a woman I know is disease free. And now that I'm married… well… it's a hell of a lot simpler to stay that way and avoid the unwelcome complications of being unfaithful, no matter how attractive some of the opportunities might be."

I often told her to leave me, but I knew she didn't believe I would ever initiate a break–up. She never believed that I seriously wanted her to go. I merely wanted it understood that I didn't need her. Needing or wanting anyone or anything invited enemies to hurt you by taking what you wanted away.

I loved playing at concerts and I would come home on a high after and talk about how good it felt to be up there on show and how well the band had performed. Yet I constantly talked about yearning to do something useful with my life. I considered what I did a waste.

"You practise for hours, then you go out there and make a magnificent sound and everyone claps, then it's gone, Fran," I said often. "It achieves nothing."

"It entertains people, Paul. It gives them pleasure. They go home feeling happy. That's achieving something."

"Yeah. They listen and clap and for five minutes they feel good, then they go home and forget they even heard it. That perfect note you worked so hard for—it just evaporates! Builders create houses for people to live in for decades. Clothes manufacturers make stuff people wear year after year. Even artists and writers create something real and lasting. Musicians? They create a vacuum. A nothing. Especially army musicians. Jesus! They put on ridiculous–looking clobber and they march around ovals banging drums and blowing horns with a clown out front waving a stick. The real stars of the show—the new recruits graduating or the blokes going off to war or coming back—march along behind waiting for their turn for a moment of glory. What a waste of effort! The whole damn show is a load of hypocritical bullshit."

"OK, I get that you don't like the parades, but you do love the concerts."

"Yeah. I play the occasional concert in the park. Nice! I get five minutes of fame and the people get five minutes of pleasure. Most of the bloody concerts are for arsehole sergeants and officers and their dragon wives playing 'let's dress up for a fancy dinner and pretend we're important'."

"You're a cynic, Paul. Can't you try to take a more positive approach to life."

"No. There's nothing positive about my life. Not my work life, anyway."

"Then maybe you should transfer to another corp. Is that an option?"

"What? Become a bloody storeman? Stuff around with those half–witted morons doing even less than musicians do? B–company! They be there when you go and they be there when you get back, except that there's no war on at the moment so there's nothing useful for any of them to do. They just train for something that might not happen until they're six feet under.

"No, Fran," I told her often, "I have to get out of the army."

"And do what?"

"Apart from becoming a professional punter—which I'm sure I could do with a little more research—I have absolutely no bloody idea."

Concert in the Park

29: CONCERT IN THE PARK

AUGUST, 1973

"I'm working Sunday arvo," I told her over dinner one Monday evening in August. "Concert in the park. You can come and listen if you like. I'm playing the French horn. First public appearance since I changed instruments. Hope I don't mess up with you there."

"You'll play superbly. You always do. How's it going, anyway?"

"Playing horn? Great. I think it's my instrument actually. It just feels right."

I paused for a minute to swallow. "I never really wanted to play cornet you know. I wanted to play trombone, but my arms were too short when I joined up."

She laughed until she realised I was serious.

"They called me 'Tarzan'," I added. "Had trouble fitting a uniform on me, I was so small. Army food and exercise changed that in a hurry."

She took the kids to the park. As always, we looked resplendent in our black trousers and bright white coats and shoes polished until you could see your face in them. The afternoon sun twinkled on the highly polished silver instruments and on our badges and brass buttons.

There was a keen crowd there. Some stood in little groups, others spread rugs on the lawns or settled themselves under shady trees with picnic hampers and wine coolers or those little Kentucky Fried Chicken dinner boxes. The music was lively and entertaining. We were enjoying ourselves. The applause was enthusiastic. At half–time, I joined her for a while.

"How's it sounding?"

"Great. But you knew that. The kids seem to be enjoying it too."

As we talked, Captain Ellis walked behind my music stand, peered at my music and frowned. Then he marched in our direction. "You are playing exceptionally well today, Musician Wilson. You've taken to your new instrument well."

"Thank you, sir," I said, without even a hint of a smile. I'd been watching the Captain's movements and knew what was coming next.

"Why do you have tenor–horn music on your music stand?"

"That's the music I was supplied with, sir. French horns have only recently been introduced in this band and—"

"Yes, but you were instructed to transpose the music for French horn, before this concert."

I considered the rebuke silently for a moment, determined not to flinch. I looked straight into the Captain's eyes, set my lips tight and thrust my chin forward, aware that my stance was arrogant and my glare challenging.

"I'm transposing mentally as I play." I focused on keeping my tone calm and unflustered, pretending confusion at a misguided rebuke; determined not to let him humiliate me in front of Fran. "Didn't you just say I was playing well?"

"I did, and you are."

"Then what's the problem, sir? Bass trombonists have been doing it for years." Now my tone was defiant and I laid heavy emphasis on the 'sir'. The Captain responded by adopting an authoritarian air.

"The problem, as you well know, Musician Wilson, is that you ignored me."

I shrugged then. "Guilty as charged then, sir. What's the penalty?"

My casual tone was a mask, and I suspected Fran knew it, but I was focused on saving face, and disguising my hatred of the man.

"Oh, for Christ's sake, Paul! You make things damn difficult for me, and for yourself."

My gaze remained fixed, challenging. I gave no response. Ellis turned to Fran.

"Can't you talk some sense into him, Frances. I'm trying to help him advance his career—move up the ranks." He shook his head and pinched his chin between his thumb and forefinger.

"Damn it, Paul, you're a bloody good musician. Excellent in fact. You're diligent, dependable, hard working. You're well liked. You could go places in the army, and I'd like to help you, but you need to lose the attitude, mate."

"What makes you think I want to go places in the army, sir?"

Ellis raised his open palms to elbow level in a gesture of despair and walked back to the bandstand shaking his head. I watched him silently for a minute, eyes burning into his back and that persistent whistled "Waterloo" tune echoing in my head.

Fran pretended the children needed her attention, so I wandered off to talk to some mates. Then the concert resumed and I gave it all I had, determined not to give Ellis an inch. Bastard could cheat me out of a promotion I'd earned, but he damned well wouldn't find fault with the way I did my job.

I knew I performed well. There was a photo of me in the local paper next day, holding the horn proudly. Fran said I looked magnificent and she couldn't understand how I could hate the army so when I obviously loved music and relished performing.

She broached the subject of the afternoon's conversation nervously that night.

"Paul, on the one hand you talk about wanting to leave the army and on the other you say it's not an option and you will probably have to sign on again. Don't you think as long as you are stuck with it as a job you might as well try to make the best of it?"

"What are you talking about?"

"You know what I'm talking about. What were you thinking? Not transposing that music like you were supposed to."

"Didn't need to. I was doing perfectly well transposing in my head. When I have to play a piece I can't transpose mentally, I'll write it."

"But Captain Ellis said—"

"Orders! That's my fucking life. Bloody orders!" I wasn't shouting, but my voice was cold and hard. "I obey them when they make sense or when the consequences of not doing so are likely to be drastic. It's all such a load of bullshit! I can do my job without some bloody up–jumped egotist with pips on his shoulders telling me how to."

She was silent for a minute.

"And can you stop folding those bloody nappies? Christ, it's nine o'clock. You never stop working."

"I have two babies to care for. They make lots of work."

"Evening work. Yeah. You have to do it in the evening so you can spend time with your boyfriend during the day."

"I don't have a boyfriend, and if you were around all day you'd know that I don't stop working. In case you haven't noticed, I clean the house, wash and iron your clothes and cook your meals as well as caring for our kids."

"Yeah. I know. And I know how long it takes and what women do the rest of the day."

She threw the nappy down and kicked the basket in my direction.

"We were talking about you and your career, Paul. Did it ever occur to you that maybe you owe it to us to try to move up the ladder, earn a bit more. It's not easy managing on the wage you bring home."

"Oh, right! Now it's about me being a fucking failure as a husband. Well, you knew what I did for a fucking living and how much I fucking earned before you married me. What, does your boyfriend have rank? Officer maybe?"

I slammed my fist against the wall, denting it badly. I would patch it later. I had become quite proficient at disguising the evidence of my violent rages.

"Stop it, Paul. Why do you act this way?"

"Why do you nag me constantly about my job?"

185

"I don't. I was worried about today that's all, and if Captain Ellis is good enough to want to help you advance your career, I think you ought to be grateful and co–operate."

"Advance my career? That's a joke! You must have a very short memory. Anyway, it's your fault I didn't get a promotion. If you hadn't helped that arse–licking idiot pass a basic maths test, I would've had the hook."

"You asked me to help him. I had no idea it would affect your chances of promotion."

"You have no idea about anything. Least of all how the fucking army works. If you did, you wouldn't believe Ellis' bullshit. It was only for your benefit anyway — a show. Big man, isn't he? Running around demanding everyone salute him and ask 'how high, sir?' when he says 'jump', and then pretending to be Mr Nice Guy when wives are around. I don't need his bloody favours."

"Fine. Go on being an idiot then, and get yourself charged."

"I managed nearly 10 years with a clean army record. I don't need you to tell me how to keep it that way. And I am not interested in bloody promotion. I have one year left in this friggin' job and then I'm done saluting jerks for ever, thank Christ!"

"And you'll do... what?"

"I've told you. I have absolutely no fucking idea. But I'll be free."

30: FIRST SUSPECT: THE URCHIN

SEPTEMBER, 1973

Nine o'clock. She would have wrapped cling–wrap over my dinner and put it in the fridge hours ago. She'd have eaten alone, washed up, and bathed the kids and read them a story. She'd be beside herself with worry by now. Bloody cops!

She was used to this—me staying out late drinking—but not on week–nights. She knew I had an early start tomorrow for a short trip away and I hadn't packed yet. I was seething.

I never let her iron my uniforms. They had to be perfect; everything had to be perfectly prepared for work before I started drinking. Fran often remarked that I was a dichotomy. I hated the army and bucked authority whenever I could get away with it, yet I was conscientious when it came to punctuality, performance and presentation. I was trained to be diligent and I was proud of the way I did my job. However much I hated my life, I was determined that for as long as I was stuck in any job, I would do it well.

I turned in the drive, cut the engine, stepped out of the car and slammed the door hard. Fran opened the back door and, in the dim porch light I saw that her face was contorted with worry. Her lips were tight and her eyes blazed. She sniffed at my breath as I pushed past her.

"Why so late, Paul?"

"I'm hungry. And I need a bloody drink."

She filled a saucepan with hot water and set it on to boil and put my dinner plate over it. It would take a while to heat. I grabbed a beer and swallowed half of it in a single gulp.

"I'll be up half the bloody night getting ready for tomorrow."

"I'll help you. You can take care of your uniforms and I'll pack the rest. So do you want to tell me about it? Obviously something is wrong."

"Oh no! Nothing is wrong. The bloody MPs drag me into a friggin' cop shop and accuse me of fraud and threaten to arrest me. That's all!"

"What?"

"Two fucking hours sitting alone at a table in a room with two–way glass, knowing they're watching me. Pistol on the table in front of me. No idea what that was about. Maybe they hoped I'd shoot myself and save them some trouble. They made me write a mate's name over and over — try to forge his signature."

"Why? What on earth—"

"Some fool had some money drawn out of his bank account and reckoned someone had forged his signature to do it. I don't know why they suspected me, except that I've known him for a long time and I often go to the bank with him on Fridays on our way to the pub. Guess they thought I saw him sign his name enough times to mimic it. Probably could if I wanted to, but I made damn sure what I wrote in there didn't look anything like it."

"So what happened? Did they finally sort it out?"

"Don't know. They came in eventually and told me they worked out they had the wrong man. Told me I could go. Showed me the forged signature. I'm pretty sure I know who did it, but I'm not gunna say."

"Don't you think you should?"

"Christ, Fran! Invite more trouble? No way! It was a pissy 30 bucks, and it's none of my business. They're cops. Let them figure it out. That's their job."

"It must have been awful, Paul."

She put her arms around me, but I brushed her away. When I spoke again, I was aware that my tone was acrid and I saw that she shivered.

"Shouldn't surprise me that I was the first suspect. That's how it's always been. Why should it ever change?"

"I don't understand, Paul. What do you mean 'that's how it's always been'?"

"It's a long story. You don't want to know, and I don't have time now to tell you. I've got uniforms to iron. Is my dinner warm yet?"

I ate in sullen silence. I ought to have rushed off to the ironing board when I was done, but instead I sat back with my eyes closed, breathing deeply, remembering, and debating whether to tell her. Finally, I looked up at her, without emotion, and began the story.

"I planned a robbery once." I said. "Payroll robbery. Me and five other guys. The pay truck picked up our pay from the bank every second Wednesday and followed the same back road across a little bridge to the pay office."

The colour drained from her face and she began to tremble, but she was struck dumb.

"The guards were armed, but we knew their pistols weren't loaded. They carried their ammunition in a separate pocket. We were going to hit them on the bridge. We planned it meticulously, but one fool lost his nerve and we had to bail. I never forgave that stupid bastard. My life could have been very different if it weren't for him."

"Different? It would've been different all right!" she said. Her tone was frenzied. "You would've spent the best part of it behind bars."

"We wouldn't have been caught." I said it with certainty. I had never considered capture even remotely possible.

"Don't be daft, Paul. Of course you would've been caught." She stared at me thoughtfully for a moment. "But it's all academic. You wouldn't have done it. It was a boyhood game, that's all. You're too honest to—"

"It was no game, Fran. It was deadly serious. To this day I regret that we didn't go through with it. It wasn't entirely dishonest, either. At least not on my part. I would've simply been taking back what was stolen from me."

"What do you mean?"

"Deferred pay. In apprentice school, they gave us a spending allowance. They kept back most of our pay as compulsory savings to be paid out on graduation. It was a fair bit of money. Enough to pay cash for a small car. I was 17 when I graduated. Still legally a minor. Those over 18, they paid it directly to them. Under eighteens, they paid it to their parents. Of course the parents either gave it to their sons or invested it for them. I assume they paid my money to my legal guardian, the State of fucking New South fucking Wales."

She stared at me blankly, struggling to understand. "Surely the Government wouldn't keep it? It was your money? What did they do with it?"

"I have no fucking idea," I said, resigned and weary. I had long since given up asking why.

"All I know is I never saw a cent of it. Not one fucking brass razoo!" [ix]

31: SETTING FRAN FREE

ARMIDALE, OCTOBER, 1973

I took leave in October. Three glorious weeks, right at the start of summer before the heat and humidity made the days uncomfortable—the best time of year. We went home to her mother and we visited my aunt and uncle. I doted on the kids. I doted on her. Away from that regimented world I hated so, the demons left me.

Her mother babysat while I took her out for a day. I bought her a new dress for the occasion, waiting patiently and even feigning interest while she tried on one after another. I complimented her figure. I told her that her eyes sparkled, her cheeks glowed and she looked just like she did the day I fell in love with her.

"Have you been told today?" I asked her at least twice a day.

We went to the races. She was the best–looking lady there and I was sure I must be the luckiest man alive. I hummed happily as we walked past the stalls and inspected the horses. I felt some kind of magical connection with those beasts, and I knew I astonished her with my knowledge. She knew I studied form, but it was more than that. I knew the animals. I read their expressions. I talked to them and they responded.

"That one's got a stubborn streak."

"How can you tell?"

"Small eyes and very small pupils. Lots of white. Usually indicates meanness."

I inspected the racing dimple—the crease along its hind haunches—and commented on its depth. I examined the forearm and thigh muscles and commented on the neck arch and the bounce in a beast's step.

I studied form guides with odd earnestness for a casual racegoer. For me, this was not just a fun day out. I wrote little asterisks and tiny numbers everywhere, underlining cryptic numeric indicators of past achievements. When I placed bets, I carefully calculated the amount to wager based on multipliers of previous losing bets and the number of losses since the last win. I tallied the returns meticulously, constantly referring to net profit on turnover as though this were a serious business venture. It was. I had something to prove. If I succeeded, I could soon be free.

The wins were substantial and the losing bets few. We left with my wallet bulging and Fran dancing on air, but I expected the profits. I was as sober as a businessman counting takings from a carefully orchestrated sales campaign. It wasn't luck. Paul Wilson was never lucky. I had studied and planned for this. It was my ticket to freedom.

She suggested asking her mum to keep the kids a little longer and going out to dinner to celebrate. I strutted into that restaurant beaming as I guided her to the chair and held it for her. When the waiter came, I asked for her favourite wine. I remembered the name. And then I asked the waiter could he please ask the band to play our song, "All I Have to do is Dream". Whenever we were apart, I would sing that song to comfort myself and I could see her and feel her beside me.

I ordered lobster thermidor for her. She'd always asked for that when we'd dined in the Bamboo Hut in the heart of Singapore. We used to go there regularly for meals. It was dark inside. The only light was in the base of a huge fish tank that ran down the centre of the restaurant. It was filled with live lobster, and they would ask her to choose the one she wanted and they would take it out right there in front of her. We were never quite sure if that was an act, but it was fun. Then they would reassemble the cooked lobster with tiny light globes where his eyes had been. Diners could see the meal coming from the kitchen—just two tiny yellow lights.

This restaurant was brightly lit, with starched white tablecloths and vinyl chairs instead of high–backed wooden pews with rustic benches between. At the Hut, you couldn't see the other diners. A single candle on the table provided barely enough light to eat by, and to light faces. Here red roses adorned the tables. The music wasn't loud enough to drown out the conversations of the other diners, nor to stop them overhearing yours. Waiters in black aprons darted about clattering plates and asking for orders in loud voices. Singapore restaurateurs could teach Australians a thing or two about hospitality.

"You look like you are miles away?" I said, smiling.

"Just thinking happy thoughts. Wine, lobster. It's bringing back memories."

A wave of sadness washed me as I studied her. "It's hard for you isn't it—army life? It's no life for a family."

"It's your life, so it's my life." She stared into her wine. "I made a commitment, Paul. And I meant it."

"Even if you live the rest of your life in misery?"

"I'm not miserable."

"No? I treat you badly. I fly into jealous rages and accuse you of things you would never do. I whine constantly about hating my job and hating my life.

192

I go out drinking with mates and leave you stuck at home alone with babies. We don't go out together. We—"

"I love the concerts in the park. Lazy, wet afternoons reading or listening to music together. We go out for ice creams and to the movies occasionally. You work for a living, Paul. Family life isn't all fun and games."

"I wouldn't know."

"No? Why, Paul? You don't talk about your past."

I ordered the demons to be still. I couldn't allow my past to intrude on my happiness now.

"Let's not go there. It's depressing." I reached across the table and took her hand in mine. "I love you, Fran. You are my world—you and those two beautiful children you gave me. I don't want us to be the way we are. I want you to be happy."

She smiled and squeezed my hand.

"I love you too, Paul. And the last two weeks have been wonderful."

WAGGA WAGGA, NOVEMBER 1973

We had been back from my leave for over a month when she finally confronted me with her decision.

"I'm going to take the kids home, Paul." she said softly, hands trembling almost as much as her voice.

She never thought of this as home. Her home town was home. This was 'camp', as if a temporary residence. Yet we both knew it was quite likely we would be here for many years.

I had been away most of the time since we returned from Singapore. She was on her own, and miserable. Soon after our son was born, she took our daughter to a specialist for tests. I was in hospital having a minor operation on my foot when she had to go for the results. It wasn't good news. They told her the child needed a city specialist's attention. How was she to arrange that?

I was sent away on jobs—twice—after they discharged me from hospital and I went again after my October leave. By the time I returned, she had made up her mind.

"Just for a while," she continued when I didn't respond. "A month or two. Three maybe. Until I get some medical care for Nicki and sort out how we are going to manage her treatment. I need a break and I need some help. I can't manage alone, with you away so much."

Prolonged silence. I sipped my beer, expressionless.

"Well?" she said at last. "Can you say something, please?"

"Say what? You're leaving me. Expected, eventually. Inevitable." My tone was deliberately nonchalant—a talking–about–the–weather pitch matching my careless stance and bland expression.

"I'm not leaving you, Paul. It's temporary."

"They all say that. I'm not dumb enough to expect you to come back. And I don't blame you either. I know this is a shit of a life and I know I'm not much of a husband."

I was sitting at the dining table, on a high–backed chocolate vinyl chair, sipping beer from a can. The dinner dishes still littered the table. Two matching high chairs perched on a plastic sheet near one wall. The sheet and trays were littered with vegie scraps and crumbs and pools of melted ice cream. She had bathed the children and put them to bed, but she hadn't yet had time to clean the mess.

It was the tiniest of cottages and she hated it. The little L–shaped kitchenette offered four tiny cupboards, three under the sink and one above. We had to angle sideways to open the refrigerator without being pressed against the gas cooker. The children couldn't play outside because the yard wasn't fenced. They were plagued by neighbours' dogs that roamed around knocking over garbage bins and tearing up gardens, driving us mad with their incessant barking and whining.

The house was at the edge of town, near the army base. There were no shops in walking distance. She had tried to get on a bus once to go to the store. With two babies, a pram and toddler seat to juggle, it was an impossible task. For some odd reason, drivers weren't allowed to leave their seats to help. She was too timid to ask a fellow passenger and none offered. So we shopped on Thursday nights or Saturday mornings, when I could take her. She stocked up heavily before I went away and just made do until I got back.

She had made no friends here. In Singapore, we lived in close quarters and wives got together regularly for social events. Here, the army wives didn't mix except at the occasional dinner dances. She walked to the local church hall once a week to take the children to Playgroup and she made a few casual friends there, but none close enough to confide in or to mix with outside meetings. The only woman she could really call a friend was our neighbour.

She was lonely and miserable, but she insisted she would never have decided to go if it hadn't been necessary for our daughter's wellbeing. She knew she could never make me believe that and she knew it was pointless to try. I had been convinced since the day we met that she would eventually leave me. People I loved left me. That was my lot. Why should she be different?

She stared for a while at the untidy kitchen. Finally, she walked over to stand behind me and put her arms around my neck. "I am not leaving you, Paul. I love you. I will come back, I promise."

I grunted and pushed her arms away roughly. I buried my face in my hands for a moment, but then I pulled myself upright again and turned to glare at her. My lips were set and my fists tightly clenched.

"Go, Fran," I spat. "Just go. I don't care. I don't want you to come back."

I stood up and threw the not quite empty beer can at the wall, punched the table, pushed two chairs over, and kicked the dining room door hard enough that my foot went right through it. Then I fetched another beer and stormed out, slamming the back door hard behind me.

For the first time in our married life, Fran left the dishes and the dirty kitchen. She went to bed and cried herself to sleep.

#

"We're doing another Sunday afternoon concert in the park," I said after dinner the next evening. I hadn't yet said a word about the conversation the night before, but I skipped the usual good morning hug and kisses before leaving for work and on returning. We had barely spoken until now.

"I'll bring the children along," she said, emotion seeming to clog her throat.

"I thought you might be gone already."

She shook her head.

"The concert is to rally support to save the band," I said in a voice loaded with disdain. "Apparently our esteemed Prime Minister, Mr Whitlam, has decided one way to cut Government expenditure is to reduce the number of army bands. Ours is one of the first to go. They are taking up a petition to try to save it. They'll be chasing signatures on Sunday."

"So I guess I should sign it?"

I shrugged. "I'd rather you didn't, but maybe you had better not be too conspicuous about refusing. It wouldn't go down well."

"Why wouldn't you support it?" she replied, puzzled.

"Because if the band is canned they have to get rid of bandsmen. That means transferring them to another corps or discharging them. It's about the only hope I have of getting a discharge application approved. And I do intend to lodge an application, on compassionate grounds. It's a long shot, but it's worth a try."

She stared at me, stunned. I talked all the time about getting out, but I knew she was convinced that, despite all the talk, I was an army musician for the rest of my working life. We both thought I was stuck with it at least until I got my 20 years up and had a pension to fall back on while I tried to find a job in civvy street.

"I thought you might be pleased," I said coldly. "You said you couldn't live like this anymore. You said you were taking the kids and going home."

"Temporarily. Until I sort some things out. I never intended it to be permanent and I told you that."

I shrugged, suppressing all hint of feeling. "I knew you wouldn't stay. I've told you. People I love leave. They hurt me. That's my lot. Why should you be any different? And now I know for sure it's me you're leaving, not our life here. Otherwise you would've jumped for joy just now."

Tears welled and she didn't try to hide them. "What do I have to do to make you trust me, Paul? To make you believe me."

"I almost did believe you. I thought if I got a discharge… but I understand now. It's me you want to leave, not the place, not the army."

She searched my expression, but it gave nothing away. I spat and rubbed at the toe of my boot, focusing on producing a mirror shine, as though the conversation was as meaningless as a discussion of what time I'd start work in the morning or what she needed me to pick up from the store on my way home.

"Paul," she whispered tearfully, "It's the place. It's the army. Don't give up your job on my account, but if you really want a discharge, apply for it. I don't know what there is for you outside the army. I don't know how we'll manage, but we will somehow. We'll figure something out. I just want to be with you. I want my family together."

Fear coiled in my belly. I wanted her. I wanted my family, but I had no idea how I could support them outside the army. I signed on again because I had no options—no education, no skills, no experience. This was all I had known since I was 15. I knew the idea of my leaving this life terrified her. Yet she knew how desperately I wanted my freedom, and we both knew there was no way she could stay here.

PART III

32: FREEDOM IS NOT SWEET

ARMIDALE, JANUARY 1974

I bounced out of the car and leapt up the back stairs, arms outstretched, enveloping her in a giant hug. "Bet you haven't been told today?"

"Not for a whole week." she replied, laughing.

"Guess I have to tell you seven times then?" I chuckled. "And then we should celebrate. I'm a free man at last, Fran. You can't begin to imagine how good it feels."

I had left the previous Saturday to drive to Sydney to be formally discharged from the army, staying a week with a friend in Mossman while the formalities were completed. I was due to start a new job — labouring with a local council — the following Monday. Freedom. Working outdoors, surrounded by open spaces. No guards at gates checking passes. No saluting. No more crowding with mobs of identically stiffly uniformed blokes into rows of hard chairs in a stuffy little room to blow and finger valves hour after hour. No ironing perfect creases and spit–polishing boots every evening.

At that final interview, I'd been ordered to drop my trousers; part of a routine medical check. I was sorely tempted to moon the pompous bastards presuming to dictate my fate, but I bit my lip and reminded myself that this was it. The deed was done. This was only a formality. I would walk away a free man.

Elation lasted until Sunday evening and then reality dawned. Through the weeks that followed, I put on a brave pretence of contentment, but I was lost, confused and frightened. I even talked about signing on again a few times, but I was quick to dismiss the idea.

We found a shabby little cottage to rent on the edge of town. The rent was cheap, but it still took almost half my pay. I took a second job as town bandmaster. It didn't pay well, but I enjoyed it and every extra cent was welcome.

We settled our little family into the cottage, and Fran started to think about establishing a permanent home. My long service and deferred pay would total enough for a deposit on a cheap house, according to her. She was determined no matter how hard it was to live on my wage, that money would stay in fixed deposit until we could buy a home of our own.

We had talked in Singapore about buying a house one day. I said blokes like me didn't own houses. She told me all her uncles battled in menial jobs on low pay, but they all owned their homes. I just shrugged and said she should forget that dream because it wouldn't happen, at least not until I perfected that betting system. Then she could have all the houses she wanted.

Money was a major problem. I was paying off a near–new car when I met Fran, but I wrote it off going back to base after a trip home to make wedding plans. There had been floods and the roads were in bad shape. I came up over a hill too fast and had to slam on the brakes. The car rolled. I was unhurt, miraculously, but the car was badly damaged. The insurance was cancelled after it was repaired and then the hire purchase company repossessed it because it was uninsured. We were in Singapore by then and knew nothing about what was happening. I ended up losing the car and saddled with a debt.

When we came back from overseas, we bought a cheap little bomb. We spent all our savings furnishing and setting up house. Then I was hit with an incorrect tax bill and had to borrow money to pay it while we argued it and begged for review. The mistake was a really dumb one by the tax office, but it took two years to sort it. When they paid me back, it was without interest. The value of a dollar had almost halved in the interim, and we had paid interest at personal–loan rates for two years.

Then there were the medical bills. Fran was told to cancel her medical insurance when we left for Singapore and it would be reinstated without loss when we returned. Treatment in Singapore was free. They didn't tell her that a child born there and returning to Australia with a pre–existing condition wouldn't be insured, so we were lumbered with the full cost of all the specialist treatment Nicki needed.

I should be accustomed, by now, to being beaten up by the establishment. It was my lot. It seemed, despite freedom, the pattern would continue. So when Fran danced in one evening, face aglow, holding application forms for government housing, I felt it my duty to crush her hopes before they rose any higher.

"But the rent would be half what we pay now, and we'd have a proper bathroom and separate laundry," she protested.

"The houses are in ghettos. People who live in those places wear a brand."

Her forehead creased and her mouth dropped open. Quizzing eyes burnt into mine. I had worn a brand for too long, and had no intention of doing so again. She, of course, couldn't be expected to understand, and I had no inclination to explain.

"It's not that bad, and it will only be until we can afford a home of our own."

"Yeah, sure. Dream on, Fran." I went and sat on the back step to brood, and she dropped the subject. She raised it again the next evening.

"Go and apply, if you must," I snapped. "I doubt we'd have a hope anyway, but the rent saving would help."

"And living in a ghetto?"

I shrugged. "I got used to wearing a brand a long time ago. Don't know why I thought I could ever change it."

Her eyes misted, but she let the remark go.

"Our neighbours are applying too," she said, forcing an uncertain smile. "They seem pretty confident."

"They should be," I replied sourly. "They're the right colour to get preference."

The neighbours were Aborigines. Nice family. Two kids about the same ages as mine. They played with ours often. He was unemployed, although he'd been offered my job and turned it down. Apparently the Aboriginal dole was more than the wage my job paid. The white man's dole was about equal. When you took work clothing, running a car to and from, packed lunches and union fees into account, we'd have actually been much better off on benefits, but I'd be damned if I'd take charity again.

The neighbours lived in a modern brick flat with three big bedrooms and all the mod cons and nice carpet on the floor. Fran had to scrub and polish worn linoleum every morning, battle with a dirty, old, wood–fired stove, and bath the kids in a laundry tub. I sugar–soaped the smoke–stained walls when we moved in, and begged paint from the landlord to dress up the kitchen cupboards. Fran made some colourful gingham curtains. It brightened the place up, but I sympathised with her desire for better.

She settled herself at the kitchen table after dinner that night to fill out protracted forms loaded with invasive and seemingly irrelevant questions.

"Typical bureaucracy," I snorted, looking over her shoulder. "They always want to know when you had your last shit and how much it weighed."

The decision was fast. The letter was sympathetic and apologetic.

"We understand that your family genuinely needs housing assistance," it said. "We regret that we are unable to make an offer at this time due to a serious housing shortage. You will appreciate that we must give preference to those in greatest need. Accordingly, your name has been placed on a waiting list. At this stage, we expect it will be up to two years before we are able to offer you housing."

Of course it went on with the usual crap about there being an appeals process if we thought the decision unfair. Of course I said, "I told you so".

I was more relieved than disappointed. I wanted better housing and cheaper rent, but not that way.

Six weeks later, our neighbours started packing to move.

"I don't get it," Fran said, ladling stew on to plates. "I just assumed they'd get the same answer we did. It doesn't seem fair, when he's got better accommodation and healthy kids and actually brings in more money than you do."

I shrugged. Since when was anything in life fair? But she persuaded me to go with her to the Housing Office to challenge their decision. I saw no point, really, but she insisted.

They showed us into a small cubicle–style office — one in a row down the side of an airless hall with waiting–room furnishings in the middle. We sat opposite a weasely little man with huge ears and a pointy nose. A brass plaque on the front of the desk identified him as "Mr Norm Higgins". His face was flushed and he sat tapping his pen on the polished timber desk and frowning, as though having to speak to us was a great inconvenience. I was sure it was. The high piles of papers scattered on his desk suggested he might have a lot of more pressing business to attend to. They probably actually indicated nothing more than that he spent more time at the coffee machine and taking smoke breaks than working.

"I'm confused," Fran said, unable to suppress annoyance. "My neighbour says he was told there is about a six–week wait. I was told two years. How does that work?"

"Obviously, Mrs Wilson, his must be a high priority case. We work on a points system, you see. We have to prioritise those in greatest need." He leant back in his chair and sucked the end of a pen.

"I see. So can you tell me, sir, how you assess someone whose income is higher than ours and who, unlike us, doesn't have a child with a condition that requires expensive medical care, to have greater need than we do?"

"I can't answer that. No. I would have to look at his file and yours. And we don't discuss comparative situations of applicants. Applicant privacy must be protected."

"Hmmm. Then I guess I'll just have to appeal."

He leant forward again, frowning. "I could, I suppose, give you some general guidance to help you understand how we prioritise. Hopefully that would assist. For example…"

He turned to me. "Are you employed, Mr Wilson? Unemployed persons are obviously needier."

"Even if their income is higher?"

"Well, it wouldn't be, would it? And of course Aborigines are always given highest priority."

"Thank you, Mr Higgins. You have told me all I need to know." Purple with anger, Fran gathered up her bag and strode out. A tense silence hung over us as we drove home and I prayed that her simmering anger wouldn't erupt in a bitter attack on me. She hated me whenever I was proved right.

"So, Paul," she began, flinging herself into an easy chair. Her puckered face reminded me of Nicki's when a request was denied, and I had to suppress an amused smile. "A neighbour who can comfortably afford a nice brick apartment with carpet on the floors and electric stove and a tiled bathroom and separate laundry, and who has two healthy kids, is more needy because of the colour of his skin and because he chose to refuse the offer of a job that pays less than the dole — the Aboriginal dole, that is. Great system we have! Really fair, isn't it?"

"What did you expect?" I said coldly. "The words 'fair' and 'system' don't go together. What do they call it? An oxymoron?"

"I'm angrier than I remember being in a long time, and you don't even seem mildly surprised, let alone annoyed. How can you be so — "

"I learnt how the system worked a long time ago," I said, strolling calmly to the wood box to fetch some more logs for the stove. "I did warn you."

#

"Shirley seems to think we were lucky to be refused public housing," she said over dinner a few days later. Shirley was a friend from Playgroup who had been studying to become a social worker before pregnancy got in the way. "She seems to agree with you — government housing communities are ghettos."

"You've got to admit you can pick a public housing estate a mile away. And you can usually recognise the people who live in them, even when they're away from home."

"That might be a bit of a stretch!"

"It's true, Fran. They're a type. You can pick them."

"Paul, some of the people who live in those places are salt–of–the–earth, hard–working, good people."

"Did I say they weren't? They're still a type."

"Anyway, as I was saying, Shirley reckons giving people houses and money destroys incentive and pride. She agrees with short–term charity, but she says long–term charity destroys the soul. She was quite vocal in her criticism of society for the handouts to Aborigines. 'Never has solved their problems, and never will,' she said."

"I think I like her. So what does she think we should do about not being able to afford a decent place to live, since she thinks we are so lucky? Does she have an answer for that?"

"No. Seems she can solve the world's problems, but not ours."

"Typical. Should've been a social worker, or a bloody bureaucrat."

"I've been thinking though, Paul, and maybe I have a solution." She took a deep breath. Her eyes were pleading. "I think we should buy a house."

I made a pretence of choking.

"I'm serious, Paul. I think we should investigate the possibility. We have some savings to use as a deposit and the repayments mightn't be much more than we pay in rent."

"Don't be an idiot. You know it's never going to happen, so why prime yourself for another disappointment?" I considered her frown for a moment before adding, "Fine. Whatever. Go be an idiot if you must. No doubt someone will convince you it's never going to happen. Just please don't ask for sympathy from me when they do".

I shoved another log in the fire and slammed the firebox door hard, then banged the kettle down on the hotplate over the firebox.

"What's a man have to do to get a cup of tea around here?" I snapped. "Can you stop bloody dreaming long enough to make me something to eat?"

#

Weekday newspapers were now a luxury beyond our means, so it surprised me to see the daily edition on the kitchen table one Wednesday, a few weeks after the moving van departed from next–door. I cracked a stubby and pulled it across to read the headlines.

"Building Society offers Subsidised Home Loans for Low Income Earners".

Fran spread a sheet of old newspaper on the table opposite me, laid out an assortment of vegetables, and dropped into the chair opposite me. Picking up a peeler, she started scraping carrots. When I made no comment on the headline, nor any effort to read on, she dropped the peeler and looked up at me, her face puckered with anxiety.

"They're offering low–interest loans for people to buy homes of their own. We could get our own place. It'd have to be cheap, but we could fix it up and make it nice. And it'd be ours."

"It's a government program, Fran," I snorted. "You'll fill in a monstrous batch of forms, and they'll send you a polite letter explaining why they can't help us and telling us in very legalistic lingo how the 'appeals' process works."

She refused to be dissuaded. I was utterly convinced this was a pipedream.

"I worked it all out, Paul," she chirped, her face alight and eyes dancing. "We can afford something up to $20,000. Even with stamp duty and legal costs the repayments only come to about what we pay in rent now."

"First," I said in an authoritarian tone, "houses in this town cost a lot more than $20,000. $25,000 is cheap. Second, we are struggling to pay the rent now, and you want to lumber us with a liability for the next 30 bloody years! And there's rates and insurance and maintenance costs on top of the repayments."

"I know, and I still think it's doable. It won't be easy for a while, but inflation pushes rents up every year, and wages. Home–loan repayments stay static. A year from now, the rent here will be more than the loan repayments, rates and insurance combined. Why worry about 30 years from now? By then, we'll be setting aside the price of a loaf of bread for loan repayments!"

"Right. Then go find a house for under $20,000," I snarled, and watched the dull, red tide of anger creep across her cheeks. Her eyes blazed and she tore at those vegetables, ripping large chunks of flesh away with the skin.

Savagely determined, Fran poured over classified ads and stalked real estate offices for months. She snapped at the children and was rarely civil with me. When she demanded it, I sullenly strolled through run–down houses, careful to point out rusted gutters and rotting timbers and warning her off with inflated estimates of repair costs. She refused to be discouraged, but gave up requiring me to accompany her on inspections.

Eventually, she found what she declared 'a gem'. She asked the agent to arrange for me to check it out, alone, after work on Friday. It was my drinking night, so I was pissed at her for making the appointment. My disinterest was thinly disguised as I trailed through the place behind an irritatingly enthusiastic agent nattering about 'potential'.

It was 30 years old and badly in need of renovation, and it was located right at the point on the highway where the semitrailers changed gears. It had two large bedrooms at the front and a small sleep–out at one end of an enclosed back veranda. The laundry and toilet were at the other end. There was a comfortable living room with a fireplace.

The large combined kitchen and dining room had an electric stove, only one tiny window facing south and admitting no light, and flooring that looked remarkably like hessian sugarbags opened up and stitched together. The back windows were rotten and the bathroom pipes leaked through the bedroom wall. The yard was so heavily overgrown that we'd have to take truckloads of tree branches to the tip before we could get a piece of furniture through the door. But it was solid and liveable. Two months later, it was ours.

Despite a prevailing chill of unidentified fear upsetting my belly, a thrill tickled its way up my spine the day we finally signed those mortgage papers and the solicitor handed us the keys to our new home. Fran whooped with glee.

#

"That sheet of wallpaper is upside down," Fran laughed, looking from the bed into the freshly papered hallway I had thought looked so lovely. "Look! The pattern is actually of vases of flowers."

"Yes, but they go both ways. Up and down."

"Uh uh. No they don't, but I agree the pattern is hard to identify. Maybe no–one will notice."

I had fallen into a tolerable routine of stumbling, frustrated, through long hard days working at a job I detested. I led band rehearsals and taught budding young brass musicians on Wednesday evenings and conducted band concerts often on Fridays and weekends. Otherwise, I spent my weekends working on home–renovation projects.

We'd removed a wall in the bathroom to repair leaking plumbing, then replaced the rusty old tub, installed a smart new vanity, and painted and tiled. Fran wallpapered the kitchen cupboard doors and made curtains for the living room and back veranda. She was now child–minding, taking in ironing and making and selling children's clothing to add to our scant renovations fund.

A month after moving into our new home, panic displaced joy when a loans officer advised that the back windows must be replaced before Christmas. With no money to pay for such an expensive renovation, I was convinced the loan would be cancelled and we'd be back in rental accommodation—if we could find any. Fran's uncle came to the rescue, offering an indefinite interest–free loan for materials he could supply at trade prices and volunteering his labour free. Another uncle arrived one Sunday morning with a new toilet on the back of his utility and ordered us to arrange to use the neighbor's facilities for a day until the concrete set after he installed it. He'd noticed a rather large crack in the base of ours.

Moving in had been a family affair too, with an aunt stocking the fridge and sliding a cooked casserole into the oven to keep warm for the evening meal and uncles coming and going with loaded cars while cousins helped unpack and stack cupboards. A member of the band—someone I had met once—lent me his truck for the move, and our landlord brought his truck and helped move heavy items. He even loaded a bed that belonged to him, insisting it must be ours as our son slept in it, and he waived the last two week's rent. I was slowly adjusting to a world where people were kind, caring and supportive. It quieted the demons and warmed me.

Transforming our shabby little cottage into a home rapidly became a labor of love. Readily mastering the required skills produced a warm glow of pride. Fran's uncle gave me tips on painting — a task I performed often, but found I detested. I learnt to lay concrete, tile and replace broken taps and doorhandles. Carpentry became a favoured pastime. I delighted in building bookcases and cabinets.

In the lead–up to Christmas, I built a magnificent doll's house for my daughter, complete with tiny balconies edged with plastic replicas of iron lace. A battery–operated lighting system thoroughly enchanted her, although she flattened the battery on the first night by refusing to switch the lights off.

Leading the town band proved a challenge, but one I embraced with vigor. The band hadn't won a contest in over 30 years. Assessing the rabble confronting me at the first rehearsal, it was easy to see why. I found myself, now, mourning the absence of the army discipline I had so detested. I quickly resolved to focus on music and avoid marching contests. To my amazement, conducting proved no challenge and the band — especially the younger members — were enthusiastic and responsive. Wednesday evenings became the highlight of my week.

"So are you going to audition for the musical," Fran asked, still staring at the sheet of wallpaper. The local musical society was planning a production of Annie Get Your Gun and advertising for brass musicians.

"Absolutely," I replied, starting to hum "You Can't Get a Man With a Gun"' as I headed for the bathroom.

The weeks flew by and the leaves began to rust and fall as I prepared to take my band to a State music contest in Gunnedah. Taking up the baton at a Sunday concert the week before the big event, I grew a full two inches. The melody washed over me, transporting me into a trance–like state where everything around me glittered and the baton was a Midas wand. The notes floated up to drift away on clouds and the crowd roared approval.

A week later, the day dawned warm and sweet. The sun set in a copper blaze of triumph behind a bus filled with rowdy bandsmen singing, shouting, laughing and applauding the triumphant bandmaster who had coached them to win three out of four events. I stepped on to the bus holding a trophy high to be greeted with waves of wild applause. On the journey home, I resolved to finally challenge the demons and apply for retraining. I had set myself free. I had proved my ability. Now was the time to start my new life — to finally pursue a career path of my own choosing.

#

"I stopped in at the Employment Office today," I said, dropping the weekend race guide on the carpet and settling back to put my feet up on our chocolate vinyl lounge. Fran leapt up and folded the paper carefully and put it in the magazine rack. The cream–wool living–room carpet was the only floor–covering in the house that didn't need replacing, and she was paranoid about anything marking it.

"I asked about the army retraining program," I continued, shaking my head at her. "They told me I was eligible when I was discharged, and the local Employment Office could give me whatever information I needed."

A triumphant beam crinkled her eyes at the corners. "That's great, Paul. What did you find out? Do you have any idea what you would like to do?"

"I told them I want to learn a trade. Do something with my hands. Carpentry maybe, or shoe repair. I have to take an aptitude test and go for an interview, then they'll process the application. Apparently I can do a short–course training program and I'll be paid to learn."

She flicked at a stray tear, obviously overcome with emotion. She had urged me many times to think about retraining.

I was quiet and withdrawn for days after, and she watched me anxiously for signs of enthusiasm, or lack of. She tried to talk to me about career options, but I merely grunted. "Wait!" I said, my face twisting with impatience, "There's hurdles to cross."

"It's important you appear eager, Paul," she warned, knowing my tendency to feign disinterest so others wouldn't know they had the power to disappoint. I merely shrugged and told her I had no intention of getting my hopes up — priming myself for yet another disappointment. When she nagged me further, I assured her that I was trying to stay positive and I would give my best at the interview. I didn't tell her about the dull, numbing bleakness consuming me, or the screamed warnings of the demons refusing to let me hope.

The days seemed to go on endlessly, but finally, the appointed day came and I dressed carefully, asked her to wish me luck, and, characteristically, left early.

Anguish burnt in my chest watching the brass minute hand edge towards the half–hour, but when the interview finally commenced, a full 15 minutes late, the knot in my stomach became a clenching fist of ice and fire. A dark–murderous rage boiled inside me. I think I called the man Simms, bidding him a terse goodbye.

#

"Paul? What's wrong?" Fran's hopeful glow dissolved to a look of haggard, wretched astonishment as I slammed the fridge door, tore at the stubby cap, and crumpled on to a chair, face working in a contortion of angry frustration.

"Intelligence test! How long is the fucking Tigres Euphrates River? What's the name of the highest mountain in the Himalayas and how high is it? How many people could answer fucking questions like that?"

"What? Why would they ask questions like that? Surely that was only a small part of it? What else did they ask?" Her voice was fishwife shrill and she was shaking.

"Oh, plenty." I said in a tone iced with contempt. "All along the same lines. And then they interviewed me. What a fucking joke! Arrogant sneers at every word I spoke, but oh so fucking polite when explaining they would have to consider what jobs I might be capable of doing, given that I had no education."

"But you did courses in the army."

"I told them. Maths and English to Intermediate equivalent, and music to a level that matched the Trinity School of Music final exams. Apparently fucking army education certificates aren't worth the fucking paper they are written on outside of the army. And then there's my age to consider. Apparently the brain cells die when you pass your 25th birthday!"

"Surely they are going to offer you some sort of retraining?"

"I have to go back next Thursday. A pencil–pusher named Wicks is handling my case. He drives a black sedan."

She made a puzzled frown. "Government issue, Paul. They all drive black cars."

"Yeah," I replied, my tone vague and distant. "They all do."

#

Escaping from that office the following Thursday afternoon, dark clouds wrapped about me and a relentless fist pounded at my brain, screaming reminders of demons' warnings and branding me a fool for forgetting lessons from my past. The strain of holding back a thirst for blood left me spent. I headed for the pub, but the beer was vile and its chill had no effect on the savage fire in my gut. I swallowed one after another, gulping them down and slamming glass and coin on the bar, glaring impatiently at the barman until he planted a filled glass on the coaster. Slowly, rage gave way to that familiar hollow feeling of having all the life sucked out of me and everything I cared for snatched away. The ale made my gut churn. When I finally staggered out, muddy–headed and choking on vomit, I was no more than a walking corpse, waiting for my body to recognise that my mind had died.

My responses to Fran's questions were rambling and incoherent, but terse and resentful. I was violently sick, ate nothing, and went to bed in my underwear without showering or washing my teeth. I was always fanatical about personal hygiene. Even on bush camp–outs, I was religious about bathing, shaving and cleaning my teeth. Fran had seen me drunk and depressed often, but I had never gone to bed unclean before.

I left for work the next morning without a word, and stayed out late drinking again. On Saturday, I slept until 11. Then I went outside and sat on the back step, brooding. I felt as though I'd been swallowed by a black monster and I was swimming about in its belly. Dark hopelessness surrounded and consumed me. When Fran called me in for lunch, I didn't answer. She came and sat beside me.

"OK, Paul. Enough. Spit it out. What happened?"

"Nothing. Nothing at all." My tone was dead. Rage had dissolved to a grudging concession of black defeat. Her face was etched with pain and fear and she was drawing ragged little breaths, but I had no strength to care.

"Something upset you terribly. What did they say?"

"That the tests evidenced that I lack the intelligence to do anything other than dig fucking ditches. I lack aptitude to be eligible for retraining. And, in any case, I'm two fucking months too old."

Her shoulders slumped as shocked confusion gave way to tears. For a heartbeat of time, I wanted to reach out and smother her; put an end to her tiresome questions and her nagging challenges; shed the intolerable weighty burden of having to provide for her and the children. But my heart turned over at her sorrow.

"Prison inmates can do all sorts of courses — even get university degrees — as part of programs aimed at 'rehabilitation'," I said in a voice as sour as green lemons. "Men who serve their country for a decade are thrown on the trash heap the day they shed the uniform."

She choked on her reply. What came out was a series of unintelligible grunts, but her tears spoke for her. She put her arm around me and rested her head on my shoulder. I shoved her away.

"God I hate myself sometimes. Why am I so bloody stupid?"

"You're not stupid, Paul. They are. You –"

"I'm fucking stupid all right. I let myself trust the fucking system."

"Come inside and eat Paul."

"Fuck off, Fran. Just leave me alone."

I was still sitting there when she went to bed that night, and she asked me how long it would be before I would wash or eat or do something to reassure her I was going to be OK. How could I answer? Year after dark pain–filled year of incarceration had locked me in a prison of hopelessness and despair.

As a jailed child, and in a stifling uniform, I counted the years to freedom. I planned and schemed and hoped. Weak rays of sunshine piercing the darkness had assured me that, one day, I would be 'OK'. But there was not the faintest glimmer of light in this cavern.

I was certain, at that moment, that unless I found and murdered my tormentor, I could never be 'OK' again.

33: REUNITED

MARCH 1974

Friday morning, I left for work as usual at 6:45 am. Two weeks before Easter, with the start of winter at least six weeks away, the early morning departures were still tolerable. The house pipes didn't freeze and the windscreen fog cleared with just a swish of the wiper blades. Two months from now I'd have to rise 10 minutes earlier to take hot water from the house to clear the ice from the windscreen. If the house pipes were frozen, I'd have to fetch water from buckets filled the night before, first cracking the thin layer of ice on top, then boiling it in the kettle. But this was the best time of year here. The fiercely dry, hot summer was over. For the next few weeks the frosts would be light and the days would be sunny and still.

Fran lifted my pyjama–clad toddler son out of the high chair, wiped his mouth and hands, and hugged him to her chest, taking Nicki's hand to lead the children to the door to kiss me goodbye. Another nine hours of monotony and frustration before two glorious days of respite. The bosses had extended our work days and introduced a nine–day fortnight. I could have taken the day off, but I'd chosen to extend my Easter break. Eight glorious days; my first real break since I started this job. What to do with it?

An opportunity to search for Simms? Search for my family? Ultimately, I supposed I would sleep late, mow the lawn, paint the dining room and spend time playing with my kids. Desire burnt strongly enough, but somehow the pressures of daily living seemed always to make responding too difficult. Fran suggested I had a subconscious desire to avoid the confrontation I feared possible if I returned home, and perhaps I did cling to the safe and familiar. My revenge plans were a closely guarded secret, and it was definitely not desire to avoid confrontation that delayed action towards that goal. I was in no hurry. Anticipation only served to make revenge sweeter.

"Wilson. Phone message. Your wife called," a clerk yelled as I walked past his office to the lunchroom. The message alarmed. Fran never called me at work, but the clerk assured me all was well as he handed me a note asking me to come home early. It pissed me off. There had better be a good reason for her asking me to forfeit my usual Friday afternoon drinking session.

211

Throughout the afternoon, I puzzled over what could possibly prompt such a request. Although she objected vehemently to my drinking, and complained endlessly, she rarely actually tried to stop my pub sessions.

She met me at the door that evening glowing with childlike anticipation, but there was an anxious tremor in her voice and she was slow to answer my questioning stare.

"I had a visitor early this morning. He startled me. For a minute I thought it was you, back for something you forgot, but the clothes were wrong and his hair was darker and straighter. He was well tanned, and a little leaner than you, and he had a distinctive from–the–bush accent."

"Are you going to tell me who it was?"

"He said he was your brother."

She seemed to lurch towards me and my gut lurched in response. I swayed on my feet like a drunk after a long binge. My vision blurred. Memories I'd fought down for nearly two decades surfaced to besiege and threaten, tearing at my heart and screaming warnings. Her eyes probed, but my throat locked.

"I told him you didn't have any brothers, but he seemed quite certain, and he was so uncannily like you. Had that distinctive Wilson chin, too."

"I have brothers. Two," I mumbled. Icy fingers squeezed my heart, quenching raging flames of desire.

"He said you had five... and four sisters." Frown lines sliced Fran's forehead and her eyes accused. "You never told me you had brothers."

"Why should I? They ceased to be part of my life when they were barely toddlers. I never expected I'd ever see or hear from them again."

"His name's Ian. He said he'd be back to see you at about seven, so we should eat before he gets here."

She went to the kitchen and turned her attention to a simmering pot. I sought refuge in the toilet and begged my stomach to be still and my head to stop spinning. I needed a drink. I wanted to run. Elation, terror, hope, despair and disbelief battled for dominance, and a voice in my head pleaded for some clarity of what I was supposed to feel.

My little brother. 18 years. He'd be 23, maybe. He was about four when I last saw him...

No more pretence. No more excuses. I had to face it now. I had to decide, truthfully, if I really wanted to go home. The demons from my past had caught up with me and wrapped me in a shroud of fear. Fear of disappointment. Fear of rejection. Fear of discovery. Fear of climbing, again, to dizzy heights of hope and joyful anticipation, then crashing again into the dark depths of despair.

I was on a roller coaster, climbing at breakneck speed in a carriage that threatened to break free of the track, and staring ahead in terror at a sheer drop into hell. I clung to the underside of a world turned upside down; thrust out of its orbit. No gravitational forces held me. If I loosened my grip, I might drift into oblivion or be sucked into the blazing heart of the sun and spat back as a pile of ashes.

I ate my meal in silence, conscious of Fran's questioning gaze and thankful that she asked nothing; said nothing.

First an uncle. Now a brother. Never my mother or my father. Why had they never come? Had they simply forgotten me? Were they too busy with younger kids to care? No letters. 18 years of silence.

I had long since stopped waiting; stopped believing. Deep inside, the hope for a sign they cared never died. I hoped somehow, some day, the emptiness and confusion would end and there would be answers and the answers would be acceptable. I hoped bitterness, rage, mourning and yearning would give way to understanding, and somehow the world would make sense.

Ian Wilson was close to my height, rough skinned and darkly tanned. He was lean, but muscled, like Dad. A wave of oily black hair flopped over his forehead. He flicked it back with a work–toughened hand, just like Dad's. He half–grinned as he introduced himself, then he shook my hand heartily and thumped my shoulder, but he had little to say. I passed him a can, and he sat down opposite me to pop it and suck from it.

I don't know how long we sat in silence, staring. What should brothers say to one another after 18 years apart? A million questions pounded my temples, demanding response, but I couldn't bring myself to mouth any of them. I was spinning out of control, yet I knew I appeared completely calm—cold and unfeeling. Eyes vacant.

At last, he broke the tense silence. His words seemed to float like a bubble that burst without leaving a trace. They echoed in my head, muzzled and vague. I opened my mouth to answer, but the sound died in my throat.

He stayed only minutes that evening, but he returned two nights later. This time we talked a little, recalling the day he had hammered spilt bullets and one exploded under my big toe. Dad wrapped it in bandages, doused it with Dettol and said it probably should be stitched, but it'd mend OK. It did.

We laughed over the memory of Rob falling out of a cart on the way to town and spending a few days in hospital with concussion, then falling out again on the way home. As a toddler, Rob never could sit still.

Neither of us mentioned my leaving. We gave Fran no clues as to when we parted or why we'd been so long apart. Neither of us spoke of the life we'd lived while apart.

"Rob is getting married on Easter Saturday," Ian said, preparing to leave after his second visit. "Come to the weddin', bro. Real casual affair. Rob'd be stoked to have you there."

Dark stillness. Only the vexing tick–tock of the clock and the faint, shallow sound of sleeping children's breathing disturbed the silence. Ian was watching me intently, eyes wide and pleading.

I stared into white froth on my beer. Fran watched my reaction, temples knotted with anxiety. I'd talked about going home and I'd said I wanted to see my parents again, but after 18 years of separation, talk is easy. I'd made no serious move to try to find them and I wasn't at all sure I wanted my family to find me.

"You can stay with Carly and me," Ian said at last. "There's plenty of room at our place for all four of you."

I considered the offer, still staring intently into my beer, afraid my expression would tell more than I wanted to reveal. I was painfully aware of Ian's discomfort. My voice, when I finally answered, was low and hesitant.

"What about Mum and Dad? Would they welcome me? I wouldn't want to make the event uncomfortable for anyone."

"Come, Paul," Ian said. "I'll tell Mum and Dad." After a moment of reflection, he added "You've got brothers and sisters you've never met. Kevin, Michael, Brian, Sandra, Helen and Julie. It's time you got to know all of them. It'll be great, a wedding and family reunion in one. It'll be quite a party."

He extended a hand, then changed his mind and placed it affectionately on my shoulder. "It was good to see you, bro. I'll see you Good Friday, 22 Laurel Ave. Ask at any service station if you forget or need directions. Everyone in town knows us."

"I might come. I'll think about it." My response was flat, disinterested. If it disappointed Ian, he showed no sign. He waved happily from the car and gave a short 'beep beep' as he drove off.

"If I'm finally going to meet your parents, perhaps you should tell me enough about your past so I don't put my foot in my mouth," Fran said nervously when Ian had gone. Despite my noncommittal reply, she was obviously certain I would decide to go. I stared into my beer to avoid her gaze, not at all sure I would.

"Paul, I know you struggle to trust me, but we've been through a lot together. Don't you think I have a right to know what makes you like you are?"

"Like what? What are you talking about?"

She couldn't answer, so she pretended to busy herself folding washing. Later, she tried again. "What should I expect when I meet your parents? Is there anything I should know about them."

"What? Like I haven't seen or heard from them in 18 years? I probably don't know any more about them than you do."

"Surely you have some memories?"

214

"Yeah, I have memories." *Crystal–clear memories. As vivid as if it all happened yesterday. Trauma stamps impressions indelibly on the brain and heightens the senses.*

"But you never talk about your past."

"I swore the day I joined the army that no–one would ever know about my past. I buried it the day I put the uniform on. Until then I was a 'home kid', unwanted, unloved, society's trash. I was determined no–one would ever call me that again."

She wrapped her arms around me and kissed my cheek, but I shrugged her away.

"Paul, you were never society's trash. You were a victim of society's failure."

"My parents were very poor. I was a bush kid, feral. The Government said they weren't taking proper care of Jen and I, so they took us away because we were supposedly neglected."

"But they left two younger kids behind? They couldn't have thought there was any danger of harm."

"Who knows what they thought? All I know is that a social worker took us into a courtroom and charged us and I remember my dad swearing at the judge and storming out in a rage. Then they put us in a black car and took us away.

"They were the days of 'the reds under the beds'. Remember, Fran? People were scared stiff of commos. We'd heard stories about what the Nazis did during the war, taking families into concentration camps. And there we were being carted off to God knows where in a black car driven by a stranger in a suit. Dad had stumbled away raging mad, but frightened, obviously unable to control what was happening. There are no words to describe the terror.

"They told us it was for a little holiday. They said we would be going back home soon. I suppose they told our parents the same lie. They put us in a horrible place where nuns beat us and cursed us and told us every day that we were scum and we had bad blood in us. We never went home again. My parents went on to have heaps more kids, it seems, and I guess maybe two less to care for was a bonus. They probably never gave us much thought ever again." He took a swig of beer and stood up. "End of story. Nothing else to tell. I went from an orphanage to the army, very much against my will, and you know the rest."

"How do you feel about the prospect of seeing them again?"

I shrugged. "How should I feel? I've told you often enough that I don't have feelings. I'm not like other people. I was trained not to feel.

"I decided in Singapore that I wanted to see them," I continued, wondering now at the wisdom of that decision, "but I don't know what to expect. Don't

215

even know if I'll be welcome. I thought about them now and then when I had leave from the army. Sometimes I'd think 'Maybe I'll go find my parents and have a holiday with them'. But I knew what a holiday with my aunt and uncle would be like. They were good to me. Their house was home. In the end, I always chose the familiar over the unknown."

"Bill never encouraged you to see them? Never talked about them?"

"No. I think he thought it was best to leave the past buried and maybe it was. I guess I'm about to find out."

34: GOING HOME

MARCH 1974:

A winding track thumped and jolted past a murky dam, across browned paddocks, and through a rusted gate jammed permanently open, its sagging bottom corner obscured under layers of thick red dirt. The fire–blackened walls of an iron–roofed shack came into view. A tired stick–woman draped in a worn cotton dress stood in the doorway. Beside her, just outside the door, a man and three boys stood in a line wearing worn but bright white shirts. The man might have stood nearly six feet tall if it weren't for his stoop. His face was rugged and well sun–tanned, but worn down almost to the spirit. His clothes hung loosely on an overly thin frame.

The woman had medium–length, dark hair — unruly, a hint of auburn competing with emerging streaks of iron–grey. She raised a hand to shield questioning eyes. The man shook his head. The boys began to run forward, but she called them back.

"They don't know we are coming, Paul," Fran said, concerned. "No–one told them."

"Ian said Rob would tell them. He would have." I spoke without certainty.

"I don't think so. Look at them. They look confused, worried. They don't know."

The car we followed stopped under a tree, alongside the shack, and I pulled in behind. The woman started towards Ian's car, then hesitated. For a long moment, she stared at me. Slowly, a hesitant smile of recognition crept across her face.

"Fred! Look, Fred! It's our daughter–in–law, and she's brought us our grandchildren."

She came at a run. As Fran stepped from the car, she raced to the passenger side door, unfolded our baby boy from Fran's arms and hugged him tightly, soaking his shirt with her tears.

"I never thought I'd see them. I never thought I'd see them. Oh my beautiful babies!"

I stepped from the driver side, opened the rear door, unbuckled the child restraint and lifted my daughter from her seat. Thrusting the child over my

217

shoulder, I walked around the car and turned to face the old man who stood silently staring, trembling, face grey. For an uncomfortable few moments, I just stood there. I sucked in a deep breath, then stepped forward to extend an open hand.

"Hello, Dad."

"Just like that," Fran remarked later. " 'Hello, Dad.' As though you had known him always and were seeing him again after a brief absence. As though there was nothing at all unusual about today."

I would have known him anywhere. It was like looking into a special kind of mirror that aged you 30 years. The hair was much darker and straighter and the eyebrows were bushier. His complexion was darker, but the facial features were unmistakable. There could never have been any doubt. This was the man who polished my shoes so meticulously 18 years ago, the man who gave me an air rifle, the man who told me endless stories of explorers and bushmen and poets. My dad. At last, I was home.

My mother came across to me. Tearily, wordlessly, she hugged me and kissed my cheek. I returned her embrace with a casual hug and a soft peck on the cheek. We swapped babies. She oohed and aahed over my bewildered daughter, and then, at last, she turned to say hello to Ian and Carly, and invite us all inside.

The shack comprised three small rooms. Outside, half a rusting galvanised iron water tank rested on its side on four piles of old bricks, forming a wash tub. Under it, a pile of ashes still glowed faintly from the morning wash. A wet trail revealed where the soapy water ran away to a small vegetable patch. The tub had been refilled with clean water for the family to wash their face and hands and dip a cloth to sponge their bodies clean. Despite the primitive conditions, I noted that they were all remarkably clean and well groomed.

Inside, the floor was neatly swept and bore no trace of food scraps. A kettle gurgled and popped on one side of a huge, old, black stove. On the other side of the room, a battered gauze–doored dresser displayed a scant collection of scratched enamel mugs and chipped china plates. The large wooden table in the centre of the room was white and lined from scrubbing. Around it stood four unmatched straight–backed wooden chairs, two with props bandaged to one leg. On the hearth stood a three–legged stool, its seat shiny from wear and its legs revealing great gaping patches of raw timber between layers of peeling green paint.

There were no windows, only hessian–covered holes in the walls with telltale stains below where the water trickled down when the rain came in. At either end of the kitchen, a hessian sack hung across an opening in a pathetic failed attempt to provide privacy to the bunk rooms beyond.

Pity vied with contempt as I puzzled the lack of basic comforts. Dad was an innovator. I pondered the probability that money for materials was in short supply, but I realised, years later, that Dad was already, at that time, a sick man.

In one room, double bunks with ragged broken springs lined both walls. In the other, two double beds stood side by side, with barely enough room to squeeze between. No wardrobe or dresser was visible. The shack was devoid of comfortable seating, but somehow, it seemed to radiate a special kind of warmth.

Fran surveyed the scene. What's she thinking now? This world was so different from the one she knew and yet, in the strangest ways, it was so similar. She returned my gaze with a warm smile. Later, she remarked that she had felt an unaccountable sense of belonging.

My mother and father. How should I address them? I had called Fred 'Dad', but using their titles somehow felt wrong. These people were strangers. I took my cue from Fran, whose use of those titles seemed so natural and easy.

Leaning against the sideboard, sipping tea from a chipped enamel cup and munching homemade biscuits from an enamel serving platter in the centre of the table, I asked three younger brothers about school and football. I asked my father about his work.

"Ian told me you can't shear any more, Dad. Do you still go out droving? Do you still have horses and dogs?"

The old man's nervousness abated slowly. His hands steadied and his colour improved. Once or twice, I saw the hint of a grin; that familiar laconic half–smile that showed itself more in the twinkling of the eyes than the upturning of thin lips or the dimpling of the chin.

His voice was deep, but soft. He answered questions tersely, like me, using no more words than necessary to address the question and appear reasonably polite. Volunteer nothing. It wasn't unfriendliness or disinterest. We just didn't see the need for detailed conversation. With people I was close to, I often conversed without either party speaking, or with half–finished sentences that made no sense to an outside observer. I found I could do that now with Dad. There was an instant connection.

Neither of us spoke of the past. Later, Ian thanked me for not uttering a word of accusation or recrimination. No reminders of the pain of our parting 18 years before or our long separation. I said nothing of the life I led as a child.

"What good would it do?" I replied when Fran commented. "There's been quite enough hurt already."

I wanted desperately to know why we were parted, but I never asked. In all the time we spent together, on that day and more than a hundred others, neither of us uttered a word about the awful events that separated us. I acted the part of the loving son returning home after a brief absence, as though I had left there to join the army or to work in another town. As though nothing was unusual. I was just another of Fred's many sons.

We stayed only a short while. Mum handed Carly a tin of cakes and a pie. "To help feed everyone," she said. I saw Fran glance at the big old wood stove and the primitive collection of kitchenware and I knew she marvelled that Mum could make pies and cakes in such conditions.

Mum kissed and hugged Fran and told her to call her Elsie. She hugged the children, then she put her arms around me and kissed my cheek and said, "See you later, son". I gave her a quick, soft hug, shook hands with my dad again, and said "See you at the wedding". I slid into the car, started the engine, and drove back in an uneasy, confused silence.

35: A FATHER'S LOVE

MARCH 1974

The clock over the courthouse entrance read 14 minutes to three when our little group assembled on the wide footpath to await the arrival of the bride. Dad stood proud in his worn, dark–grey suit and starched white shirt. He wrapped his arm about Mum and beamed admiringly at her. She was dressed in a smartly tailored purple satin suit—made by her, we learnt later, on an old treadle sewing machine with tools limited to a pair of scissors, needle, thread and just two pins.

Fran remarked that she was stunningly beautiful. Later, she admitted wondering how she might have formed that impression of an anorexic woman with wispy, untamed hair, hard, wrinkled skin and a gummy smile that showed a scattering of misshapen nicotine–stained teeth. But when you looked at her, you felt always compelled to focus on her eyes. You could look right through those eyes into the depths of her soul.

She won a beauty pageant once, or so the rumour went. Somewhere in the archives of photographs held by Dad's relations—no–one in the family ever met any of hers—there was a picture of a stunning, magnificent young woman. I secured it after her death. It now hangs on the family photo gallery wall in our sitting room. The woman in that photo is the woman I remember as my mother. The eyes and a familiar gentle voice were all that was left of her now.

Rob and Valerie had opted to marry in the village, rather than in the nearby regional centre, and I was relieved that Dad and I would not be forced to enter the big stone courthouse we recalled with such horror. Over the past few weeks, I had finally told Fran of the events of that awful day in 1956, and just a little about the life that followed.

The courthouse in the little bush town was a quaint, unpretentious white weatherboard structure with a galvanized iron roof on which the rain often sang so loudly that proceedings inside could not continue until the weather improved. The bride was fashionably late… five minutes. Dressed in a simple street frock and low–heeled shoes, she broke with tradition by entering on the arm of her groom. We had caught Rob reluctantly and clumsily trying to fasten his tie as he stepped from car to pavement to join Val, looking more than slightly affected by alcohol and pretty damn stoked at the prospect of claiming Val as his wife.

The registry office was too small for the gathering accompanying bride and groom, so Fran and I hovered uncomfortably just outside the door, near enough to hear most of the proceedings, but not close enough to hear the bride's nervous whisper and the groom's stumbling recitation of promises. Ian stood beside Rob as best man, similarly casually attired and looking equally uncomfortable, his tie crooked, his neck and face ruddy from a hasty dash from the pub on the corner, where he'd stopped off to ply Rob with a generous dose of liquid fortification.

With the exception of her mum, a stout German woman with a stentorian voice and heavy accent, Val was unaccompanied by family. Ian's wife, Carly, stood beside her as maid of honour. None of my younger brothers and sisters were invited to attend, although they joined us later at the reception.

When the ceremony was done we all migrated to the bowling club—a similarly unpretentious timber building set between two manicured lawns, with most of its seating on a long, wide veranda covered with shabby green Perspex. We dined on sandwiches, salads and trifle, and large hollowed–out cob loaves filled with savoury dips, with broken lumps of bread on the side for dipping. Blokes gravitated to the bar and spent the entire evening perched on high stools exercising their elbows with 10 ounce weights, while the women gathered around tables outside.

A large group of townsfolk joined in the festivities. In this town, celebrations were open to all without specific invitation, and in any case, it would have been impossible to exclude those who exercised their usual right of use of the facilities. There was no formal booking or allocated function room. Uninvited guests weren't a problem, though, because everyone threw in for the catering and we all paid our own way at the bar.

As we entered the reception hall, Mum migrated towards me. Reaching my side, she took my hand. "My son," she whispered in an ecstatic tone. "My wonderful eldest son." She hardly released my hand or left my side for the duration of the celebration. Over and over she introduced me as "My eldest son". Surprise was evident on many faces, and some were brash enough to ask, "Where have you been hiding him?" or "I thought Ian was your eldest? Where has Paul been all these years?" Others opened their mouths to speak, but were cut off with her enthusiastic "Don't you think he's handsome?", "Isn't he charming?" or "And did you meet his beautiful wife and my two gorgeous grandchildren?"

Mum handled all the awkward questions with calm confidence. "Paul joined the army when he was only 15," she said to some, and "Paul and his wife live a long way away," to others. Something in her tone or expression seemed to warn against further inquiry. Although folks might reasonably wonder why they hadn't met me on a previous visit, either the answers, or her demeanour as she gave them, seemed to shut down conversation on that topic. She would squeeze my hand and beam proudly at me, proceeding with a brief commentary on the ceremony of the day, or asking the inquirer what she thought of the bride's attire.

Once, when I pulled away briefly to retire to the gents room, she commanded me to come right back and told me firmly that now she had found me again, she intended never to let me out of her sight.

Fran said later that after I'd gone, she sought her out and told her how happy she was to have such a beautiful daughter–in–law and how fortunate it was I had a good woman to love and care for me.

"She told me she didn't look after you as well as she should have," Fran said, her eyes misting. "She said it was such a relief to see you cared for and happy. She said it so matter–of–factly, but when the words were out, her face twisted with pain and she stared at the floor."

I didn't reply, but I knew that my expression spoke volumes. I struggled to tolerate my mother's pretences. Eighteen years and no attempt to make contact. Someone was to blame for me being taken away and it sure wasn't my father's fault.

"I said I was sure she did her best," Fran was saying. "I told her babies don't come with a 'How to be a Mum' manual. There were tears in her eyes when she answered. She said how good it was to have you back and I could have no idea how much she missed you. The days go on. You do what you have to do. You get through, somehow, but she said she cried herself to sleep every night since you were taken."

"She never tried to get us back."

"I asked her why, Paul. I wanted to swallow my tongue after I said it. How could I be so insensitive? But she didn't seem to mind the question at all. Do you know what she said?"

I shrugged, unsure whether I wanted to hear how my mother had replied.

"She said, 'Many times. Fred walked over 70 miles, once, to the Home we thought they were in, but they told him the kids weren't there. Social workers visited, and we told them we wanted the kids back. We asked them what we had to do, but they just told us the kids were better off away. In the end I decided perhaps they were. You've seen how we live. What did we have to offer them?' "

Love. A sense of belonging. An identity. A feeling of worthiness.

Fran was still rattling on. "It must have been so hard for her, Paul. I can't begin to imagine how any woman could cope with losing a child, but what matters is that her son has come home. And it's clear she couldn't be happier."

I didn't answer. My head swam with questions I would never ask, and accusations and recriminations I would never utter. She had her son back, but her son was a man who no longer had any need for a mother—a man besieged with doubts that she had ever really been a mother, because she had failed to protect me. I struggled to suppress an awful sense of having suffered the ultimate betrayal, and yet I wanted desperately to love her.

#

We visited my family again a month later. Fred was still noticeably uncomfortable in my presence and nothing we could say or do seemed to put him at ease. Three months later, I brought him up to stay with us for two weeks, hoping we could get to know each other better. He was a delight to have around the house. The kids adored him, but his nervousness around me didn't abate.

We talked, drank beer and even went to the pub together. Fred met my friends and engaged in casual conversation with them, but when we returned home, he retired with no more than a polite goodnight and a haunted look that suggested he was afraid of me, and would rather be anywhere else but in my home.

The third evening Fred was there, I had a band rehearsal scheduled. Fran was struggling with dinner dishes and demanding children, and concerned about my father's obvious discomfort. I shouted at her that I couldn't find a clean shirt to wear and stormed into the kitchen yelling at her that I was going to be late for the rehearsal.

"For Christ's sake, leave the fucking dishes and find me a clean shirt and iron it," I pulled a chair back from the table, slammed it against the wall, and thumped down to polish my shoes.

Fred regarded me thoughtfully for a minute, frowning. Then he stood up and walked calmly to the kitchen and fetched a tea towel from the hook above the sink. He walked back to where I sat and flicked the towel hard across my left ear. Then he leant down so his face was close to my ear and hissed, "Iron your own bloody shirt. And don't speak to your wife like that again".

He straightened up, walked back to the kitchen and, to my astonishment, began drying dishes. I guess I had always envisaged my father as somewhat chauvinistic and very masculine—not the type to volunteer for women's work.

"I'll do your kitchen duties for you tonight," he snapped, "but in future, get off your arse and help your wife. She's got enough to cope with without you expecting her to be your servant. Wilson men treat women with respect."

I ironed my shirt, pulled on my shoes, fastened my tie and stormed out without a word to either Fran or my father, slamming the door behind me.

In the morning, I sat down across the table from my father, still chafing, and concentrated intently on my breakfast. Fred's face creased and he spoke hesitantly. "About last night, mate. I'm sorry. I had no right — "

His quivering tone shocked me, but I recognised the opportunity his uncertainty presented.

"Why?" I asked, looking up with a wry smile. "You're my father. It's your job."

A sigh of amused relief. Fred nodded cautious approval, and there was a rare softness in his look that spoke of a deep, hurting love for the little boy he had lost, and the adult son he had at last found.

He adopted an authoritarian air, then, and with heavy emphasis on the word 'son', he said, "Well then, son, I hope you were listening to me".

He laughed when I said, "Yes, Dad" in a meek and contrite little–boy voice, and he came around the table and patted my shoulder affectionately. The tension was broken.

Later, I realised that I'd apparently given Dad licence to tell me off whenever he thought I was out of line, but I made no complaint. The order of our relationship was restored, and I couldn't imagine anything that could make me happier.

Dad went out in the afternoon, and he wasn't back when I came home from work. When an hour had passed and he still wasn't back, I worried he might have got himself lost, and went looking for him. I found the silly old bugger in the pub, sitting on a bar stool, holding court. He was bragging to everyone who would listen about how important his son was, being the town bandmaster and all.

"That's nice, Paul," Fran said when I told her about it that night.

"It's bloody embarrassing is what it is," I replied. "Jesus! I don't think I'll ever be able to show my face in that pub again."

"He's proud of you. Surely that pleases you?"

"Yeah, well, he can tell me privately or keep it to himself. He doesn't need to go making an idiot of himself in front of half the bloody town."

"I'm sure no–one thought he was an idiot."

"I'm sure no–one there gave a damn about me being the town bandmaster. It wouldn't have impressed them one iota!"

"It impresses your father, and that's what matters."

The memory of his words swept over me like warm rays of sunshine. "Yeah," I agreed, "I spent a lot of years wishing I had a father to impress.

"But he's still a silly old bastard," I added, laughing.

JUNE 2010

Ern's eyes pricked with emotion. I was accustomed to emotional reactions to this part of my story. It was a big deal, at the time, but it wasn't until decades later that I really appreciated the significance of that period of my life, and the torrent of emotions that swirled around us all as we struggled to reconnect and to reconcile the joy, the anger and the pain.

I felt the need to discuss something a little less intense, and talking of my father's pride in my musical accomplishments stirred a recollection of one of the happier chapters of my life. I told him of my triumphs with the town band and performing with the local musical society.

"I did well with the youngsters too," I said, glowing at the memory of a particularly impressive success. "A parent woke us at 2 a.m. to tell us her son, who I was tutoring privately, won several events at a major eisteddfod. She was so excited she couldn't contain herself and had to bring me a thank you gift on her way home."

"You clearly had impressive ability, Paul. Surely you could have pursued a career in music outside the army?"

"Without formal qualifications, there was nowhere to go with it. Ability didn't cut it, any more than the worthless bloody army certificate I worked so hard for. I taught music at a TAFE College in Lismore years later... filled in for a mate who was ill. I proved myself to be a damned good teacher.

"I could have gone a long way in the profession without even a shred of ability if only I'd had a piece of paper with the right words written on it. Ultimately, I was pushed out of the town band and replaced by a guy with a university degree. Forged, it turned out. He couldn't blow wind up my backside, but they paid him 10 times what they paid me and they helped him get tutoring positions at private schools to supplement his income. Band never won a contest under his leadership, and they never apologised when they found out his qualifications weren't genuine either."

I didn't tell Ern about the dozens of other jobs I believed I could have done well, nor the dozens of failed applications I submitted for jobs I was confident I could handle with ease. Had I told him, I would have had to admit to both of us that it was an inability to believe in myself—let alone to communicate confidence—that deprived me of dozens of opportunities.

For a time after the reunion with my family, a fragile bubble of hope had shimmered inside me that my father's love and approval might finally quiet the demons and the pattern of my life might at last change.

Self–doubt holds you prisoner, but I thought surely love could set me free. The denial of retraining devastated me, but my father admired me and I threw myself into life determined to vindicate his pride.

PART IV

36: THE "MATRON" VISITS

ARMIDALE, JUNE 2010

Paul parked the Roller at the gate of the hobby farm. The house was obscured now by trees, and the sign on the gate was elegantly embossed rather than just roughly painted. The property name remained unchanged, and the house—despite a small addition and some cosmetic improvements—was still recognisable as the one he had constructed all those years ago.

He and Ern walked up the long drive to find the current owner in the front garden. When Paul explained he'd built the home more than thirty 30 before, she was pleased to indulge them with an open invitation to tour the property, and then to join her inside for coffee.

When Paul showed Ern the little creek on the back boundary, a platypus obligingly slid out from its hideaway to sun itself. Walking back, he showed Ern the spot where the pumpkin patch had been, and the place where he'd built the pigsty. Then he stood with Ern on the little front porch where he had greeted Ede Tuck nearly 30 years before.

ARMIDALE, JUNE 1980

"Paul Wilson!" Ede Tuck exclaimed, throwing her arms around me and hugging me hard, then laughing that deep, resonant, Welsh laugh that made generous layers of flesh roll and her eyes dance. I was instantly transported back to another era, hearing the Ohio Matron's happy singing as she went about her chores and tasting the rich cream–filled cakes, still warm from the oven, that she greeted me with after school every day of my early teenage years. I heard her telling me to "make your lips like a chook's bum" to blow into the cornet mouthpiece when I was first learning to play.

It was a wintery Saturday afternoon and Ede and her son, Peter—my Ohio 'brother'—stood, with Peter's wife, shivering on my front porch. It was over a decade since I had seen Peter. I hadn't heard from Ede Tuck since I joined the army.

229

Ede introduced me to Peter's wife and I stepped back and beckoned them to enter. I led them through to the kitchen where Fran was clearing the table after lunch.

"Fran, this is Peter Tuck and his wife, Helen, and..." I hesitated a moment, feeling rather foolish, then stumbled over the words, "I don't know what to call you. Matron doesn't seem right anymore and –"

" 'Mum' doesn't work for you now, and 'Mrs Tuck' is way too formal for someone you used to call 'Mum'," she laughed. "Why not just call me Ede. That is my name after all."

I considered her reply silently.

"It's all right, Paul," she laughed, hugging me again. "You are all grown up now. Those old rules don't apply. And my, how you have grown up! A home, a family. How old are your children? You didn't introduce me to them yet."

She fussed over the children while I asked Peter where he was living now and what he was up to. He had changed corps, been promoted to corporal and was stationed in Perth. He had two children, about the same age as our older two. Fran had presented me with another daughter four years earlier, and Helen was pregnant with their third.

"Cup of tea?" said Ede, looking up. "Sit, Fran. I'll get it. Just point me at the makin's." She took command of our kitchen with the same happy confidence that dealt with a thousand boyhood crises and challenges during my early teenage years. Within minutes we were all seated around the dining–room table with Frances and Helen smiling silently while two brothers and their mother laughed over precious memories of childhood, struggling to fill each other in on events since they last parted.

"I visited Garry Simpson yesterday," Ede said. "Things are not going too well for him marriage–wise, I'm afraid. I'm so happy to see you with a lovely family and a nice home, Paul. You deserve to be happy." She winked at Fran. "He was always one of my favourites, you know. I shouldn't have had favourites and I tried not to let it show, but this auburn–haired, freckle–faced squirt, with his cheeky grin and devilish eyes, won my heart. He was a good kid, and he was good company. He used to stand in the pottery shed for hours talking to me while I worked."

"I loved watching you," I said, remembering. "An artist at work. Loved those stories too—about you working in decryption during the war."

"Paul has told me such a lot about you," Fran said. Since reuniting with my family, I had begun to open up about the happier chapters of my past.

Ede laughed. "Should I be worried?"

"He paints you as a very special lady."

"Perhaps I should be embarrassed, then?"

"I only told her what you did for me. I've often wondered where I might have ended up if you hadn't come into my life. I think I was pretty messed up when I arrived at Ohio."

"It took us three weeks to get a word out of him," Ede said softly, addressing Fran. Her eyes misted and her forehead creased. "He had us very worried. We were required to report that he was seriously disturbed, but they would have sent psychiatrists to take him and lock him away."

"I used to call him 'Monkey'," Peter laughed. "He was a runt when he came there. Bald patch on the side of his head. Emaciated, and wanted to sleep on the floor for some reason. Scared of pissing the bed, maybe, or not being able to make it to required standards in the time allotted. Wouldn't speak either. Shit scared of something. Dad made me take him to my room and show him my stamp collection and comics. Reassure him. Get him to speak. I didn't want to, but we became mates and we were inseparable. He's my little bro', and I'd fight to the death to protect him if the need arose. Even now."

"As if I'd need a wuss like you to protect me," I said, punching his arm lightly and reaching in the fridge for two stubbies. "Look at you. All flab and beer gut."

"That's gratitude!" Peter replied, twisting the cap. "Cheers, mate," he said, clinking the bottle against mine. Then he turned to Fran again and his tone changed. "Mum and Dad loved those boys, " he said, his voice warming with fond recollections. "Referred to them as 'their boys', and demanded they be treated with respect and kindness. Dad was tough. He ran a tight ship, but he cared and it showed."

Peter and Helen excused themselves mid–afternoon to do some sightseeing. Fran started preparing dinner. She had invited Ede, Peter and Helen to stay and they accepted eagerly. I took Ede on a guided tour of the house and our little hobby farm.

"You've done an incredible job here, Paul. You always were good with your hands," she said, running her fingers over the cedar–panelled feature wall in the living room. I was tempted to reply it was a shame her husband didn't appreciate my talent enough to let me cultivate it, but I kept the thought to myself.

"So, tell me what else you've been up to since you left the army."

"Not much to tell. I work in a shit job I hate, but it pays the bills."

Her face puckered with concern. I was still working on the electricity lines and I hated it. I had consented to complete a short course to become a qualified electrical linesman, mainly for the extra pay and the chance of a place on the on–call roster, which meant a generous annual bonus and occasionally some well–paid overtime. It was dangerous work. I tried to keep it from Fran just how dangerous, but in town one day she was embraced by a teary friend who had just heard a newsflash on the car radio. One of my workmates was electrocuted. His first name was Paul. She had misheard the surname. I didn't tell Fran I had handled that light choke just minutes before it killed him. I didn't tell Ede how dangerous the job was either.

"I took some time off a couple of years back," I said, trying hard to sound more cheerful. "I had renovated a little cottage in town and we sold it and bought this land—eight acres. It's an idyllic spot. The back of the house overlooks the creek that forms the back boundary. The creek is inhabited with eels and platypus. I'll show you shortly.

"It's blissfully peaceful out here," I continued, smiling now, although it was still a little forced. "A mile off the main road with only a handful of neighbours, all a considerable distance away. I hired a mate, on daily rates, to help me build this place to lock–up stage and I moved the family out here. Then, after I started working again, I worked nights and weekends to finish the place. It was a labour of love and I think it was the only thing that kept me sane."

I didn't add that, during the day, I went through the motions of living mechanically, without feeling. At night, I either hammered, sawed and sanded until I collapsed from exhaustion, or drank myself into oblivion.

"You never went on with your music?"

"For a while. Until some up–jumped academic decided the town bandmaster should be someone with formal qualifications. They brought a fellow up from Tassie who supposedly had a uni degree in music. I stayed on and played under him for a few months, but I quit after he told Fran I could develop into a competent musician under his tutelage."

The acid in my voice discouraged reply, but the sympathy in her eyes told me she felt my pain. I decided some happier conversation was in order and changed the subject. I pushed the living room sliding door open and ushered her out. We walked towards the little creek on the back boundary. I hoped the platypus would be out, but I couldn't see any. A few eels darted about just under the water's surface.

"Remember the time I tried to run away?"

She nodded and laughed.

"I found my parents a few years back, and three brothers and three more sisters, plus the two brothers I knew existed."

"Oh Paul! That's amazing." She smiled broadly, but her expression changed to concern as she asked, "And how did the reunion go?" Long experience with State wards would have taught her that going home is often a devastating experience.

232

"Good. Really good. Fran gets on well with Mum and Dad. My brothers are great."

She was studying me intently, searching out my secrets.

"My brothers and sisters had good parents. They grew up OK. Adore Mum and Dad. Doesn't seem like there was any good reason to take me away." I tried not to sound bitter. When she didn't reply, I forced a smile and continued, "But all grey clouds have a silver lining. If they hadn't taken me, I wouldn't 've met you".

"I remember the day you arrived at Ohio," she said in a wish–I–didn't voice, her eyes watering. "You were so pathetically skinny. All battered and bruised. I don't know when I've seen a little body in such dreadful condition, and in my line of work I saw a lot of abused children."

"It wasn't that that hurt me, though, Ede. I was a survivor. Resilient. I could have avoided a lot of beatings, but I stood up for myself, even when it cost me."

She nodded and I knew she remembered times at Ohio when I defended myself despite the price.

"It was the loss of identity. The loss of a place to belong in the world. I see my brothers so at ease with themselves — comfortable in their own skins. They know who they are and where they fit in the world. Me? I don't know where I belong in the scheme of things. My father was a drover, a shearer and a horse breaker. Good with his hands and in touch with nature. That was me when I was little, a bush kid, feral. When they took me away, they took away the right to be me."

I resisted the urge to add that I didn't belong in a uniform, jumping to attention every time someone barked a command.

"And it turns out there was no good reason for it. I had loving parents. Dirt poor, but decent, caring people who worked hard and gave their kids all the stuff that really matters."

She took a hanky from the pocket of her cardigan and wiped her eyes.

"One day I'll find the bastard who did that to me," I said. I was conscious of clenching my fists and thrusting my lower jaw forward. "Geoffrey Simms. I am going to find him one day and kill him."

I waited for a shocked exclamation or a sharp rebuke, but instead Ede reached across and closed a hand gently over mine.

"And why would you want to destroy your lovely family and your good life by doing something like that?" she asked mildly.

"Because he deserves to pay for what he did. He wrecked families."

"Not knowingly or intentionally, Paul." She gazed into my eyes and I was a young boy again, eating chocolate cake and listening to her gently explain why I couldn't go home to see my dad.

"Paul," she said thoughtfully, "Geoffrey Simms was a pathetic, ignorant little man doing a job the way he was instructed to do it. A bureaucrat following instructions, that's all. He didn't mean to harm anyone."

"How can you make excuses for him?" My tone was harsh, but it elicited no reaction.

"I don't excuse what he did. It was terribly wrong. It was cruel and it caused children pain that no child should suffer. It tore out mothers' hearts. It is hard to conceive a more dreadful crime, but it wasn't his crime, Paul. It was faceless men in back rooms making decisions they were not qualified to make and giving instructions they weren't qualified to give. Men who write policies to cater to the interests of self–serving power groups. Simms was nothing more than a vehicle—a man doing his job, the only way he knew how."

She let me think for a while before continuing.

"Paul," she said softly, "you have suffered terribly—suffering that would destroy many strong men, but you have come through it. You have made a life for yourself. You have a family who love you, a nice home, a job. You have won the respect of good people, and now you have two choices. You can try to forgive those who caused you so much hurt, or you can invite pain and suffering back into your life and the lives of your wife and children. You can let the desire for revenge destroy you." She stared meaningfully into my blazing eyes, willing me to unset my jaw and relax my gripped fists.

"Geoffrey Simms was a misguided little man following instructions," she continued, lecturing me now. "Those who instructed him were blind and ignorant, and far too powerful for their own good and that of the society that empowered them. And you… you are a good, intelligent, strong man who has survived against the odds. You've shown the world those nuns who branded you were wrong, and Geoffrey Simms and the judge in that Children's Court were wrong. The faceless men were wrong. There are better ways to manage situations like the one Geoffrey Simms sought to manage, but that poor, ignorant man could not conceive a better solution."

For a moment, I felt my shoulders slump a little, and my fists opened. Perhaps I had been carrying this dead weight for too long.

"Guess I'll stop looking for Simms. The bastard's probably dead by now anyway."

A little breath of air escaped her lips and a relieved smile lit her eyes, deepening her dimples. I let her enjoy her little win. She was a good woman and I didn't want her carrying my burdens, but a dark, murderous anger still boiled my blood. If the bastard was dead, I would blow up the Department he worked for, and murder all his heartless, self–righteous colleagues.

I needed revenge, and someday I would have it.

37: ANOTHER LIFE ENDS

SEPTEMBER, 1984

"Where are you going to mail it from," Fran asked, folding a letter carefully and pushing it into an envelope with gloved hands. She fixed a typed label to the front. No return address. It was unsigned.

"Maybe Ebor," I replied. "It's real pretty down there this time of year. We could pack lunch, make a picnic and return the typewriter on the way."

"Does subversive activity put you in the mood for a picnic?" She seemed alarmed by the thought.

"Subversive? Is that what you call it? I'm trying to save lives here."

"By writing anonymous letters on a borrowed typewriter and handling everything with gloved hands so no–one detects where it came from? Why all the secrecy? It's not as if you are doing anything wrong. This is what Workplace Health and Safety Boards were created for. They can't function if people don't speak out when an employer breaks the rules."

"I told you. The union rep said he'd make sure I was fired if I rocked the boat on this."

"Good for him. What a hero! His life isn't in danger."

She pressed the envelope closed and laid it carefully on the table, then removed her gloves.

"I don't think I ever told you about the conversation at the Christmas party last year," she said. "A group of us were discussing that death in Inverell and saying how worrying it was to have our husbands working in such dangerous conditions. Bruin was eavesdropping. Comes over and declares he doesn't know what we are complaining about. The council pays a fortune to keep you all well insured."

"Bastard. But about what I'd expect from that mongrel. He'll get his."

My mates and I were climbing 40–foot poles in freezing weather and blazing heat. Some of the poles were old and quite unstable. A large number of them were marked for replacement, but a bright young engineer, eager for advancement and keen to demonstrate his skills at reducing expenditure, designed a prop to hold them and claimed it made them quite secure. What was more disturbing, though, was that he adapted another piece of equipment, called a 'red devil', to back–stay the poles while we were climbing them. Red devils were hollow metal tubes pegged to the surface of the ground. He had them used as a substitute for heavy, well–anchored buried logs.

The red devils were intended as a temporary stay only. I verified with the manufacturer that no–one should ever climb a pole with a red devil used as a back–stay, but my employer insisted it was safe and necessary. I battled with the union rep to recognise the danger and take action. He didn't climb.

"I'm on a good wicket here," he said when I asked for assistance. "I'd really prefer not to rock the boat, and I'll see you fired if you make any more waves about this."

"Your fucking union forced us to strike over changes to the medical benefits scheme," I replied in a voice thin with fury, "and we struck for a pay rise so insignificant that it would take three years to recover the pay we lost by striking.

"Your union boss mates failed to oppose a judge's declaration that our job wasn't dangerous. No danger money should be payable, despite several serious accidents and a couple of deaths in recent years across a relatively small number of linesmen employed in the State. But you guys agreed with the employer that because workers' compensation premiums were high for 'such a dangerous job', the employer could deduct the premiums from our superannuation contributions. I was promised my contributions would be matched dollar for dollar, but what have I got in my super account? Sweet fuck all. Don't you rock the fucking boat, mate. You just stand by and watch your mates die."

The union rep held firm, and the dangerous work practices continued.

Apart from the danger, I found the work boring and my workmates incapable of stimulating conversation. When, occasionally, one of them came up with a bright idea to improve efficiency, it was dismissed with contempt, then adopted and credited to a boss who claimed it as his own. One worker did manage to force acknowledgement of his innovation. He was paid the grand sum of $50 for designing a device that ultimately saved millions. The result, of course, was that morale on the job was poor and most of the workers suffered through the day thinking only of the beer, sex and home comforts their pay packet afforded them at the end of it. The only upsides to the job were that we often worked in the bush, and on wet days we sat in the shed playing cards for hours while the rain pounded on the roof. We secretly prayed it would last for days.

I posted the letter, reporting the illegal use of red devils to Workplace Health and Safety, at a post box in Ebor. Afterward, I took the family for a drive out to the gorge and we ate a packed lunch by the roaring waterfall, then sat listening to the birdsong and replying to their calls. I enjoyed mimicking them and watching their reaction. I was good at it too. Fran was sure they thought they'd found themselves a mate.

"Listen," I joked. "That's a Dr Arthur bird. Hear him? He's singing out 'Dr Arthur, Dr Arthur'," and when the crow called I told her it was singing out "Get faaaarked," and I called to him not to be so vulgar.

"Storm birds are singing," I remarked. "Some substantial stormy weather looming. Most people think their singing means rain coming, but actually their singing indicates a period of heavy storms. Did you know that? Look, the tree bark is tinged with red. The drought is about to break."

"How do you know this stuff?" Nicki asked.

"My dad was a bushman. I remember him telling me these things when I was barely old enough to walk and talk."

Fran smiled, but there was a sadness in her eyes. "You missed out on a lot, being separated from him for so long, didn't you?"

I shrugged. "I guess there were some compensations, but I missed him terribly. I never forgot the things he taught me, or the way I felt when he took me out with him and explained the secrets of nature."

As expected, the letter sparked an investigation, and quite a furore at work. The bosses had us all lined up one morning while they ranted on about the trouble the letter caused and how misguided it was—because they would never allow unsafe practices. They assured us they would find out who did it and whoever it was would pay. I struggled to fake dismay and disapproval.

Three weeks later, the rains hadn't yet come. The late spring days dawned crisp and fresh and ended with a refreshing chill that invited Fran and I to light a fire behind the garage to grill chops or sausages. We huddled around the fire with the children watching the last of the sunset and the rising of the moon. The days were warm.

At work, we were replacing poles on a line in the bush some 40 miles from town, out near a gorge. I was enjoying the bird serenades, sucking in the clean scent of new growth, and taking morning tea and lunch around a campfire, toasting my sandwiches and boiling billy tea. Nearly two miles of wires terminated on a pole located near the edge of a cliff that dropped into a deep ravine. The pole was anchored with wires to a red devil pegged on to the ground as a back–stay. I was up there working one day when I felt it leaning. That wasn't uncommon, but this was different. Disquiet graduated to alarm and a dull thudding in my head crescendoed to incessant hammering. My limbs tensed and I was suddenly ice cold.

There was no time to think about demounting. The red devil had let go and the pole was gliding smoothly, almost gracefully, towards the edge of the cliff. I was strapped firmly to the high side of it.

Time stopped.

The ground rose and the world tilted. The pole pressed through the air. I felt like I was on one of those thrill rides at a fair, only there was no safety stop.

The air whistled as the pole pushed through. Somewhere in the distance I heard a bloodcurdling howl. The ground was rising, rising. Suddenly, there was a slowing, and then the movement stopped. The heel of the pole had caught in the ground and was fighting against it, pushing at the soil, demanding freedom. I was a few feet above the ground now. Strangely, I felt no fear—just a cold certainty that my life was about to end. I had a vision of my mangled self, splintered and minced, torn face death–grey.

Then the ground moved and the heel of the pole broke free. With a thunderous crack, the pole crashed hard against the earth. My heart leapt into my throat and its wild pulsing choked me. My lungs screamed for air. I crouched on the pole a while, incredulous.

Am I alive?

A confused stew of voices; hands reaching out to touch my head. I unbuckled my belt. The world spun. Voices rattled commiserations, cursed and blasphemed. Contorted faces peered down at me, at the pole. Someone wandered over to inspect the red devil, tugging at the dislodged wires.

I climbed slowly off the pole slowly, shaking violently. I stood for a moment, testing my legs. I waved my arms, leant forward, swung back, turned from side to side and felt my face. A trembling hand pressed at my temples, pleading with my head to stop throbbing. At last, convinced I was still whole and in the world of the living—not wherever we go when we cross over—I jumped into the boss's truck, drove back to the depot, and scratched my resignation on the bottom of my time sheet.

When I arrived home that afternoon, Fran had elderly aunts visiting. When I told her I had quit my job, their look of horror might have challenged that of a spinster discovering Napolean's severed penis.

"And what will you do now?" one asked in a disapproving tone. "Jobs aren't easy to get. I should think you would be grateful to have one."

"Sell up, move to the coast and go on the dole," I replied without thinking. I was more concerned with demonstrating my contempt for her and her lofty expectations than for indicating any genuine intentions, but after I said it I decided it actually sounded like a pretty good idea. I'd put in 20 years paying taxes for the privilege of slogging my guts out in jobs I detested, while beach bums bludged on the system and went surfing every day. And all up I had very little more income to live on than they did, despite putting my life in danger every working day.

Enjoying their shocked reaction, I added, "Become a bludger and a beach bum. I reckon that's something I'd be good at".

Fran was devastated at having to leave her home, but we sold it for more than twice what it cost us. Two months later we moved to Ballina. It was a place I remembered fondly as the scene of a wonderful childhood holiday, and close and similar to Pottsville—a little paradise where I had spent some of the happiest days of my teenage years.

I didn't think much about employment opportunities before making a choice for relocation. The cold climate had been messing with my health, so my doctor suggested we look for a place where the temperatures were less extreme. The other determining factor was a somewhat misguided notion that returning to a place where I'd once been blissfully happy could fix all my woes.

38: BUSINESSMAN PAUL

BALLINA, MARCH 1986

Fran snapped the lid on the esky and lay back on the picnic rug to soak up the glorious early autumn midday sun. Lulled by the music of children's laughter, I suspected she might have drifted into a blissful daytime sleep if not for the sounds from the transistor I held to my ear. I was listening intently to race calls and I knew she considered the sound an irritating drone.

"This promised to be such a great day out, Paul," she said, clearly annoyed. "The kids have been looking forward to it all week. Why do you have to spoil it by spending most of the day with that infernal thing pressed to you ear, scratching on a bloody form guide?"

I ignored her question, but lowered the volume slightly. She shrugged and laid back, appearing to doze.

"Yes!" I shouted, jolting her from a state of half–sleep. "Twenty–to one, you little beauty. My bank just reached 40 grand."

"Your mythical bank" she corrected.

"I've been working this on paper for a long time now and it never fails. One day soon I'm going to do it for real. Watch it make me very rich, but if you keep complaining and putting me down, you won't be sharing it."

"I just wish you could put it aside on days like this, Paul. It's a family day out. We don't have many and the kids need your attention."

"The kids are fine. Listen to them. They're having a ball. Young teens don't want their father joining their games."

She sat up and hugged her legs, resting her chin on her knees. "Thankfully, they are having a great time, otherwise I might be tempted to pack up and go home."

I don't know how long she sat there like that, but at least two more races were called and I lost on both. It didn't faze me at all, but I switched the radio off after the second loss and declared there were no more system horses running in this meet.

"Peace, at last," Fran said, lying down again.

"I want to take out a second mortgage, Fran," I said suddenly. "I know it's possible. The house is worth a fair bit now it's renovated and we owe very little on it."

She drew a deep breath and I prepared for yet another violent argument.

"It should be my decision. I did the work," I said defensively, recalling exhausting months of sawing and hammering late into the evenings.

"Yes, and you did a superb job too."

I had renovated the first little old cottage we bought, installing a smart, modern kitchen and replacing the rusted tub and cracked basin in the ugly, damp cell of a bathroom, then tiling walls to make it sleek and modern. I taught myself carpentry, painting, concreting, tiling, and even the basics of plumbing. I transformed a run–down old cottage to a lovely modern home.

Then we'd sold it and I built a country homestead. My skill and dedication had astonished her, given my inexperience and the absence of any form of tuition or help. It broke her heart when I quit my job and we had to sell, but we'd made a healthy profit on it.

When we arrived in Ballina, I wanted a big, old, loved house wrapped in worn timber and iron verandas and ivy creepers, built in the days when proud craftsmen carved their souls into elaborate picture rails and mantels. In the end, though, we bought a late–model brick and tile that had been dreadfully abused and neglected and I was forced to renovate again. I complained bitterly, but I enjoyed the work. It was a distraction, and the finished product gave me a feeling of achievement.

The house nestled into the base of a hillside on half an acre on the outskirts of the town, surrounded by fruit trees and adjoining a koala habitat. The kids spent their weekends on one of Australia's most beautiful beaches, still virtually undiscovered despite strong white–foamed breakers crashing on to clean golden sand. I bought them a kayak and they canoed up and down the river pretending to be pirates or explorers, reminding me of brief periods of happiness in a miserable childhood.

"So," I said emphatically, "I've been figuring out this business plan, and I want to take a loan out to—"

"No, Paul!" she snapped. "I don't care how much you've won on paper or how reliable you think this system of yours is. It's not happening. We've been through this. We are not risking our home to bet on bloody horses. End of discussion."

There was an uncomfortably long silence. My fists were clenched and my face was set hard. I was avoiding her gaze and trying to swallow my anger. Finally, I spoke again.

"Who said anything about betting?" I said. I paused a moment. "I want to take a second mortgage to start a business."

She sat up and spun round to face me. "What sort of business?"

"A craft business. Metal spinning. I've done some research and I can buy a machine for a few grand. I've read about the process. It's not that hard."

She seemed lost for words. I studied her expression.

"I've always been good with my hands, Fran, and I like making things. I worked in shit jobs for 20 years and hated nearly every bloody day of it. With no education or trade training, I've got no more hope of finding a fulfilling job here than I had when I left the army. Less, probably. I don't want to spend the rest of my working life doing something I hate. I might as well have stayed in the bloody army. At least it paid a decent wage."

I opened the esky and helped myself to a beer and sat staring at the label. My pulse raced. I studied Fran's anxious face and silently prayed I'd find a way to make her understand how desperately I wanted this chance.

"What do you plan to make?"

"Junk jewellery, souvenirs, badges. There's heaps of stuff this machine can turn out."

She considered my reply silently, understandably confused. I'd been secretly researching this for months, but it must have seemed to her that this came out of nowhere. She needed time. I agreed to drop the subject for the moment, but over the days that followed, I continued to plead. Eventually, she relented.

Three weeks later, she met me one morning on the wide steps of the local bank. We walked arm–in–arm down the long corridor to the manager's office to listen to the compulsory reading of legal cautions and loan terms and nervously affix signatures to a 'Second Mortgage', adding $20,000 to our existing debt. The banker solemnly handed us a cheque book and explained that we had a $20,000 overdraft. Interest would be charged only on the largest outstanding balance during any given month. Fran left there white–faced and shaking. I couldn't recall when I'd felt so optimistic and so happy.

Five months on, the money had almost run out and I had sunk into the depths of despair. Fran sat at the table one stormy Friday evening, peering over loss statements, telling me tearfully I would have to quit. I remained stubbornly determined to ignore all signs of defeat. I ripped up financial statements and threw them at her.

"Piss off with your fucking numbers. You're so negative. All you want to do is tear me down."

She knew that deep down I fretted and worried. She heard me tossing and turning at night. She knew that I worried about her. She found me on the verge of tears one day, after a casting failed. "I didn't want you to know, Fran." I said quietly. "I knew how it would upset you."

243

Then, one windy late September Wednesday, she came home to find me whistling as I slid a bottle of her favourite champagne into the fridge. I turned to her with eyes dancing and my face glowing as I pulled a shiny badge from my pocket and flashed it at her joyfully.

"Look closely, my darling! You are looking at our ticket to business success," I said, dropping it on the table.

It was odd shaped — a curved section with a long tail on which the words "Harley Davidson" were engraved. It was shiny silver, not real silver of course. Polished monkey metal. It twinkled in the sunlight, so the words were hard to read. She seemed incapable of sharing my obvious enthusiasm.

"Well? You are supposed to be excited."

"What is it?"

I gave an exasperated sigh. "A motorbike badge, for Harleys of course. I took an order today for 500 of these at 20 bucks a pair from a bike shop in Tweed Heads."

She made no response, but just stared at me doubtfully.

"Five thousand dollars, Fran, and I can fill this order in two days."

She turned it over thoughtfully. I struggled to suppress frustration.

"Five thousand dollars," I repeated. "We based the business plan on taking less than half that each week, and if the badges take only two days to make, I'll still have plenty of time to produce other stuff. And best of all, Hopo insists it must be all cash dealing."

She sat forward with a start. "Why? Is there — "

"He's a bikie, Fran. He sells to bikies. It's a cash business, but it's a great business. These guys love their bikes. They spend a fortune on them. Hopo reckons he can't get enough of these things. I can make a thousand a week with ease. More maybe." I studied her expression, bitterly disappointed by her lack of confidence.

"I'll deliver the order next Monday" I said brightly. "Come with me, Fran. Meet Hopo. He's quite a character. You'll enjoy a day out. We can go shopping after. It's a while since you've been to a city to shop, and I know you love it."

She nodded silently, apparently not trusting herself to speak. I understood her fears. I struggled to believe too, but I had an order in my hand and a promise of more to come.

Hopo's shop was in a back street, a rather grubby–looking shed–like structure with a dozen shiny Harleys lined up out front. Fran hated bikes, but she couldn't help but admire the gleaming chrome–spoked wheels, the brightly coloured duco polished to a mirror shine, the long, plush, leather seats, and the shiny handlebars standing high and proud.

Inside, racks of spare parts of every description lined the walls and the smell of leather and chrome mixed with the pervasive stink of nicotine.

Exhaust pipes, leather seats, handlebar grips, wheels. Along one wall, T–shirts and leather gloves. Up the middle, racks of heavy–lined leather jackets.

A streak of light from a high window danced over shiny helmets—silver, red, purple, deep blues and greens—all lined with deep–black leather padding. Boxes of decals and badges rested, tilted on the diagonal to display their contents, against the front edge of a wide wooden counter. No cash register—just a tattered–looking docket book with a worn blue carbon sticking out from under the top page.

Behind the counter, Hopo! Long uncombed hair, scraggly beard, heavily pocked face with a deep, angry scar running down the left side from forehead to chin, and a huge crooked nose. His chin rested on an arm painted in reds and blues and purples—every inch of flesh from bare shoulder to wrist covered with complicated designs featuring skulls and dragons and eagles and flames. An unbuttoned navy shirt—frayed at the shoulder where the sleeve ought to have joined—only partly covered a hairy painted chest. Even leaning over the counter, he towered over me. Thick, solid muscle pushed out tattooed skin. I hoped he didn't notice Fran's involuntary shudder.

"Wilson!" he exclaimed, straightening up and extending an enormous swarthy hand.

"Hopo. Meet my wife, Fran."

He looked her up and down with an evil grin. "Lucky guy. She's got curves in all the right places."

I ignored the remark and placed a large box on the counter. Hopo lifted the flap and thrust his chin forward as he peered inside.

"I'll need a minute to inspect and count them," he said. "Want to make yourself and that pretty little sheila a coffee while you wait?" He pointed to a grubby sink set into a wooden bench littered with chipped cups, half–full coffee jar, and a jar of sugar caked and blackened from repeated dips with wet, soiled spoons.

"No thanks. I want to watch you. Can't risk you stashing a few under the counter when I'm not looking and then accusing me of short–changing you."

"You wouldn't short–change me, mate. I'd knock your bloody block off if you tried," Hopo chuckled, but his tone was cold and warning. He started examining the pieces, one by one. He set eight aside, pointing out what he claimed were imperfections. I saw no flaw, but I didn't argue.

Fran whispered a complaint that her legs ached and her mouth was dry, but she had no appetite for his coffee. She was scanning shelves loaded with an astonishing variety of male jewellery, clothing, badges, wall plaques, miniature bikes. Everything embossed with the word "Harley".

At last, Hopo was done. He reached under the counter and pulled out a large metal box. Fran gasped when he opened it. It bulged with 20, 50 and

100 dollar notes. I reckoned there must have been 50 grand in there. Hopo carefully counted out 5,000, then made a show of returning 100 to the box. He pushed the rest of the pile across the counter.

"Another batch next week?" I said, ignoring the small deficit in the payment.

Hopo nodded. "Told you, mate. Keep up the quality and I reckon I can move all you can make."

"He scares me, Paul." Fran said, driving away.

"He scares me, too," I admitted, "but he's OK as long as you don't cross him. He's got a reputation for being pretty nasty if he doesn't get his own way, and he's got some pretty unsavoury friends. Apparently some of that cash comes from drug dealing, but I prefer to know nothing about that."

"God, Paul. Do you really want to do business with a guy like that."

"For five grand an order? You bloody well betcha!"

The orders came through regularly, mostly for 200 at a time after the first three. Hopo frequently objected to non–existent flaws and short–changed us, but it didn't matter. I returned from delivery trips with my wallet bulging. Fran dashed nervously from parking lot to bank door with bundles of cash, after extracting a few notes for the cash tin hidden in the back of the pantry. By the end of the following year we had paid off the business loan and I'd persuaded Fran there was enough spare change for me to pursue my long–cherished dream. I set aside five grand, opened an account with an SP bookie, and started to work my betting system.

39: CHRISTMAS HUMBUG

DECEMBER, 1987

I was doing another Hopo delivery three days before Christmas. Fran was wildly excited that, for once, we wouldn't do Christmas on a pauper's budget.

"Take me and the kids with you, Paul." she pleaded. "We can do some Christmas shopping. You can distract the kids while I get their presents and then we can all go out for lunch." She waited for a response, but when I was silent she continued eagerly. "That was one of the best things about Christmas when I was a kid. We always went shopping together and bought lunch out."

"Christmas! Bah humbug!" I said with a chuckle, adding, "Sorry, guess I'm a bit like that character, Scrooge, was it? But for different reasons. I hate all the fuss and bother and the crowds. Do we really have to battle crowds of Christmas shoppers?"

"Don't be such a wet blanket, Paul. We've always made Christmas special and fun. Remember that first one, in Singapore? We were so damn homesick, I cooked enough to feed 10 and we showered each other with so many gifts to try to make up for being alone and far from family, and then we made love on the living–room floor all afternoon."

"I remember. It's still bah humbug." Then, after a pause, "OK. OK. If it will stop you nagging, I'll take you with me and we'll have lunch, but you can sit in the car while I do the delivery. I'm not taking you inside that place again." My forceful tone caused an involuntary shudder.

"Fine. I don't like Hopo anyway, but why is it such a big deal?"

"I overheard a conversation a few weeks ago. I didn't like it at all."

"What –"

"Told you he ran drugs, didn't I?"

"Yeah."

"He had an unsavoury–looking fellow in there and they were talking about some woman Hopo had taken up with. It seems folks think he murdered her husband. Police interviewed him, but they couldn't pin anything on him. Happened six years ago, apparently, so I guess he thinks he's free and clear so he can be a bit careless about who he boasts to. I'm sure he didn't mean me to hear though."

247

"Shit, Paul! Murder! And you're going to keep doing business with him?"

"Yes, I am. It's none of my business, but I saw the way he looked at you and I don't want him deciding he fancies you better than whoever it is he apparently thought was desirable enough to kill for."

We set out early, kids all dressed up for a fun day out, planning what gifts to buy for each other, and Fran chatting happily about ideas for Christmas gifts for relatives. I was in a cheery mood, almost excited in fact. I told Fran I was planning to buy something really special for her, so she would have to take the kids off somewhere after lunch and let me organise surprises for all of them. "And not to see Santa either," I added. "I want to take photos of them, and you, on Santa's knee."

"The kids are way past that," she laughed, "and you definitely won't get me up there."

"Then how will I know what you wish for?"

"You just said you already had a plan."

"I do."

"So give me a hint."

"You'll just have to wait, my darling. You are just like a little kid at Christmas, and I'll enjoy watching you struggle through the next few days in agonising suspense, wanting desperately to sneak a peek and not quite game."

We stopped to buy ice creams before heading out to Hopo's, and I left the kids to wait in the car with Fran while I finished my business. I thrust a large box under my arm and headed off into the store, whistling merrily.

They were all getting impatient when I finally emerged, still with the box under my arm, and holding the envelope Hopo had given me. My expression was, no doubt, as grim as his had been when he greeted me. I threw the box into the back of the car, slid into the driver's seat, slammed the door hard and thrust the envelope at Fran.

"Merry bloody Christmas," I spat.

"What's this?"

"A fucking Christmas card from Hopo. What do you think? Read it."

The envelope had been torn open. She extracted a soiled and tattered page and carefully unfolded it. The letter was addressed very formally to Mr Hopo Niles, Tweed City Harleys. It bore that elegant, distinctive Harley–Davidson emblem at the top, and the print at the bottom declared the signatory "Director, Brand Management and Intellectual Property Protection, Harley–Davidson Australia."

"It's a warning about selling knock–offs, Fran. With a very polite explanation of Harley–Davidson's licensing and quality–control terms."

She stared at me blankly.

"The badges I make. The real deal cost $90 a pair. I couldn't hope to produce a genuine product at that price, not with the licence fees they charge and their quality standards. Under patent law, they could take me for everything we own and more for making imitations."

She was speechless, terrified. It was bad enough that we hadn't been quite honest with the tax man. She excused that, because the tax office shafted us early in our marriage and we figured it owed us. But…

"Patent infringement? A patent owned by a company as powerful as Harley–Davidson? Shit, Paul!"

"Surely you must have realised the deal wasn't quite legit? Jesus! How gullible are you, Fran?"

"You're dealing with a drug–dealing bikie suspected of murder, making illegal product for him to buy from you for cash out of a tin that must contain around 50 grand in cash bills? Paul, have you completely lost your senses?"

"Can you show me a way to earn a decent living legally when the system has been shafting me since I was eight years old?" I paused for a moment to compose myself. My caustic tone lightened a little.

"Christ, Fran. Don't go getting all self–righteous! We live in a dirty world. The people who get on well in it don't do it by being proper and nice and law abiding. They do it by playing in the grey. And that's all I did. The very pale grey, actually!"

"They don't do it by getting into bed with drug–dealing murderers, that's for sure!"

I started the engine before replying, then answered with far more certainty than I felt.

"Hopo isn't the problem here. Dealing with him is perfectly safe as long as the deals are on his terms. I don't argue when he claims to find a flaw or when he miscounts an order. I take what he's happy to pay me, smile, shake hands and say thank you, and I keep him well away from my woman."

"Not nearly far enough away for my liking," she said sharply. "So what now? Where do you go from here?"

"Hopo won't be placing any more orders, and I can't risk looking for other customers like him. I have to stop, Fran. It's too risky."

"Of course you have to stop. You should never have started."

"And if I hadn't, we'd all be sleeping on the street instead of planning lunch with Santa Claus." I slammed my fist into dashboard and glared at her. "And if you breathe a word about any of this to anyone, it won't be Hopo you'll have to be afraid of."

My vicious tone no doubt transported her to an earlier time. Jealous rages, violent outbursts ending with broken china, holes in walls, and Fran engaging for days in futile attempts to mask a bruised cheek, split lip or black eye with

249

makeup. It was all a long time ago, before I was reunited with a father who told me emphatically, after reprimanding me for raising my voice at her, that women were to be revered and honoured, treated with tenderness, and never spoken to in anger. My mother had added softly that for all the hardships she endured, she had seldom suffered a harsh word from her husband and he had punished his sons severely if they ever dared to show her disrespect.

Despite the reconciliation and my dad's influence, the demons still hadn't left me. I still feared those I loved always deserting me, and I talked constantly of women betraying men and couples being incapable of staying faithful. Just a month ago, I had told her that my aunt and uncle separated, and I asked her when she would leave me.

"I won't," she had replied, but I countered with the comment that my aunt had been telling my uncle that for nearly 20 years.

"You see, Fran. Everyone I love lets me down. Everyone I trust betrays me."

She knew I loved my aunt. What could she say? She tried to assure me that the failure of their marriage didn't mean my aunt was deserting me, but there was no way to convince me. Ultimately, I didn't give my aunt the chance to show me that I was mistaken. I cut her off, declaring that she was not worthy of my affection any more than she deserved her husband's.

Fran watched me nervously, afraid to speak, and clearly distressed that the kids could hear. They sat in the back, white-faced and silent. I wrestled with remorse and rage. Finally, she summoned the courage to break the intolerable silence.

"What will you do, Paul?"

I pulled away from the kerb and started towards the mall. "Guess I'll take these kids for lunch and shopping. Get this bah humbug business over with," I said. "Wouldn't want to spoil their fun."

"I meant —"

"How will I earn a living, now that I've been fucked by the system again? The business wasn't viable before I met Hopo. It won't be viable after we part company.

"My racing system failed, Fran. I've been agonising for weeks over how to tell you I lost the whole bloody five grand. Nothing I do ever works out. Never can. The system has been screwing me since I was a little kid, and it will continue to screw everything I try to do. Some people are born to live shit lives. Obviously I'm one of them."

40: THE POWER OF FAMILY LOVE

OCTOBER, 1988

Despite the beauty and tranquillity of that beachside paradise, I continued to languish and waste after closing the business. I rose late, lingered sullen and morose over breakfast, stared blankly at the television set, snapped at the kids and battled with Fran over anything and nothing. Fran urged me to take up music again, but the trumpet rested in its case at the back of the wardrobe. My reading interest denigrated to mindless paperback westerns I could devour in an hour and never needed to finish reading anyway, because they were written to a formula with both action and ending entirely predictable. Fran complained that my conversation, when I consented to engage in any, consisted of nothing but whining, criticism and complaint. I was entirely unresponsive to her efforts—or my children's for that matter—to engage my interest. Finally, fed up after months of watching me fritter away the days and shun her every attempt to motivate me, Fran snapped.

"You have responsibilities, Paul," she screamed. "We have children to feed and educate. You need to find a job."

"I had a job, Fran," I replied. "One that damn near killed me. Remember? What if I had died? "

I punched the wall and kicked a dent in the kitchen door.

Over almost a year of unemployment, my mental state had steadily declined. However unsatisfactory and unfulfilling line work might have been, it had been a distraction. I had worked our little hobby farm before the move, too. I brought home four poddy calves and raised them and let them mate. I held the children, delighting in their innocent amazement while they watched in awe the miracle of birth. Now and again I'd fished for eel and we skinned and boiled it and dipped slices in batter to fry. We'd raised chickens, and the children delighted in fetching the eggs. When a hen went broody, they waited and watched anxiously for the tiny fluffy chickens to emerge.

The children had loved the farm, and I had loved watching them grow up there. It reminded me of my days at Ohio—happy days when I had ambitions and dreams to cherish and I believed in myself and the things I could do. I'd been happy here as a child, too, but it was the scene of a beach holiday, and I guess I was intent on treating my life here now as one long vacation.

After my business failed, I tinkered in my shed on occasion, but without purpose. I sat in front of the television set from before dinner to late into the night.

"You are so clever with your hands, Paul. Can't you find some good use for that talent?" Fran pleaded.

"What do you suggest, Fran? Make Harley–Davidson badges, perhaps? Or should I try for adult training in leatherwork or carpentry? I was too old and too stupid at 25, when the army owed me paid retraining, remember? What hope would I have at 39, huh?"

"Do something with your music, then."

"God, Fran! What's wrong with your fucking memory? My music qualifications aren't worth the fucking paper they're written on. I sat exams in the army, but I might as well have spent my time on a fucking desert island cracking coconuts! All that wasted effort. For what?"

"Paul, there must be something you can do. You can drive. Get a taxi licence."

"Spend my days dodging maniacs and being abused by fat bitches with snotty–nosed whining kids, rude, impatient businessmen always in a hurry, or drunk teenagers emptying their guts on the way home from the club at two in the morning. I'd last five minutes. I'd lose it completely and kill a passenger before I got through my first day."

"There must be something. I can't stand seeing you like this. It's driving me insane, and it's disruptive and distressing for the kids. Your bad temper scares me. If you don't pull yourself together and –"

"What? You'll leave me? Well go on. Piss off, Fran. Just bugger off and leave me in peace."

"You realise you're destroying yourself?"

"So clear out and let me get on with it."

"You don't mean that, Paul."

"Don't kid yourself, Fran. You think I need you? You think you can hurt me by leaving. You've forgotten a lot of things, it seems. People come and people go in my life and once they go I never think of them again. I don't need anyone. I can be happy in a bull's–head tent in the middle of nowhere. All I want is to be left alone."

"Fine. I'll leave you alone, but you can leave, Paul. This is mine and my children's home, and I'm not giving it up. If you want to spend your life wallowing in self–pity, go do it somewhere where it won't ruin mine and our children's happiness."

I stood up and threw my chair across the room, then stormed into the bedroom, thrust an open suitcase on the bed and began carelessly throwing clothing from the wardrobe. I pulled drawers from the dresser and tipped their contents into the case, thrusting them upended on the floor as each was emptied. Slamming into the bathroom, I dragged drawers from the vanity and upended them. After selecting items from the medicine chest, I swept an open hand across the shelves and sent their contents smashing into the basin below. In my rage, I found the sounds of shattering bottles perversely comforting.

Misty visions of nuns and scowling soldiers with stripes on their sleeves appeared. I wished they would take form so that I could punch their faces in. I wished Wicks — the employment officer who denied me retraining — would appear. I wanted to push him down, squat on his pot belly, clench my fingers around his bulging red neck, stare into wild yes, and slowly… ever so slowly… squeeze the air out of him. I wanted to hear him gurgle and splutter and squeak, and see the colour drain from his whisky–reddened cheeks and watch his goggling eyes begging for mercy. Maybe I would ease my grip, now and again, just enough so he could ask me why and utter a plea, and I could reply with a mocking laugh and increased pressure. I would not explain myself — never let him know how his abuse of power had hurt me. Even as he breathed his last breath, I would not give him the satisfaction of knowing how he made me suffer.

I kicked the front door shut behind me, thrust my suitcase in the back seat of the car, and booted the car door closed. Folding myself into the driver's seat, I revved the car motor mercilessly, grated the gears, and careered — tyres throwing up clouds of thick dust — down the back road to the highway. At the corner, the speeding vehicle skidded to a stop, and then, with another wheel spin, I took off and swung on to the highway.

Nearly 12 hours later, now outwardly calm, I turned into a government housing estate and parked in front of the neat little cottage Mum and Dad now called home. The Housing Authority had moved them from the shack shortly after Rob's wedding, in response to intense lobbying by Carly.

"Paul! What a wonderful surprise," Mum said, hugging me. "Fran and the kids not with you?"

"Fran's working. Couldn't take the kids out of school," I said, trying a little too hard to show no emotion.

I hadn't planned to visit my family. The decade–old Holden wagon I'd taken such pride in restoring often seemed to have a mind of its own. It knew its way home — not that I'd ever regarded my parents' house as 'home'. I still had mixed emotions when I thought of Fred and Elsie. At first I'd found it awkward calling them 'Mum and Dad', but when I observed Fran using those titles with ease I followed her lead and I discovered delight in hearing them call me 'son'.

Whenever I visited my folks I made small talk and helped out with household chores. Occasionally, I'd play my trumpet for Mum and Dad, and it thrilled them. There was love in my mother's eyes when she looked at me, and pride written in the creases of Dad's half–smile. When they spoke to me, it was as if to a son from whom they had never been parted, but there was an awkwardness in my responses. I worked hard and successfully to hide it, as I had always worked to hide every emotion. Paul Wilson was a polished pretender.

My brothers had become mates. I drank with them and joined their fishing and shooting expeditions. I went with them, sometimes, to the shearing sheds to watch them work the sheep to make mountains of soft, oily fleece, but there was always a distance between us. Fran and I did not belong to that parched, dusty place. There was no air of possession when I surveyed the wire–fenced paddocks littered with black bubbles of sheep dung and dry, cracked cow pats hosting beetle colonies. It was with the apparent discomfort typical of a city slicker that I swiped at the bothering flies and pulled my shirt collar high and my hat low over my pale face to block the savage western sun. And I caught the mildly contemptuous glances of my deep–tanned, bare–chested brothers. So like them that I was often mistaken for one or the other of them, I was nonetheless a misfit among the cockies and the shearers. I didn't speak their language. I didn't understand their culture. I was a foreigner in this land of my birth and I could never think of it as 'home'.

We rarely spoke of my childhood, although Dad told me he had once walked over 70 miles each way to try and see me, only to be told I wasn't there. I remembered that day—the lockdown—the nuns' report of a vagabond peeping tom. I had glimpsed a shadowy figure through the window as they marched us upstairs. Had I known it was my father I might have called out, and he might have heard me, but they sent him away.

When Dad asked me about my life, I told him I got on just fine. Fred winked and said, "Resilient you are, like me. I always knew you were a chip off the old block. I knew you would be OK."

I would never do or say anything to compound my parents' suffering or to reduce their joy in having me back. From arrival to departure I played my part to perfection, but whenever I left there I was an actor leaving the stage. And yet, I was uncomfortable in my own world too—like the immigrant struggling to assimilate, yet craving to return to the motherland. It seemed there was nowhere I could feel at ease, but now, with my marriage ended, there seemed no place else to go but back to the first family I had lost.

"So what brings you out here at this time of year?" Dad asked.

I shrugged. "Just felt like seeing my bros, and doing some fishing." My tone was deliberately nonchalant.

"Your brothers are working."

"I'll find ways to amuse myself. Maybe I'll go out to the sheds with them, and I'll see them on the weekends and in the evenings."

Dad shrugged, went to fridge and fetched two stubbies. He handed one to me and sat down in front of the television set. I sat down opposite him.

"Who's winning?" There was a rugby league game in progress. Mum busied herself preparing the evening meal while Dad and I sat watching, very occasionally cheering a player or disputing a referee decision, but not in any conversational exchange. Very few words passed between us.

I went to visit a brother after the evening meal. I came back late, heavily inebriated, to announce that I was going to the sheds next day to watch the shearing. Mum nodded and said, "I thought you might. I packed a lunch for you just in case. It's in the fridge, and there's an esky in the laundry and some ice bricks in the freezer".

I said goodnight and promised to try not to wake her leaving in the morning.

"You forgot to take your lunch, son," she said, when I came in the following afternoon. She placed a pot of tea on the table and went to the cupboard for cups.

"I took it, Mum. It was really good, thanks."

Puzzled, she pulled a lunch box from the fridge and held it up.

"Must 'ave grabbed the wrong one. I had a chicken leg and two sandwiches and a piece of fruitcake."

"That was your morning tea," she replied. "This one was lunch."

I laughed. "Geez, Mum. I went for a day, not a week."

"I'm used to feeding workmen," she replied. "Your brothers work hard so they need plenty of fuel to keep them running."

I shrugged, but said nothing.

"Never was out of work a day in me life apart from when I was sick," Dad said. "Boys neither. Tough sometimes, findin' work out here, but we do. E'en if the pay and conditions is lousy an' we 'ave t' travel a'ways."

I suspected my father's statement might be loaded, but I gave no reply. I hadn't told my family I wasn't working, and I couldn't imagine any way they would know.

I visited my sister the following day. Sandra was the young Elsie — auburn highlights in a mop of tightly curled golden–brown hair, finely carved features, radiant complexion, and those same talkative eyes. All that distinguished her from our mother was the absence of stick limbs and wrinkles and that slight sagging of the shoulders that had for so long borne the weight of guilt and almost unbearable sorrow.

"God, Paul! What are you doing here?"

"Visiting family."

Did everyone have to demand explanation?

"Fran and the kids with you?"

"No. Just me."

Puzzle lines appeared briefly on Sandra's forehead, but she composed herself quickly.

"Want a cuppa?"

"Wouldn't say no."

"So what are you doing for a quid these days? Not just being a beach bum, I hope! Lucky bastard! Living in paradise!"

"I'm working on an invention," I replied, ignoring her 'too close for comfort' comment and hoping she didn't have extrasensory perception or access to a gossip hotline. I knew Fran would never expose my secrets to my family.

Always innovative, and quick to find inventive ways to manage challenging tasks, I had twice tried my hand at inventing for commercial return. Not long after I left the army, I came up with an idea that, in hindsight, might have made me quite wealthy had I understood, back then, about intellectual property protection and commercialisation. Struggling with a dramatically changed routine—no longer working until the early hours of the morning—I'd installed a television set in the bedroom and formed the habit of going to sleep with the television on. It drove Fran crazy, but I couldn't go to sleep without the distraction. In a quiet room, my mind raced and the demons plagued me.

Back then, the television channels shut down in the very early hours of the morning with a rather loud pop. Inevitably, it woke Fran. She complained endlessly about the interruption to her sleep. To solve the problem, I made a timer that plugged into a power point and turned off the power at a pre-set time. It was clumsy in appearance, but it worked a treat and I used it to impressive effect for a couple of years to switch off the television after I fell asleep. When it wore out, I took it to the local electrical store, showed them the concept, and asked if such a device was available for purchase. It wasn't then, but within months the highly successful Krambrook timer appeared on the market.

During my time on the electrical lines I invented a service termination clamp for securing electrical lines to poles and houses. The device in use at the time was awkward to apply, especially in cold weather. I came up with a novel alternative. This time I followed all the right pre-commercialisation processes to test it and assess its appeal to those who would use it.

The market for such a device was tightly defined. A single distributor sold all devices of that type to electricity authorities nationwide. I approached the company and demonstrated my invention. They were impressed. For a brief moment I dared to hope that they might license it and made excited calculations of how many they sold annually and what the royalties might be. Ultimately, they announced that they had just invested hundreds of thousands in new machinery to make the existing model. Regardless of the superiority of design of a possible alternative, they would need to continue marketing the existing product exclusively for nearly a decade to justify their investment. They suggested I might talk to them again in eight years' time. Eight years later, I had moved on.

My answer to Sandra wasn't exactly a lie. I'd been nurturing an idea… even tinkering a little, but my efforts hardly qualified as 'doing something for a quid'. I felt my cheeks flush a little as guilt stabbed at my heart and chiding voices shouted in my brain.

"Do you really make money from inventions?" she asked.

I shrugged. "It's hard, and it's risky."

Guilt gnawed at me now. Its incessant chewing made my heart gallop and my chest hurt and my head throb. Silence hung heavily, broken only by an occasional hushed slurping or gulping sound as we swallowed tea and the odd soft thud as a mug was placed on the table between sips. Tension magnified the sounds. I searched for words that might be appropriate to speak to break the awkwardness.

"Mum and Dad would have been thrilled to see you," said Sandra.

I just nodded. Then a random thought crystallised and suddenly became a burning question.

"How was it, Sandra," I asked, "that after 18 years I could walk back into your lives and for Mum and Dad and all of you it was as if we'd never missed a day?"

"Because you were always there, Paul," she replied. The response was quick and unhesitant, but she paused after and I noticed that her eyes were watering.

"You were always part of us. Mum and Dad talked about you every day. Told us how much they loved you and talked about the letters they wrote you, the occasional little gift they sent. Talked about how one day you and Jen would come back and we'd be a family again."

Letters? Gifts? I never received any.

Fran's mother had told me the nuns burnt the mail in the fireplace in the living room. It was disruptive, they said, for children to stay in contact with a family to whom they could never return. My mum had sent me a little battery operated boat once, but the nuns put it away and gave it to me months later. It was the only gift I was ever given in all the years I spent at St Patrick's. I was never told where it came from. I found out when I was 30. Mum asked, just out of the blue one day, if I liked the gift she sent for my ninth birthday.

The boat was broken when they gave it to me, but I'd fixed it, and I'd thought myself very inventive. Pity I couldn't put that talent to some productive use.

"They never gave up hoping," Sandra was saying, unaware that I was lost in recollections. "And they never stopped trying, despite all the knockbacks. I often wondered where they got the strength."

I looked up, and my face asked the questions I could never bring myself to speak.

"I remember the social workers coming to visit," Sandra said sadly. "I was only a little kid, but I remember it so well because Dad would go quite crazy after. One time, he thought he was back in the war, so he got his rifle and laid down behind a little hill. Mum was scared he might shoot one of us. He seemed to think we were all Japs."

I shuddered. The tales of torture I'd heard in Singapore came flooding back. It hadn't occurred to me that the effects, so long after, could be that dramatic.

"There was that one time," Sandra continued, "when they wanted Dad's consent for you to join the army. He raged about the place for days after screaming 'No son of mine is going in the bloody army. They're not putting no bloody uniform on my boy, not after what I went through'. He was so angry us kids were scared to go near him.

"He begged the officer to send you home," she said sadly. "I think they told him you didn't want to come. You were dead keen to join the army, with or without Dad's consent."

"Lying bastard," I said, and refilled my tea.

"There was another time, a bit later —"

"Later? Why would they come again later?"

"I think you were being sent to Vietnam or something. That was the time Dad really went berserk."

My jaw dropped. "He knew about that posting?"

"He knew pretty much everything, Paul. Mum and Dad somehow kept up with everything you did. Social workers in the early days. Later, they had a spy somewhere."

Uncle Bill? Why wouldn't he tell me he was in touch with them?

"Yet they never tried to make contact after I was grown–up," I said, struggling to maintain an even tone. "After I could make my own choices about replying."

"They insisted you had to make the first move. When you made no contact, they figured you wanted nothing to do with them. They said they couldn't blame you for that, but I know it broke their hearts."

"They had a shit of a life, Sandra. A real shit of a life!"

"They made the best of it, Paul. I never heard Dad complain, and he always told us to treat every day as an adventure and a challenge. Mum always said the only real failure in life was hurting someone, but Dad said it was not having a go."

I smiled. "I remember them saying that stuff to me when I was a little kid, before they took me away. And one time, in the pub, after Dad ripped into me for yelling at Fran, a few beers made him suddenly very philosophical. He looked up at me and said, 'Let me give y' a little fatherly advice, son. I know it's prob'ly far too little, but hopefully not too late. Young blokes have such big ambitions, and hopefully you can realise some of yours. But if y' can get through life without doin' anyone any harm, feed your kids, and treat your wife like a woman should be treated, you've done OK. For the rest of it, jus' make the best of what fate deals out. In the end, the only real choice any of us gets is what attitude to take an' how to treat others'."

Sandra smiled. "That sounds like Dad. He's a smart man, you know? Given half a chance, he could have achieved a lot in his life."

"Yeah. I remember him making whips and breaking horses. He was bloody brilliant with animals, and such a hard worker. Guess he just never got a lucky break, poor bastard. And then they took his kids away."

Sandra reached across and put her hand on mine. "He won through in the end, Paul. He got his son back."

"Small compensation, though. Look at him, Sandra. Look at Mum. What reason have they got to get up in the morning?"

"Mum would say she's blessed. She lived to see her sons and daughters making a success of their lives and giving her beautiful grandchildren to spoil. What more is there for people like us, Paul? Different for you maybe. You had opportunities — music school, boxing lessons, overseas travel, a chance to buy a house of your own, go into business. Mum and Dad couldn't do more for us than feed and clothe us... and love us."

I studied her expression. Her words echoed, feeding my guilt.

Maybe that's what's made me so discontent? I tasted a more fortunate life, but it was so plastic... so hollow.

"Guess that's what was missing for me, Sandra. Their love. In the end, I think that's all that really matters. Feeling safe and cared for. Belonging."

Sandra sniffed and ran the back of her hand across her cheek.

"You always had their love, Paul. Now you have the chance to feel it. Enjoy!"

Ian organised a barbecue on the weekend. Dad, not in the best of health of late, was settled in a rocking chair on the veranda with a rug over his knees. A thick haze of smoke hung in the air and the aroma of grilling meat competed with the smell of hops and malt as we cracked our stubbies. Fred dozed a little. When he woke, Carly was seated beside him. He reached across and touched her hand lightly, and I somehow felt, rather than heard, his faint whisper.

"Look at that," he said, "My six sons all together. After all those years apart, it's near enough to make a grown man cry." He had never seen all his children together, and this was only the second time that he'd seen all his sons together.

Talk of the war was taboo around Dad, but he talked to me about it that day. He told me how it was in prison. He laughed about catching cockroaches and swapping them with the Japanese guards for rats, because rats were more to his taste and more nutritious.

"You were in Singapore, yeah?" he said suddenly, turning to me.

"Yeah, Dad," I said, glancing at Ian with a look of concern. I wondered if I ought to be changing the subject, but remembering didn't seem to be distressing the old man. "For some of our time there, Fran and I lived in what used to be the Changi prison camp."

"There was a lovely Chinese gal. Used t' work in the prison," he said, smiling at the memory. "Hired by the Jap guards, but she used t' smuggle mail in and out and bring medicines t' sick prisoners. I had shrapnel wounds in both me legs when I was captured. Real bad. Infected. That little gal brought a bottle of grubbies in and put 'em into the wound t' eat the infection. I'd a' prob'ly died otherwise."

He turned and looked at me earnestly. "Don't y' go telling y' mum, but I think I was a little bit in love with that gal. She was my angel of mercy. She was very beautiful."

A shrivelled and stooped old hawker bearing baskets of children's clothing shuffled out from the depths of my memory. When I told Dad I'd bought baby clothes from his angel, a single tear rolled down the old man's cheek.

#

An idea was forming in my mind as I drove back to Ballina, contrite, and determined to repair my marriage. I struggled to focus, but Sandra's quotes of my parents' advice played over and over in my head like a broken tape on a player with no off button. The fear demon drifted in, but I blew it out with a deep breath, reminding myself of Fran's loyalty and tolerance over so many years. Then it drifted in again and reminded me that everyone has a breaking point. Had she finally reached it?

Please God let her give me one more chance. I won't blow it again.

The guilt demon whipped me and shouted curses at me for not having my father's strength of character, mocking me for not accepting the faith so that my prayers could be answered. I reminded God that He had deserted me when I was just a little boy, long before I knew about faith. I cursed Simms for denying me the benefit of being raised by a man who would have taught me how to treat a woman. I cursed the nuns for making me hate women, and turning me against God—if there was one.

I stopped the car, got out, and stood leaning against the passenger door watching the sun sink behind the hills, painting the sky around them brilliant pink and soft orange, and turning the hills from green to grey, then a menacing black. And then the yellow moon climbed into the sky and its light danced over the black hills. All my guilt and fear disappeared behind the horizon with the sun. Hope rose with the moon, and I got back into the car focused on my idea.

My youngest daughter had given us a scare when she was very small. I found her, late one night when Fran was fast asleep, lying grey and deathly still in her cot. Thankful for my first–aid training, I revived her. For years after, I read everything I could find on sudden infant death syndrome and conceived wild ideas for devices to alert a parent of worrying changes in a baby's vital signs. As I drove, an image of the ideal device presented itself. I began to mentally dissect it and examine the componentry. I detoured to Brisbane and a specialist electrical store, and arrived home with a supply of tools and parts and brimming over with excited anticipation.

Fran asked no questions. She was well accustomed to me taking time out to battle my demons. When I emerged victorious, she celebrated privately and prayed my tormentors would stay away. She welcomed me home and helped me unpack. I hugged her and kissed her and told her I loved her deeply and I could never leave her. Then I told her that my sister had talked some sense into me and things would be better from now on.

Two weeks later, she leapt for joy when I announced I'd seen a job ad of interest and planned to apply. It was casual work—only two days a week and lousy pay—but it was something. In fact, it was something I believed I could actually enjoy.

I applied for the position of swab steward on the race track thinking I hadn't a hope of success, but I had always loved horses. Although I rarely wagered money after that one disastrous experiment in which I lost the entire five grand, I was still committed to the belief that the system I'd developed could potentially win millions. I followed it religiously, calculating the winnings on paper. I know it drove Fran mad, because it became quite an obsession.

At the job interview, I was asked three times if I could ride a horse. I hadn't been on one since childhood. Although the men on the committee seemed unconcerned with my negative reply, I was worried it had destroyed my chances. Eventually, frustrated with the repeated questions, and rather aggro with the ugly bitch who kept interrupting an otherwise intelligent interview with stupid challenges, I looked squarely at the inquirer and said, "I thought I only had to collect their piss. I didn't think the job involved riding the bastards".

There it was again—that self–destructive arrogance that always seemed to get in the way of building a career. To my surprise, this time it impressed. The job required someone who could assert authority. That had never been me, but I fell into the role comfortably and enjoyed the job. I discovered an affinity with animals, and, like my dad, I handled the most difficult horses with ease.

"Dad was the horse whisperer," I told Fran. "He could break a wild horse without ever touching it. He'd just walk up to the animal and talk to it softly, give it something to eat maybe, and in minutes it would be following him around the paddock. He was a bloody good horse trainer. Had a way with them. Maybe I've inherited some of that talent."

Fran smiled, pleased to see me confident there was something I could do well.

If only the job was full–time and paid better.

Between race days, I worked in my shed with an intensity Fran had never witnessed before. At the end of the month, I showed her some complicated drawings and announced my desire to consult a patent attorney. The designs for my SIDS Alert—a watch–like device for babies, intended to send a signal to an alarm device worn by a parent if a baby's vital signs changed unfavourably—was complete.

I was certain this invention was destined to be a success.

41: TWO DEATHS, AND A HOPE

1989

I never wrote letters, and seldom received any, so it must have surprised Fran to find an envelope bearing my handwritten name in the Thursday morning mail. It was from my Ohio 'brother', Peter. A short note advised that his mother, Ede, had passed away a few days earlier and was to be buried in Perth the following Saturday morning.

"I'll book a flight for you," Fran said, wrapping her arms around me.

"Why?" I replied coldly, shrugging her off.

"Your best friend's mother just died. Surely you want to be at her funeral?"

"I'll send flowers."

"She was your mother too, for three years. You loved her, Paul. All the stories you told about her and the way she cared for you at Ohio –"

"She wasn't my mother. She was my carer. She was paid to look after kids who had no–one else to care about them. She did her job well and she was always there when I needed her. She was there with a broad smile at breakfast. When I came home from school, she was there with a big slice of cake. When I came in from footie training in the afternoon, she was there offering a drink, and a band aid if I'd scraped my knee or elbow. She was there in the library at night or in the pottery shed when I felt like talking about my day or listening to her war stories. Then one day I had to move into another world, and she wasn't there anymore. That's not a mother. Mothers are for ever. She was no more a mother to me than my birth mother. I feel sorry for Peter, but otherwise her death is of no concern to me."

Fran looked distressed. "You don't mean that. It's a cover–up. You do this when you're hurting."

"Hurting? Why would I be hurting? You forget. I'm not like other people. I don't have feelings. I learnt not to feel when I was very young—especially not to feel upset at people going out of my life, whether by dying or otherwise. That's all my life was. People coming into it and people going out of it. If I let it affect me— "

I stood up and walked to the fridge to fetch a beer. Fran watched, speechless for a moment. "You could have written to her. From Balcombe. You could have visited in the holidays."

"Why? What interest would she have in me? Dozens of kids came and went from her life. She was paid to look after them for a time, that's all. Then they went away and another kid took their place."

"That's not how it was for the Ede I met, nor for the Ede you described to me when you talked about your years at Ohio."

"We can't afford the plane fare. Does that reason suit you better?"

"Why do you act this way whenever something upsets you? You're so gentle and caring when things are going well. Then something bad happens and you're someone else."

Guilt weighed heavily on me. I tried to thrust its weight from my shoulders with a shrug and a silent reminder that Ede was only a part of my life for a brief time, but a niggling little pain stabbed at my heart. I secretly longed to hear her melodic laugh and see those big breasts heaving, the abundant flesh on those warm arms rippling, and Welsh eyes dancing as she passed me a huge slice of chocolate cake.

"I'll order flowers," Fran said. "What would you like written on the card?"

"How should I know what to write? Write whatever you please."

I sat up late drinking and Fran knew I was grieving. I loved Ede, but, like my own mother, she had suddenly ceased to be there when I needed her, and it hurt too much to allow myself to care.

#

"Dinner!" I said, before Fran could ask the usual irritating question. I waved a fresh fish in her face.

"Bet you bought that at the Fisho on the way home."

"Actually, our daughter caught it. Funniest thing you ever saw. I tried to show her how to cast the rod, but she flicked it into the shallows not six inches from her toe and the hook went straight through the poor fish's top lip. Must be the unluckiest flathead this side of the equator."

"Did you boys catch anything?" she laughed.

"A hundred and twenty bucks on an eight to one winner." I drew a deep breath, waiting for the rebuke.

Nope! Just that look!

"It was one bet, Fran, and it was a sure thing. I don't study form so intently for nothing. I keep telling you I could make a fortune with this system."

She turned her attention to the fish. I moved behind her, wrapped my arms around her and fondled her breasts.

264

"How about I take you out tomorrow and buy you a sexy new dress, then take you somewhere nice for dinner?"

"How about you don't! Thank you for the thought, but we can't afford it. Not even with a windfall. How about you promise me you won't risk our hard–earned money betting on racehorses, and you'll take the kids out more often."

"I'll take the kids out more often. We had the best day, Fran. It was great."

A blanket of happiness wrapped itself around me that Saturday night as I watched Fran preparing that fish dinner.

"Have you been told today?" I asked her, "You're beautiful."

"Compliments will get you everywhere," she laughed, "except forgiveness for betting on horses. By the way, someone phoned for you earlier. I wrote the name and number on the pad by the phone."

I recognised the name and hastened to dial the number. I hadn't told Fran of my audition two days earlier for a role as one of the lead trumpets in a Bavarian band. It was enough for one of us to suffer another disappointment.

"Paul! I've been waiting for your call." Wilf said. He sounded upbeat. Could I dare to be hopeful? "Can you come in tomorrow? I'd like to organise a vest and hat for you and give you some music to rehearse. Your first gig is next Saturday night."

I was dancing with Fran, singing "The Chicken Dance" and floating on air, when Rob rang.

"Dad was flown to Dubbo Hospital this afternoon. It's bad, Paul. Real bad."

I was on the highway inside an hour and I drove all night without a stop except for petrol. I stayed with him three days, barely sleeping—catnaps in the chair beside him. On the third day, Fred rallied. He sat up and ate and talked with us.

"Don't you boys have something better to do than just sit there? Like fetch your old man a smoke and a beer, maybe?"

"I said I would come visit you again soon," I replied. "You didn't have to resort to scaring us all half to death to get attention, you old bastard."

"Hey, you! A little respect for your father please," he boomed, responding exactly as I had hoped. There were audible sighs of relief at the quickness of it and the strength in his voice.

"Sorry, Dad," I said with pretended contrition, failing to suppress a chuckle. Fred caught the silent conversation between my brothers and I, and said, "Cheeky buggers, the lot of youse," and then he laughed and it was deep and hearty.

"Go home, son," he said, addressing me. "Doc says I'll be back home by Sunday. Bring the family out to visit, eh? And bring that trumpet. You know Mum loves to hear you play."

I'm not sure how I managed to drive home, but Fran was beside herself waiting for me. Rob had phoned to ask her to call him as soon as I arrived. He told her I was in no condition to drive and he had begged me to stay and rest. I would never tell Rob—because he would insist on paying—but I really couldn't afford a motel bed. The car was way too cramped for sleeping. Besides, I was desperate to get my music and practise. I had to make a good show of my first performance.

Too tired even to eat, I collapsed into bed and was asleep almost before my head touched the pillow. I had been asleep only about an hour when Fran ran to answer the phone. She caught it at the start of the second ring, but I heard it and leapt out of bed. I entered the kitchen to hear her whispering. She put the phone down and looked up to see me standing there, and her eyes told me. She hugged me close, and for—I think—only the third time since they took me away, I cried. This time I felt no shame.

We were on the road within hours. I drove for 13 hours, so consumed with grief and the need to be with my mother and family that I wasn't aware of being tired.

We passed through the government housing estate on the way to Ian's house. Living in that estate, Mum and Dad finally had electricity, running water and a proper bathroom. Mum was in heaven. I felt a little ashamed recalling how I'd complained when Fran suggested we apply for government housing.

We gathered at Ian's house to discuss funeral arrangements, and I felt strangely lost and disconnected from my family's grief. I was suddenly painfully aware that the man whose funeral we were planning was virtually a stranger. The stories my brothers told of growing up in his company left me feeling distant and empty, and asking myself if a man, once cut from his roots, can ever really reconnect.

I went with my mother and held her while she viewed my dad's still corpse, all dressed up in his worn ill–fitting suit with his thin hair slicked over his forehead just the way he used to wear it. I took her home to dress for the funeral and found a coat and tie in my father's wardrobe for one of my younger brothers to wear. Then I joined my five younger brothers at the little local church to carry my father to his grave.

Jen came to the funeral. She didn't want to. She insisted she had no parents. "A mother and father are supposed to take care of you," she said, with tears in her eyes, "those two strangers didn't do that for me."

I had seen far too little of Jen since Fran and I married. Living so far away and on a tight budget, with both of us busy with our own lives and families, there were few opportunities to get together. We talked on the phone regularly. Jen told me over and over that I was her rock. She didn't need to be close to me; she just needed to know I was there if she needed me. I always would be. I had never forgotten my promise to take care of her.

Her husband had insisted she should come. I was delighted to see her, but she stood aloof, near the cemetery gate, not wanting to join the others to throw flowers in the grave. I went to her when they started to cover Dad over.

"Go back to the others, Paul," she said. "You belong with them."

She paused to look into my eyes for a moment, then added angrily, "Have you forgotten what we suffered, and who caused it? He betrayed us, Paul".

It took me a long time to answer. My stomach churned and my head spun as I mentally phrased my reply, experimenting with a dozen ways to say it. At last, I took her hand and started to lead her to the graveside. She resisted, but I pulled her firmly along behind me and wouldn't let her go. The others had propped a single floral wreath against a small white wooden cross and stepped away by the time we reached the little mound of freshly turned red–brown mud.

"Stand here with me, Jen," I said, "and say goodbye to our father."

"I told you, Paul, he's not —"

"Jen, listen. Dad did the best he could with what he had. He loved us, but he let us down. He wasn't able to protect us. Would I have done better in his shoes? Would you, as a mother, if you faced the challenges our parents confronted? I don't know and neither do you, but I know this, Jen." I drew a deep breath.

"We were dealt a bad hand. We had a shit of a life as children and we didn't deserve it. No child should suffer as we did, and the pain continued long after we became adults. Maybe it will never really end. But we have to choose now. We can put it behind us and get on with making the best of the rest of our lives, or we can let the past ruin all our tomorrows. Me? I'm taking the first option. I'm going with my brothers and sisters now to toast my father's life, and then I'm going to take my wife out to dinner and celebrate the first day of the rest of our lives—lives that are going to be very full and very happy."

#

I acted the part well at Dad's funeral, and after, but if it passed comment it didn't escape my attention that not a single sympathy card was addressed to me. Few of those to whom my parents had bragged about their eldest son knew me, beyond a cursory 'hello' on the infrequent occasions of my visits. The sympathisers' children had grown up with my brothers and sisters. Dad had worked with them and for them. For most of the years they knew our family, I did not exist outside the privacy of the home in which my removal was so deeply mourned.

Those who did know me seemed to assume I had come to terms with my loss a very long time ago, or maybe that the death of a man they believed betrayed and deserted me was no great tragedy. No doubt my stoicism supported that view.

In reality, the void left by the loss of my dad was all the more painful because I had missed out on so much of him. I had been given just a few short years to get to know him again, to make up for all the time we missed and the special occasions we ought to have shared. Now the opportunity was gone. I was left with an irritating, irrational voice asking me over and over, "After all you endured, how could he leave you again?".

I fought the nagging feeling of betrayal, but it took months to recover from the dreadful emptiness overwhelming me. The hatred for Simms returned and the demons urged me again to find him and kill him. An awful hunger for revenge was accompanied by a burning desire to destroy the establishment and everyone who supported and endorsed it.

I finally told Fran, after the funeral, how for so long I had nurtured an ambition to find Simms and kill him. She dismissed my claim with the comment, "If he walked into a pub and stole your beer, you would do no more than threaten him".

"I was trained to kill," I protested, popping the cap off another stubby. "If I wanted to, I could kill a man without a sound and without a shred of evidence left behind."

"Bullshit, Paul. You couldn't and you wouldn't. You were trained as a musician, not a killer. Maybe, if you'd gone to Vietnam. Now you wouldn't even volunteer, even if someone tortured you to try to make you."

"That's one thing you got right! Fight for this fucking country? No fucking way. Look what this grand nation did to Dad. He goes off to war at age 20 to defend the cause of freedom and protect his fellow Australians. Comes back broken, beaten, half–starved and disease–ridden after suffering torture most Australians couldn't even begin to imagine."

I sat at our dining table, sipping beer and gazing through the kitchen window at the kids romping in the yard, remembering the sneer on Simms' face when he saw the humble shack my father called home.

"Then that Simms prick and an arsehole fucking judge take the most precious goddamn things in his world in preference to helping him get the pension benefit he's legally entitled to. Took his kids away, for Christ's sake! Killed any shred of self–respect the poor broken bastard had left. Broke his wife's heart and sentenced them both to a life of misery." I took a deep swig of beer, but the ale didn't drown the rancour. "You think Simms didn't deserve to die? And I'll bet the mongrel never saw a uniform let alone action. Probably faked disability! Or if he did join, he was in B–company, or he sat in a plush office with pips on his bloody shoulder and made dumb decisions that cost the lives of good men."

"I think he probably deserved a lot worse than death, Paul," Fran whispered. "Death would have been far too easy, but you were right when you lectured Jenny at the funeral. Take your own counsel. You don't fix the past by destroying yourself exacting revenge."

"You think I don't know that? That's what makes it so fucking hard to go on living in this shit society. There are no fucking answers, are there? The rich and powerful shit on the helpless and there is absolutely nothing anyone can do about it apart from resort to violence that gets you condemned and crucified. No wonder there's terrorism and massacres. Some of those blokes the world condemns should be recognised as heroes."

Fran was drying the lunch dishes. A cup clattered to the floor and she spun to face me. "Surely you don't condone killing innocent people?"

"I feel sorry for innocent victims, but I suspect sometimes people who get shafted by the stinking corrupt system and the bastards who serve it just have to find a way to make their message heard. I'm here to testify that there aren't too many options available that don't hurt innocents. The real murderers are the mongrels who drive people to such desperation that they lose control."

She stood there, open mouthed and bug–eyed, quivering, but she ought to know me well enough not to be shocked. To the outside world, I presented the image of a man who had it all together and was in total control. There were a few who knew I'd lost it occasionally under the influence of grog and taken my frustrations out on my wife. No–one would regard me as a violent man, nor one who condoned violence, but I found it impossible to imagine that Fran was unaware of the burning desires I fought constantly to suppress.

One of the benefits of the family reunion was that it was much easier to pretend I'd had a normal upbringing. Those who knew my story simply dismissed it as one of those sad and unfortunate things that happen and you have to get over. Everyone suffers hardships. You get past it. Most would have said confidently that I had gotten over it very well. No criminal record; 10 years of army service with a clean conduct record; a respectable citizen earning an honest living, paying off a home and raising good kids.

Those who knew of him would declare it a pity that my father wasn't strong enough to recover from his trials as successfully and blame him for the tragedy of my childhood. Few would ever condemn the system or those who served it.

"Jen and I, we've often talked about what we suffered as kids," I said, rising to discard yet another empty and help my wife sweep up the broken china. "I guess it never occurred to us to think very much about what Dad must have endured, but he suffered so much more than I did."

"He was the adult, Paul. You were the child. Kids think their parents should be in control of the world. Mums and Dads are fixers. We don't see them as helpless or suffering, so we blame them for not preventing our hurt. It's natural."

"I never blamed Dad. Jen did, but not me. I don't know why. I just always assumed everything was somehow Mum's fault, although I never let the thought be known to either of them and I know now that neither of them was to blame. Their kids were their whole life, Fran. The only good thing to come out of a miserable existence," I said sadly. "That's all it was after that Simms bastard destroyed their world. They just existed."

The back of her hand touched my cheek ever so lightly, silken fingers sliding gently towards my chin.

"So are you going to resign yourself to doing the same, or take your own counsel? Remember what you said to Jen?"

"The SIDS alarm, Fran," I said, a current of hope suddenly surging through me. "It will save babies' lives, and making it will save mine. This time, Paul Wilson is going to achieve his dream."

42: BETRAYED AGAIN!

JULY, 1993

Four–thirty a.m. The stars were retiring, and just a sliver of low moon peeped from behind clouds that wrapped around the distant hills. A bare hint of soft pink tinged the horizon with promise. Save for the careless thunder of the surf, all was silent. The morning bird chorus hadn't yet begun.

The fax machine beeped and hummed, spewing curled pages on to a slowly growing stack on the floor beneath it.

"Damn nuisance idiots sending bloody advertising crap in the middle of the night again," I muttered, "Can we turn that thing off at night or move it somewhere else, Fran?"

"Turn it off? No! U.S. companies send their faxes during their daytime and our night. Move it? Where do you suggest, Paul? If I can make this business work, I might be able to afford to move out of that pokey little office and into decent–sized rental premises, but it will take patience."

"Something I'm very short on," I mumbled, rolling over to put my back to Fran. I hated being woken early in the morning.

Fran had started a computer software business about a year earlier. Compelled to take a crash course in computing to secure any kind of work in a low–employment area, she'd found those strange new-intelligence machines intriguing. Rich with promise, they were enthusiastically embraced as the harried business owner's salvation — an end, at last, to burning midnight oil labouring over accounts records.

Ill–advised software selection and user illiteracy too often meant a wasted investment on a pile of hi–tech metal and plastic assigned to reside under a desk or in the back corner of a storeroom. Fran saw her opportunity and grasped it thirstily. She partnered with U.S. companies to source software and knowledge. While not yet returning a profit, she was compiling a growing client list eager to convert written–off spending to productive capital investment by mastering database tools to tailor their own software.

The little office next to our master bedroom had been transformed into a busy hub, cluttered with books, software boxes, files, cartons, and the beloved green–screen monster that so captivated her that I often found her tapping at its keyboard long before rooster call.

While Fran obsessed over disks and danced with excitement at new software releases, I poured over volumes of legal–speak documenting the proposed terms for commercialising my latest brainchild, the SIDS alarm.

I had answered an advertisement offering free legal services and sourcing of commercialisation partners or capital in return for a percentage share of profits. Warwick Griswold, the young, glossy–haired attorney, was well presented, and his references seemed sound. His offer was compelling. When I related the story of finding our younger daughter, then aged 11 months, in her cot ashen-grey and barely breathing, Warwick needed no convincing of the market potential of an alarm device.

Seven a.m. The morning sun bathed the house in light and warmth and silvered the dew on the lawn outside Fran's office window. I was awake, but resisting the conscience–voice reminding me the night was done.

"The fax is for you, Paul," Fran called from her office, "and it's not advertising. It was sent from Switzerland."

I leapt out of bed and headed for the shower. Fran often worked in her pyjamas until mid–morning. I had never shed deeply ingrained habits. Routine was king. However late I rose, and no matter what excitement awaited, I began the day religiously with a shower and breakfast, deferring all work and leisure until after the morning meal and wash–up was done.

At half past the hour, I sat at the kitchen table pouring over an offer from a Swiss company of a $2 million loan at half a per cent interest — principal and interest to be repaid from profits.

"But they want to add 15 additional technical functions, Fran," I said, frowning. "That will make the alarm device hideously complicated and it will most likely price it out of reach of the average family. The whole idea was to make it so affordable that no mother would want to be without one."

"So tell Warwick that part of the deal isn't acceptable."

"And what about the rest? Do we really want to be $2 million in debt?"

Fran shrugged. "I guess we'll have to ask Warwick to explain the terms. When's he back?"

"Six weeks, I think."

"Guess we postpone any decisions until then. There's no rush is there?"

I folded the document and placed it carefully in a desk drawer.

"Racing in Murwillumbah today, Fran," I called. "You haven't forgotten?"

"I've packed lunch for you, and I filled the car with petrol on the way home from the shops yesterday."

"Have you been told today?"

She laughed and kissed me lightly. "Save it for after the race meeting, my darling. I think a little celebration is in order. I'll make a special dinner. You, lover, can supply my dessert."

For perhaps the first time in my life I was genuinely happy. My relationship with Fran was good. My children — exceptionally mature and level–headed for their age and thankfully staying well clear of the student temptations — were excelling at school and university and planning bright futures. I enjoyed my job at the race track. Swab steward collecting horse urine may not sound like a rewarding occupation, but I loved those beasts and it was satisfying to know I could persuade even the most difficult of them to respond to my commands. The pay was lousy, but I was acquiring a wealth of knowledge that would one day see me achieve my long–cherished ambition of devising a betting system to deliver consistent profits. Talking to trainers and jockeys was steadily adding to my wealth of knowledge about those elusive factors determining when and where a racehorse will win.

I loved being part of the town band. The occasional paid gigs with the Bavarian band were pure ecstasy, although sadly they were far too infrequent to boost my income to anything close to respectable. Fran and I were living on hope, and my hopes rested with Warwick Griswold, the patent attorney who partnered with inventors to find ways to convert ideas to reality.

Humming happily, I backed the car out of the drive and turned on to the highway.

#

"A prominent Lismore patent attorney was last night arrested on fraud charges."

The regular Channel Nine newsreader was on vacation and his novice stand–in struggled to hide her inexperience. Sitting stiffly at her desk in her crisp linen suit, hair a flicker of fire and eyes slightly glazed, she read with nervous precision, too focused on presentation to expose any emotional response to the story she relayed.

"Warwick Griswold partnered with over 30 inventors over the past six years promising to lodge patents and arrange commercialisation loans or investment. Promising lucrative deals for clients, Mr Griswold induced them to borrow tens of thousands of dollars to secure patents and pay up–front costs to facilitate contractual agreements. But Griswold never applied for the patents and the contracts never eventuated. Instead, Warwick Griswold sold intellectual property and patent rights for any genuinely promising inventions he stumbled across, and fleeced millionaires for hundreds of thousands with promises of shares in companies he claimed could produce fuel from water or electricity from vapour, regrow amputated limbs and cure deadly diseases. Police were waiting for Griswold at Brisbane International Airport when he returned yesterday from a trip to Switzerland. He has been charged with thirty–two counts of fraud. Police say they estimate Griswold stole more than $3 million from clients and investors."

I stared numbly at the television set. The demons taunted me. I reached for my beer and noticed my hands were shaking slightly. I felt cold.

Fran came to me, looking wretched and haggard. She put her arms around my neck, but I pushed her roughly away. Glistening tears rolled down her cheeks.

"What can I say, Paul?"

"Say you should have known better than to hope, Paul Wilson. And stop blubbering, Fran. It's not as if it's anything new. Snafu! Situation normal. All fucked up."

I walked to the fridge for a stubby, then changed my mind and fetched a large bottle of vodka from the pantry. Fran sighed and said goodnight.

#

It was mixed emotions and a good deal of trepidation that I listened one evening, two months after Warwick Griswold's arrest, to my wife's suggestion that we up stakes again, and make a third dramatic life change. Our youngest child was about to graduate high school. The other two were already studying away from home.

"We can't afford to keep three kids in university, all living away from home, Paul," she said. "If we move to the city, they can live at home while they are studying."

I didn't know how to respond. I honestly didn't know what I wanted. Not to leave the Bavarian band, nor to give up stewarding. But the combination of those two occupations with the intermittent casual work I was picking up didn't pay the bills. Fran struggled to make a small profit in her little business and the hours she worked to achieve that were crazy. She had some sort of plan for another business in the city. We both figured that, from a financial perspective, things couldn't be much worse.

A month later, an agent posted a 'Sold' sign in our front yard and we loaded a removal van and moved to the city. I struggled desperately to find a shred of hope to cling to, that the pattern of my life might yet somehow change. Hopes and beliefs die, but the fire of determination still burnt strong. I had a point to prove, and I had yet to exact that long–awaited revenge.

43: GOING PUBLIC

ADELAIDE, JUNE 1997

"I'm an inventor," I declared. It wasn't a lie. So what if I omitted to mention that I had never actually made a dollar out of inventing and my paid occupation was embarrassingly insignificant? One thing retired army musicians never did—well, probably most men never did, in fact—was retreat from a pissing contest. And pissing contests were a significant feature of Australian Army Band Corp reunions.

This one was in Adelaide. I hadn't been to one for several years and Fran had never been to South Australia, so we decided to go. As long as I didn't have to reveal too much about my current employment status, I figured I could enjoy a few beers and plenty of good laughs with old mates.

Peter Tuck was first to ask the inevitable question and I was well prepared for it. I practised my public pose as diligently as I had practised music in my youth. Well, maybe 'pose' wasn't quite the right word. I didn't actually pretend to be something I wasn't. It was more what I didn't say—the lack of significant clarification—that might be said to mislead just a little.

Peter opened his mouth to ask for more information, but the waitress intruded just then with the hors d'oeuvre tray. Then some of our other mates from those heady young days in uniform joined us to drink and laugh over somewhat distorted and often exaggerated recollections of past exploits.

"Remember the day that pommy sergeant couldn't remember the command 'Fix Bayonets', and yelled out 'Knives on guns put?'" someone laughed. "The entire platoon cracked up!"

"What about that time Ray Waldon lost it after the drum major ripped into him? He threw his trombone high in the air and it somersaulted, split apart and crashed to the ground. We all watched in horror. It all seemed to happen in slow motion. First the trombone turned over and over, glinting in the sunlight, then first one piece then the other somersaulted and dropped at the drum major's feet. Everyone was certain Ray's career in army bands was over."

"So what happened?" someone who hadn't been there inquired.

"The drum major marched him into the boss's office and told the boss what happened. The boss just looked at him and said very calmly 'Then get him another one'."

Disbelieving stares.

"True story! The boss knew the drum major had been on Ray's case for a long time."

Someone recalled a time, in Korea, when a group was stealthily creeping through the jungle, alert for any sign the enemy might be lurking. One of the group, renowned as a bit of a comedian, said, "I think we need some suspense music just now" and hummed the first few bars of Beethoven's fifth, as used in the movie The Longest Day.

"That was Viv Law," Peter said. "One of the nicest blokes you could ever wish to meet." I nodded agreement. Vince had been a very special friend.

Sam chimed in then, having been with Viv when it happened. "He was about six yards in front of me in the 'J'," he said. "He looked around through the bushes and called out to me in a loud whisper. I said 'What?', then he said 'What we need is some dramatic music', and he did the boom boom boom baaah thing. I nearly drowned, 'cos we were up to our arses in a swamp."

I recalled our compulsory sports afternoons in Singapore. An angry sergeant eventually put a stop to our antics, but for over a year we chose between card games, chess, darts or 'tennis'. Someone had produced an article comparing the physical exertion involved in having sex with playing several sets of tennis, so the newlyweds among us — and singles who could find obliging partners — often opted to play 'tennis' in bed, and signed off declaring we had played eight sets.

We had some good times. Peter had done his 20 years, as had most of my mates, and I envied them the security of their army pension. I wondered, listening to them and remembering, just how I could have hated the life so much when we'd had so much fun.

What if I hadn't left? Where would I be today?

It was a question I didn't want to ponder, because, in hindsight, that decision had cost so much. Twenty–four years of struggle in jobs I hated, on lousy pay. Twenty–four years to realise the things I hated so much about army life were part of life in general. Authority, fools in power making decisions they aren't qualified to make and screwing up the lives of others. Inflated egos, senseless rules, jobs that are only occasionally satisfying and more often involve boring routine. Actually, the job of an army musician was far more stimulating and fun than most, and a lot better paid than anything I'd done for more than 20 years after. And the mateship! We were trained to stand shoulder–to–shoulder against any enemy, and although we might be out of contact for decades, most of us would still defend a buddy to the death if the need arose. When challenged by outsiders, we could team up to hold successfully against a formidable enemy, but among our own the ego contests were fierce and unrelenting.

Well, I was an inventor. I invented or modified tools for every job I tackled and created all sorts of little gadgets to automate household tasks and enhance my own and Fran's lifestyle. I'd invented three potentially commercial devices and patented two.

My next invention, a year or so later, was to be more successful. It would lead me to embark on what Fran and I would come to refer to as our 'wild ride' in the heady world of international big business. It would be hard to find a more unlikely couple to run a global information technology company, but we were to find ourselves, at the height of the so–called I.T. bubble, courting global industry leaders and counting millions.

At the time of Peter's question, though, I was substantially unemployed, completely unmotivated, and lacking any realistic prospects for improvement in my situation, had I been at all inclined to want to make any. Overall, life was tough and unfulfilling. My self–esteem was at rock bottom. I eased off the drink because I couldn't afford it, but I craved it when those frequent waves of depression washed over me and when boredom and frustration overwhelmed me — and that was most of the time.

After years of struggling to make a decent profit selling software and services, Fran had hit on an idea that seemed destined to succeed and, having had to quit my job as a steward when we moved to the city, I was working as her 'gofer'. I spent my days running errands, photocopying courseware on a single–shot photocopier, and laboriously manually collating and binding lesson books. I certainly wasn't going to confess my true occupation in a pissing contest. Despite never having made a dollar out of inventing, I wasn't telling any lies.

By the time we were alone again, Peter had apparently lost his earlier train of thought and thankfully didn't ask again about my occupation. Instead, he inquired after Fran. Peter was divorced. He could never leave Helen while Ede was alive, and he reckoned he'd suffered years of marital misery until his mother died and he was finally free to make the break. I suspected it was more likely Helen who suffered. Peter was always a bit of a cad, and I suspected Ede knew it.

He'd transferred corps about the time I got out and he did pretty well for himself. After discharge, he worked as a hospital orderly and then trained as a paramedic. He also ran a band for disabled kids, but he wasn't paid for that.

"Of course you knew Mum passed away a few years back, didn't you?" Peter said, as an afterthought.

"Yes. I sent flowers. I wanted to go to the funeral, but there was just no way we could get to Perth at the time."

Peter nodded.

"And your mum? Is she still alive?"

"Yes. Still fit. Misses Dad, but one of my brothers lives with her and she always has a stack of grandchildren around.

"She came up to stay with us for a while after Dad died," I told him. "The kids were ecstatic. They adore her. Fran sorted out her pension entitlements. Turned out Dad had never received a veteran's pension, even when he became invalid. Bloody shiny–arsed pencil–pushers never bothered to tell him he was entitled. Fran fought to get Mum a war widow's pension, and finally succeeded. She got $11,000 back pay and to her it was as good as winning a million in the lottery. They'd been moved into government housing when Dad got sick, but she had very little furniture, and no conveniences. She bought her first washing machine, a vacuum cleaner, a microwave oven and a new lounge suite. She was in heaven."

"It's hard to imagine a woman in Australia still living without those conveniences into the 80s."

"She's a tough old bird. Never complained, and it doesn't seem like the hard work did her any harm. She's full of energy and has a wonderfully happy disposition."

While she was staying with us, and later when I went out and spent a few weeks on my own with her, I finally got to know my mother and to really appreciate what a remarkable woman she was. Dad had lectured me about treating women with respect and my mother told me that as tough as her life was, she seldom suffered a harsh word from her husband. It wasn't due to Dad's upbringing. Elsie was a gentle, patient woman, but she had a fire in her belly and a very firm way of enforcing her high standards in the home.

She was totally unselfish—generous to a fault—and she had a wonderfully positive and forgiving attitude to life and people. The only time I ever heard her utter an unkind word about anyone was when my daughter told her she had been to Japan on a school exchange program. Mum could never forgive the Japs for what they had done to Dad. Anyone else's transgressions were forgiven within five minutes of being committed. She would state her opinion very matter–of–factly and quite openly—never behind anyone's back—and she would have nothing further to say ever again.

"Actually, I think your mum and mine were a lot alike in many ways," I added. "Maybe that's why it was so easy for me to call Ede 'Mum'."

Peter smiled broadly.

We chatted on for a little while about my brothers and sisters, their families, Peter's kids and mutual friends. Then a loudspeaker buzzed, announcing the evening's formalities were about to begin. Thankfully, there weren't a lot more questions about my occupation. Those that were asked were deflected with the same practised response and without elaboration. The next reunion I attended, my status had changed so radically that I relished the questions.

NOVEMBER, 1998

"Four more orders in the mail and two on the fax machine. That's over $14,000 already this week!"

Kaylee, Fran's bubbly young personal assistant, had started work part–time, shortly after Fran started writing her computer training course. She seemed completely overwhelmed by the success of it. She had been with us several years now—moving to full–time work before the end of the first year. It seemed she would never cease to be astonished at the way orders flowed in and courseware flowed out.

"And I just took another order over the telephone," Fran laughed. "Looks like your job is secure for another week."

"Steve called while you were on the other line. He wants you to call him back a.s.a.p." Kaylee said, "He said he has good news."

Minutes later, Fran danced out of her office singing. "Prospectus approved, Paul. Call the printers! We are going public!"

It was 1998. I had just turned 50, Fran had been marketing her training course for eight years and the sales just kept growing.

I had conceived yet another invention. I'd never taken more than a passing interest in computers, but using an innovative mechanical approach, I believed I'd worked out how to copy protect digital music.

When a friend first suggested looking for venture capital, Fran had no idea what the term meant, but she went to a seminar on 'Becoming Investor Ready' and came back bubbling with enthusiasm. Business plans were based on the projected profits from expanding Fran's training business, but flavoured with the excitement of potentially solving a major global dilemma by allocating a sensible percentage of turnover to research.

Fran wrote investor offers and mailed them, then for months received letters of rejection one after another. Then an offer came through, followed quickly by several more.

"Are they all going to be like this? It won't be our business at all. We might as well sell out and be employees."

"I suppose they figure if they are putting up the money, they should own the goods."

"Do they have to be so insulting? Look at this! 'Ideas are everywhere. We need to be confident that you will match our investment of dollars.' If ideas are so easy, why don't they come up with their own instead of wanting such a big share of ours?"

I shouldn't have been surprised when Fran came to me one day announcing that she had figured out a better way to fund business expansion. By now, nothing Fran did should astonish. She'd started marketing her training courses before they were written. A 'market test', she called it. When the orders flooded in, she couldn't bring herself to tell customers there wasn't actually a product yet, so she told them she would send a lesson a month for the next year.

Eager customers cheerfully handed over deposits and signed authorities to charge their credit card each month, when another lesson would be sent. Super–charged with electric energy generated by the combination of desperation, determination and ecstasy at the results of her sales campaign, Fran toiled by lamplight in the early hours of the morning. Still clad in PJs and fuelled with nothing more than strong caffeine, she persevered until late morning, before turning her attention to marketing and boring, but essential, administrative tasks.

This continued for a full year, while I alternated between panicking over the possible consequences of her failing to deliver, and panicking that she would crash and burn. I feared a physical collapse, or perhaps a psychological transformation from mad (which she had admitted to being for some time, but with a craziness that thankfully didn't interfere with her capacity to function) to incompetently insane.

If I hadn't cooked and compelled her to eat, she would have starved. Despite my incessant pleading she refused to sleep, but seemed quite capable of coping without it. Such is the power of the human mind that the body can, it seems, run on adrenalin for extended periods when either need or desire is strong enough.

By the end of our first year in the city, Fran had 22 happy graduates, 73 students at various stages of learning, and was taking regular orders for her 1,500 pages of courseware at $1,400 a sale. From then on, she pursued one seemingly ludicrous idea after another to grow the business and by some miracle, they mostly worked. The dollars just kept flowing. She hired an assistant and bought a duplex copier. Eventually I rejoiced at being rendered redundant as course–maker with the purchase of a $60,000 fully automated digital printer.

I then graduated to resident graphic artist, teaching myself photography and how to use 'Photoshop' and discovering talents I never dreamt I had. Adrenalin, it seems, can also stimulate creativity and power the mind to reach spectacular levels of knowledge absorption and skills mastery. Or perhaps the reality was that earlier assessments of my intelligence were flawed and my mental capacity had always been quite adequate to meet the challenges of retraining, if only I'd been given half a chance.

The music industry was struggling, at the time, with the losses caused by CD piracy. As a former musician—sympathetic to the dilemma this presented to struggling artists—the problem both disturbed and intrigued me. After listening to our son recant a television show about how the Egyptians used scrolls to send encrypted messages, I conceived an idea to prevent copying of music CDs. I explained in detail to Fran how I proposed to work with a team of programmers to implement it, and Fran said she was determined this invention would succeed. I knew if there was a way, she would find it.

"We can take the company public, Paul. Sell shares."

"What? On the stock exchange?" I laughed, a cruelly sharp, ridiculing cackle rising almost to hysteria as I tried to envisage Fran and I as members of the Wall Street suit brigade.

"No," she replied, lips twisting in an indulgent sneer. "There's such a thing as an unlisted public company. You sell shares privately, through brokers. I have spoken to a broker and he says it might cost us $100,000 or more to produce a prospectus, get it approved, and then we can sell shares to the public."

I took some convincing. The idea seemed more than a little far–fetched. The idea that people like Fran and I could travel such a path seemed, quite frankly, about as feasible as flying in a rocket to Mars. But once persuaded that this seemingly wild scheme was actually feasible, I struggled to contain my excitement.

The stoic Paul Wilson, who didn't experience normal emotions, recalled how it felt to stand on a little dais after winning a backstroke race. I had feelings, and it felt grand!

We suffered months of agonising anticipation waiting for a broker to find initial investors to fund the first stage of expansion, then spent months in and out of lawyers' offices painstakingly reading and amending the prospectus. I was appointed chairman of the company.

I rehearsed declaring my occupation as 'Chairman of a Public I.T. company', and put my talent for inventing to good use designing CD duplication equipment and perfecting efficient production processes. Well–to–do, well–educated entrepreneurs and directors of successful corporations treated me with respect, even showing admiration for my skills. I basked in the glory.

After Steve's call, I called the printers and told them to start the presses. Then Fran and I proceeded to work through a list of people who had given early indications of interest in investing. Within the week, cheques were flooding in.

"Here's one for $50,000," said Kaylee.

"And another $100,000." Fran exclaimed. "Must be nice to be so wealthy that you can risk that much in a start–up I.T. venture."

It was the height of the I.T. boom. Computing innovations were solid gold. The world was possessed of a madness that, just a few months on, would result in one of the biggest stock–market collapses in history and would see I.T. companies worldwide closing their doors and advising shareholders to write off their losses.

For now, though, Fran and I were counting millions and planning first–class travel to visit the leading corporations of the I.T. world, offering my invention for sale.

44: I TOUCH THE BRASS RING

OCTOBER, 2000

"Ladies and gentlemen, please fasten your seatbelts, raise your window shades and prepare for landing."

It was 20 minutes to five on a cold Monday morning. Fran and I were steadily descending through a classic London pea–souper towards the bobbing landing lights of Heathrow.

"I hope the hire–car people are efficient and the hotel is easy to find," Fran whispered. "I'm desperate for a shower and a proper sleep."

We had spent an exhausting week in San Francisco meeting with executives of leading I.T. companies — right at home, astonishingly, among Wall Street suits. Then we'd gone on to spend a week in Boston with a marketing consulting firm whose job was to teach us to elevator pitch to overcome the inherent distrust of the dour, tunnel–visioned egotists who decided which technical innovation would drive the next big wave. Now we were preparing to present our remedy for music CD piracy to the specialists in copy–protection technology. They were talking a $100 million deal if I could impress them, and our Boston tutors were confident their training had equipped me to sway the most challenging sceptic.

Sondal had already tested the technology. "We have good news and bad news," the head of their technology testing division had said in a call several weeks earlier. "We've cracked the protection."

After two years of painstaking research, repeated testing and costly modifications, I refused to be disappointed. "Really? Then I would be very pleased if you would tell me how and send me your copy to examine. I'm sure we can strengthen the protection further if necessary."

"I doubt it's necessary, Mr Wilson. The good news I mentioned is that it took an investment of over $1 million and eighteen months of our most skilled cracker's time to break it."

Hours later he called back, embarrassed. "It seems I spoke too soon, Mr Wilson. We duplicated the disk and it appeared to be a valid copy. When we played it, the sound was all broken up."

I laughed and danced with Fran. We filled the room with champagne froth and dined on prime rib steak and I told Fran I knew all along that they hadn't cracked it. I had been watching the time to see how long it would take them to figure it out.

#

"Lunch," said Fran, bouncing out of bed in our room at the classic old Tudor Inn in the heart of High Wycombe, after a welcome morning nap. "A genuine English pub lunch, and then some sightseeing. What do you say to that?"

"Fine for you. I have to negotiate strange roads and English traffic!"

I was as eager as she to explore our surroundings. I had drooled over the settings of English television shows and yearned to wander down narrow cobblestone lanes, past century–old houses, and drive past rolling green pastures littered with the poetic remnants of ancient castles. I was interested in the cathedrals, bridges and Trafalgar Square, but quaint little villages with their picturesque old stone-and-thatch pubs, patchwork fields, hedgerows and lakes that inspired the early poets held more appeal. England was a feast for the artist and a symphony for the writer, and Fran and I were in our element surrounded by its ancient beauty.

At the something–or–other–Arms, a 17th century whitewashed stone and shingle–roof structure with flagstone floors, we lunched — or gorged, for the servings were enormous — on sausages and mash. Ignoring Fran's reminders that I was driving in a strange country, I washed mine down with a half–pint of bitter and was not entirely surprised to discover that I still hated warm beer. I hadn't swallowed ale warm since Singapore, but at least English bitter tasted better than that vile Asian Tiger. We basked in the warmth of two roaring open fires while lunch settled, then began an afternoon trek through the poets' paradise.

The following day, a fellow director — an English banking executive who commuted regularly between offices in London and Sydney — met us in the hotel lobby. We braved light snow to set out for the London offices of Amcorp, detouring for a quick tour of famous landmarks on the way. I snapped pictures of the guards at Buckingham Palace, and we stood in the sleet to listen to Big Ben announce the hour. We stopped briefly at the Tower Bridge and we braved the weather again to climb the steps of Westminster Abbey.

The warmth of Amcorp's office was welcome, and we were greeted with an amazing feast of cold cuts, gourmet sandwiches, fruit salad and wines. I declined the offer of wine, partly because of the early hour and partly because I was wary of the warm, inebriated glow slowing my reflexes. It was as well

I did, because the questions were challenging. Interestingly, though, the only real objection to our technology was that it was too secure. According to one of the evaluating panel, some minor flaw in the protection is necessary to keep the Chinese Mafia or some similarly powerful vested interest group satisfied.

"The objective, Mr Wilson," a poker–faced financial director declared, "is not to stop the big commercial pirate groups, but rather to block copying by Mr Average-Home-Computer-User and the small to mid–range copy houses. Preservation of the status quo is essential to economic stability, and ensuring the continued viability of enterprises run by major criminal elements is an essential element of that endeavour."

Fran and I stared at him bug–eyed, but later we agreed that we ought not to have been surprised. The world of commerce was a dirty, corrupt place where the dollar was king, and ethics were in short supply.

Fran and I returned home via Korea and Hong Kong. In Hong Kong, I ordered four new tailored suits and a smart–mustard coloured suede sports jacket that I christened my 'Jack the lad' jacket, and delighted in wearing for years after. Fran had silk blouses made and a smart red power suit that looked stunning on her. She wore it, always, to meetings that promised to be volatile. Somehow it bestowed an aura that thoroughly intimidated her opponents.

We took an evening cruise on the Hong Kong harbour. Colourful reflections from hundreds of neon advertising signs danced over the water to light the night—a commercial war in technicolour. Every major global corporation appeared to be represented.

Boats of every kind drifted serenely. Luxury cruise boats laden with tourists idled across the harbour, cameras flashing from the decks. Paddle–boats and steamers and tugs loaded with stores chugged busily to and fro. On shabby little junks, clothes lines across the rear deck displayed family underwear, and wizened old Chinese gentlemen cleaned their teeth and spat toothpaste over the side, while women leant painfully down to fill washing buckets from the filthy sea.

I marvelled at the contrast between steel and glass towers scraping the skyline along the foreshore—accommodating suited businessmen and elegantly dressed ladies in plush offices and decadent hotel suites—and the grubby little hovels. The streets were crowded with crippled and stooped paupers who spent their days begging or slaving in market stalls or the back rooms of tailor shops, struggling to feed ragged little urchins sucking at mothers' breasts or scrounging for scraps in hotel garbage bins. It occurred to me, again, that I had enjoyed a fortunate life by comparison with these pathetic creatures, and it amazed me that many of them wore wide smiles.

We returned home from the trip to a conditional offer of purchase of our technology for $USD100 million. I was an inventor, and it seemed I was finally to see the fulfilment of every inventor's wildest dream.

45: ALWAYS AN "URCHIN"

Fran and I stood in the Tech Ventures reception lounge in stunned silence, staring vacantly at the dozers digging deep trenches on the construction site across the road.

Digging. Digging.

We were digging for answers.

How could the investor pull out now?

He'd had his pen poised over the cheque form. A $100 million deal, and all we needed was a piddling $200,000 to put the finishing touches to the product. Packaging, mostly. The technology was tested and proven. The risk was virtually nil.

"You must know more than you're saying, Kel. Please!"

Kelvin Hodgson, our investment broker, was reluctant. He'd been sworn to silence, and his sources were valuable to him.

"Does he not trust the buyer? Amcorp are among the world leaders in the industry. Surely their credentials are not in doubt?"

"No, Paul," Kel replied. "The investor has complete confidence in the prospective buyer, and that the offer is genuine."

"Then what's the problem?" I said, in a more demanding tone than I intended. "Christ, Kel, it's a measly 200 grand—for 20 per cent of $100 million. And the development is so close to complete. What's his problem? Does he think we aren't up to finishing the job, or is it just cold feet?"

Hodgson bit his lip. "I was sworn to secrecy. I really didn't want to be the one to tell you this, but due diligence inquiries turned up a significant problem. No-one can invest in Tech Ventures until it's resolved."

"What? What are you talking about, Kel, for Christ's sake, don't talk in riddles. Spit it out."

"The grant application Fran lodged. Was it all above board? It was, wasn't it?"

Embracing the promise of a $100 million licence sale of our copy–protection technology, Fran had sought to take advantage of Federal Government assistance for exporters, applying for an Export Market Development Grant.

Robert Johnson and Frank East had reviewed the application. They raised no concerns, but advised Fran that the application processing would take some time to complete.

"Of course it was. What kind of question is that, Kel? You know us!"

He nodded thoughtfully, then drew a deep breath.

"There's to be a police investigation, Paul. Apparently the assessor picked up on something in the substantiating material that disturbed him. He suspects fraud. He's asked the police to do some digging — check it out and make sure it's all clean. The investor won't move until their investigations are complete, and who knows how long that might take? These things don't happen in a hurry."

"So while Johnson fiddles and police procrastinate, we eat steadily away at our working capital reserves and watch our world slowly crumble," Fran said despairing. She'd suddenly started to sway. I was staring at the construction machines.

Digging. Digging. Digging for what? What could they possibly think...

Fran turned milk white and her legs caved. I caught her going down, but my head was spinning too. The room inverted and the furniture was floating. The persistent sound of dozers digging increased to a deafening roar, and a policeman holding handcuffs swam towards Fran — swam through air.

The walls turned dull grey and the carpet lifted and floated away, leaving a bare cement floor. The window shattered, a million tiny shards of glass showering Fran and Kel. Bars appeared. Kel was outside them. Fran was inside, pressing against them, sobbing. I was with Kel, on the outside, reaching in. I smelled fear.

"Paul, thank God you're here. Everything will be all right now."

I shook my head.

"I can't help you, Fran." I said. "But now, at last, you believe me. The world is an evil place filled with evil people. Only a fool trusts. Only a fool strives."

"But I'm innocent. The application was honest. I did nothing wrong."

"Yes you did," I said, overcome, now, with weariness and furious that I'd allowed myself to forget who I was and what world I was doomed to live in.

"We are both guilty. The guys at Amcorp warned us, but we forgot how the system works. We caught a glimpse of the brass ring, and we were gullible enough to believe the powers–that–be would let us rise above our station — that ability and honest toil could place that ring within an orphan's reach."

#

MARCH 2003

The war in Iraq was in full swing. Gallant sons and daughters were again called to sacrifice themselves for political expediency and the preservation of wealth and privilege. In daily papers, reports of U.S. forces taking control of Saddam International Airport vied for attention with announcements of stock–market gains and with Labor politicians' gripes about the claimed slow destruction of Medicare.

Nothing changes. The world had made no progress since I contemplated battle in Vietnam—no progress, in fact, since my father marched off to be incarcerated on foreign shores. But after endless months of idling away the hours reading propaganda and scanning race guides, it seemed that Fran and I might finally see an end to the nightmare war between Tech Ventures and the bureaucracy.

When Hodgson first broke the news, we counted how long Tech Ventures might survive, and took bets on how long it would take for Johnson and his mates to satisfy themselves that their nonsense suspicions were unfounded. Days became weeks and weeks became months. Ultimately, Fran lost patience. She wrote to the Commissioner of Police and Federal Attorney–General demanding the investigation proceed immediately and threatening class action by shareholders if delays caused the company further damage.

I was delighted when two detectives arrived at our office. I welcomed them warmly, rejecting their advice to call a lawyer and giving them open access to files, computers and staff. Detective Sinn replied that he ought not to be surprised by the reception. Fran had somehow managed to have a minor investigation prioritised over investigations of drug importation and prostitution rings.

More months passed. Endless police interviews exposed no clue to Johnson's motives or purpose.

"Mr Johnson's claimed concerns remain a mystery to me, Paul," Sinn declared. "I can find no irregularities, and I've told him so, but his department is my client and without his agreement, I can't close this matter."

Johnson steadfastly refused to let it go.

"I'd like to do something a little unconventional, but only if you and Fran agree. It might be uncomfortable for you, to say the least," Sinn said in a phone call one late May morning. "I'd like to bring Mr Johnson to a meeting at your office and ask him to question you directly. Tell you exactly what his concerns are and let you respond."

Fran and I replied that we would relish the opportunity to challenge our specious accuser.

On June 3rd, 2003, Robert Johnson entered the Tech Ventures boardroom with his head bowed. Refusing my extended hand, he pushed right past the others to take a seat at the end of the table and stare intently at a carving of a maple leaf on the edging around the boardroom table. Detective Frank Sinn of the Australian Federal Police followed him, greeting us with hearty handshakes and a broad smile.

There were four on the Tech Ventures side of the table. Dan, the lanky but distinguished looking ex–politician had taken over from me as chairman a year earlier. Dylan, our fresh–faced young technical director, sat beside Fran and I along the east side of the room, facing a row of Dobell prints and with framed company registration certificates, partner agreements and award certificates behind us. Fran wore her red power suit and I suppressed a smile, admiring her. At 55, she was still slim and attractive, with just a hint of salt in her hair giving her a mature, distinguished look. She had a reputation as a kind, gentle woman until crossed, but a potent adversary and one who inevitably had right on her side and would not tolerate evil.

"Well, Mr Johnson," the detective said, when all were seated with introductions complete. "You may now begin your questioning."

Awkward silence. Johnson continued to stare at the maple leaf, colour rising in his neck.

"Mr Johnson?"

Heavy silence. Fran's eyes blazed at Johnson and Sinn's face worked in an uneasy contortion of frustration.

"Mr Johnson, I warned you this would be your last opportunity to ask these questions you say you need answered. At the end of today's meeting, I am going to close this investigation."

Silence. The detective fiddled with his notebook.

"Mr Johnson," Fran addressed him now, and her tone caused me to draw breath sharply. "You have made a very serious accusation and —"

"There was no accusation made, Mrs Wilson," said Detective Sinn. "Mr Johnson raised concerns."

"Concerns? Concerns?" she shouted. "Let me tell you about our concerns, Detective Sinn."

I kicked her under the table and Dan made a face at her, but she ignored us.

"Mr Johnson comes in here just when we are about to close a $100 million deal and accuses me of falsifying a government grant application. Grounds for accusation? I have no idea. He interviews me twice and then goes away without a word. The next thing I know there are police interrogating us and our staff and searching our computers and files for heaven only knows what and our business is frozen. Instead of closing an amazing deal that will make all our shareholders rich, we are struggling to survive until Mr Johnson satisfies his claimed 'concerns', which he will not articulate and which it appears, from his behaviour today, were never valid to begin with."

"I didn't cause your business to be frozen," Johnson snivelled, without looking up. "You were free to keep marketing product."

"We are a research and development company, Mr Johnson. The product the company was founded on became obsolete due to web technology changing the landscape in computer programming. We turned our focus to music copy protection—the product that underpinned our public offering—because it promised our shareholders a return of 20 times their investment. We were on the verge of finalising a deal when you intruded."

"So what stopped the deal?" Sinn asked in a tone that implied genuine curiosity.

"It was subject to the addition of several product features. We had an investor willing to fund the research to add those features, but he pulled out because the due diligence process uncovered Mr Johnson's allegations. We couldn't secure investment capital to fund the necessary further research until this matter was resolved."

Sinn nodded, then addressed Johnson again, this time in a forceful tone.

"Mr Johnson, I consented to arrange this meeting because no matter how many times I tell you I can't find any evidence of irregularity, you keep telling me your concerns are not satisfied. I am giving you one final opportunity to ask questions. You have exactly five minutes, sir, and then this meeting, and my investigation, is over."

Johnson continued to stare in sullen silence at the maple leaf.

Your name should be Simms, I thought, suppressing a murderous rage and reminding myself that I had yet to exact that long–planned revenge.

"Tapped phones, bugs in our living room," Fran shouted. "God, you have put us through hell, Johnson. And now you sit there like a pathetic, wimpish little schoolboy who was caught out lying and —"

I kicked her harder this time and motioned to her to be quiet. Sinn frowned. "The police didn't bug your home or your phones."

"Someone did," I said. "An amateurish attempt too. A bug fell out of the overhead light in our living room."

Johnson reached for a folder in a pile on the centre of the table, upsetting the pile in the process. He began thumbing through it, seemingly without any real purpose.

"If I could just take some of these files away with me —"

"Absolutely not! Those files are company property and valuable," Dylan roared. "Tell us what you are looking for and we will locate it and copy it for you."

"He doesn't know what he's looking for. His purpose seems to be to cause total disruption and he's achieved it. He's killed $100 million deal, wiped out a business, and caused shareholders $5 million in losses. And now he's sitting there dumbstruck and unable to think of a single legitimate question to ask." Fran was on her feet now. I feared any moment she would go right across the table and punch Johnson.

"I'd like to leave now," Johnson said in a sheepish whisper. "I feel like I'm being railroaded."

"Railroaded?" Fran screamed. "You feel like you are being railroaded? You snivelling little bastard! Do you have any idea how much damage you have done with your careless accusations and stupid baseless assumptions?"

Sinn closed his notebook and put it and his pen in his top suit pocket. "I think we are done here. I am very sorry to have imposed on you and I thank you for your co–operation. I will file my report."

Johnson bolted from the room without even pretence of courtesy. Sinn lingered a while and I noticed Johnson pacing nervously about the parking lot, obviously impatient to make his escape.

"I must say, Mr and Mrs Wilson, it was quite an experience for me, meeting you. When I announce myself, most people can't get to the phone quickly enough to call their lawyer. An offer of coffee and an open invitation to inspect files and computers at my leisure was not what I expected at all."

"When one has nothing to hide, Mr Sinn, there is no need for lawyers and no reason not to assist an inquiry in any way possible," Fran replied.

"And Mr Wilson, thank you for introducing me to the internet Wayback Machine. It will prove very useful in future investigations and it certainly made it easy to respond to Mr Johnson's incorrect claim that Market Tactics never existed."

I wondered again how a senior detective with the Australian Federal Police could not know of the existence of a website that archived nearly everything ever published on the World Wide Web.

Sinn shook hands then and apologised again for the intrusion. It wasn't his fault, of course, and he had done his best not to cause disruption. I stood at the window and watched them drive off.

It was finally over. Months of police visits, interviews, employee questions, stress and living under a cloud of suspicion, and we still hadn't the faintest notion what it was all about. Johnson never gave even a hint of the reason for his suspicions and Sinn was far too professional to disclose why he had been called in. The thickset, greying detective with kind eyes questioned us politely, asked to see documents, apologised constantly for having to intrude and disclosed absolutely nothing.

Johnson drove away in a sleek black sedan, taking all our hopes and dreams with him.

It was over; all of it. The resolution had come too late. Tech Ventures closed down, the liquidators claimed the last of the cash reserves and assets in payment of their claimed fees. Their invoice exceeded their quote by a factor of five and totalled, coincidentally, precisely the amount they calculated the company was worth at the time of closure. Harry, the company accountant, said that was normal practice.

The $600,000 debt the company owed Fran and I in unpaid salaries was written off, along with debts to other directors. There were no other creditors. The shareholders were politely advised their shares were worthless and they may be entitled to claim a tax loss.

My fingertips had touched the brass ring, but a shiny–arsed bureaucrat snatched it from my grip and removed it to dangle seductively just beyond my reach. I cursed my stupidity for forgetting who I was and what I was destined to be.

All that I desired… black car departing.

I was left with that old sensation of emptiness—that same hollow ache I recalled feeling when the black car left me at St Patrick's all those years ago.

Cold.

Naked.

Exposed.

All my tomorrows lay out in front of me like paving stones forming a path through the gauntlet: a tortuous, purposeless path without any end.

#

Dan phoned the following Wednesday.

"I had a call from Mr Johnson's boss. I've been making some quiet inquiries, Paul, using my connections. I want to know what that inquiry was all about."

"And?

"I'm meeting with him at 10:30 today. I told him I wanted you and Fran with me, but he was emphatic that he wouldn't speak to me with either of you, or Dylan, present. I think it's disgraceful, but I want to question him so I've consented to go alone. I just wanted you to know. He's cautioned me that everything he tells me is absolutely confidential and I mustn't breathe a word of it to you or Fran. I'll play his game just long enough to get to the bottom of this. I'll stop in on the way back from the meeting."

He arrived at our house just after noon. Fran made chicken and salad sandwiches for lunch. Dan's demeanour gave nothing away, but there was keenness in his greeting and when Fran asked if he cared to eat first and talk later, he was quick to state his preference to talk while we ate.

"So," Fran said when we were seated, "What did you find out?"

"When East and Johnson came in for the second interview, did he ask you where Market Tactics conducted their seminars?"

"Yes, and we told them we didn't know the address off hand, but would look it up for them if necessary. They said it wasn't important." I answered.

"We gave them the taxi vouchers from the hotel and back, and we described the place in some detail." Fran added.

"Hmmm." Dan paused to sip his coffee before continuing. He looked somewhat careworn now, as though the morning meeting had been too much for him. "Fran, apparently the invoice from Market Tactics had an address on it which included a suite number."

"It did. In the U.S., they often quote a suite number when using a post office box or a secretarial service for receiving mail. Market Tactics sold out just after we went over there. They closed their Boston office and relocated to the buyer's offices in New York. They used a post office box address to finalise collection of payments, etc., because they no longer had a physical address."

"Did you tell Johnson all that?"

"Absolutely. Why?"

"Because Johnson wrote in his report that he asked you if the address on the invoice was the address of the place the seminars were conducted and you confirmed that it was."

"That's a lie and I can prove it. Check our records. The meeting was fully minuted."

"Well, it seems they flew a detective to Boston to check — twice — and he took photos of a post box. Johnson then sent the photos to the Federal Police with a statement that you were claiming to have attended seminars in a post office box."

I prepared to restrain Fran. I don't know what I expected her to do. She liked and trusted Dan. None of this was his fault. He had been wonderfully supportive throughout. He could have done as Johnson's boss made him promise to do — not tell us what he had discovered. I knew, though, Fran was furious enough that if Johnson or East were here now, they would be in mortal danger.

"And that's the sum total of his claimed 'concerns'?" I asked Dan.

"Apparently. Combined with the fact that Market Tactics didn't exist at the time he started assessing the claim." He shifted in his seat.

"They had sold out already. That was fully explained also."

"I'm sure it was. I'm satisfied both Johnson and East were thoroughly incompetent, and I said so, but unfortunately there's very little we can do about it now. I doubt they'll even suffer any penalty. It'll be put down to an unfortunate mistake."

I didn't trust myself to respond. I had suffered too much as a result of pencil–pushing bureaucrats' unfortunate mistakes.

Dan shook my hand warmly, and hugged Fran. "I don't know what to say. I wish there were words to help you feel better about all this."

"It was good of you to tell us, Dan. I know it wouldn't have been easy to make a promise you had no intention of keeping."

"It was a promise they had no right to ask for. I will never consent to supporting wrongdoing and I won't apologise for doing what I have to do to try to make things as right as they can be. I just wish I could fix the mess these fools have created with their incompetence."

"Not incompetence, Dan. Lies. Johnson knows what was said in the interview."

He didn't respond. He had been part of the system for a long time. He knew how it operated, and he was no ordinary politician. His integrity had cost him dearly in that profession.

He turned at the front gate. "By the way," he called back to us, "It's small comfort, I know, but they've approved the claim. Of course nothing will be paid now that Tech Ventures is no more, but at least no–one can question your honesty."

46: THE TRUTH REVEALED

DECEMBER, 2007

I didn't watch the news on December 11, 2007. Once almost addicted to current affair shows and documentaries, I had long since lost confidence in reporters who danced to tunes played by commercial interests and distorted truth for the benefit of lobby groups and power clusters. It wasn't until sometime later, in conversation with a friend, that I heard of newly installed Prime Minister Kevin Rudd's momentous announcement that an apology would be made to Australians who were stolen from their homes as children.

I did watch, tense and angry and with gut churning, at 9:30 the following February 13th when Kevin Rudd made his very public address to the Australian Parliament, apologising for the profound grief, suffering and loss suffered by stolen Aborigines.

On the morning of February 13, I was forced to again relive that terrible day in 1956 when everything familiar — everything safe — was suddenly snatched away. I revisited the awful playground in which I stood, lonely and terrified, counting the Sundays, believing that after just a few more I could go home. I suffered, again, the terrible beatings, often for no reason at all, inflicted by the people I was supposed to trust to keep me safe. I relived those days in the schoolyard, branded 'home kid', rejected and cast out; and the desperate yearning for home and family — for the world I was born to.

They had loaded a battered 12–year–old boy and a tiny suitcase filled with shabby, ill–fitting clothes into a sleek black car and taken him far away from his sister — the only family he had left. My 16th birthday had passed before I saw her again, and but for Uncle Bill, I might have lost contact with her for ever.

They handed me over that day like a freight consignment. I was signed for and duly delivered without a word of attempted comfort or reassurance, after being indoctrinated to believe I was too rebellious to be allowed a home among decent people, and threatened with torture and persecution until I finally conceded and fell into line.

I remembered the horror of signing away eight years of my life at age 15, leaving, yet again, everything familiar in my life for a new and frightening world; a different prison.

I recalled the awkward uncertainty of the day I at last went home, wondering if I would recognise my parents. I had rehearsed my greeting, consumed with fear of rejection and terrified our meeting might validate the nuns' condemnation of them, and thus of me. My brothers thanked me for my performance that day. No–one would ever know the strain the actor endured, nor the awful struggle whenever I was around them: battling to reconcile my craving for a mother's affection with a simmering contempt for a woman whom I thought had so dismally failed in her obligation to protect me. Wanting to belong, yet afraid to be part of a world I was taught to shun; wanting forgiveness and to forgive; wanting to know, yet afraid of knowledge. Consumed by undefined guilt and fear, emptiness, and endless confusion.

A tape recording in my head replayed the words I heard my mother utter from her deathbed—words of love and pride. I cried that day, concealed in the darkened hallway of my mother's home. When my wife came and wrapped her arms around me, I buried my head on her shoulder and mumbled, "Did you hear her, Fran. She said she loved me and was proud of me. I've waited nearly 50 years to hear her speak those words."

Ten thousand happy memories had dulled my pain. Love had healed wounds and faded scars, but nothing can ever adequately compensate.

Jenny phoned me shortly after the speeches ended.

"How many stolen Aborigines did you know, Paul?"

"None," I replied coldly. "I shared institutional dining halls and bathrooms with more than a 120 homeless children at different times. Four had Aboriginal blood. I estimate at least a quarter of the kids I knew were stolen. Many, most likely—like you and I—taken from parents who wanted them and would, if not crippled by deprivation and social injustice, have cared for them competently and loved them well. Every one of those was white."

"A woman talked of swinging on a gate, hugging a dirty rag doll, crying for her mother," Jen said. "That was me, Paul. It was my story. A black woman told the tale and claimed it as her own, but that little girl was me," she sobbed. "Do you remember, Paul? You do, don't you? It was me!"

I remained silent, listening to her soft sobbing, wishing I could hold her and comfort her.

"Aborigines were stolen, I'm sure," I said, "but they've not only had their plight acknowledged, they've been richly compensated. Their entire race—not just those who suffered. Free adult education, free legal help, preference for subsidised housing, special business and employment grants, higher rates of study subsidies for children, the list goes on and on. What do we get, Jen? Not even recognition."

"Apparently, it's all about the reason for taking kids, Paul. Aborigines win sympathy because they were taken for no better reason than that they were black."

"I've read plenty of claims that they were taken more for their own protection, because their tribes rejected mixed–blood children, or because they were neglected or abused. But what difference does it make, Jen? Kids like us were stolen for no better reason than because families were poor—because our parents didn't understand their legal entitlement to a pension and no–one cared enough to help them. Was that any less of a crime? And while Aborigines born into privileged families lined up for generous handouts, we stumbled through life scarred and bruised, with neither a helping hand nor even truthful acknowledgement of our plight. We don't exist."

"Do you think they will ever acknowledge that it happened to white children too?"

"I doubt it, Jenny. It's not politically expedient, is it?"

"I guess not. I feel sorry for the Aborigines. I do. But — " Her voice trailed off.

"It's not their fault, Jen. It's the white and privileged mixed–blood activists, the politicians and the system."

"Positive discrimination. That's what they call it, Paul, but it's racism, and it's wrong."

"I told myself I'd forgotten the trauma. I told myself the suffering had ended and I was healed. But inside, something has never seemed quite right. I envy my brothers their security, their self–confidence—their relaxed, friendly acceptance of life and people. I wonder what I might have been, had I been allowed to be me."

"I had won, Paul. I had put it all behind me. But today — " She sniffed. There was an uneasy silence, and then I heard her sobbing.

"We survived, Jen. That's what matters. We survived and we made good lives for ourselves. We have partners who love us and good kids who respect us. We've done OK, in spite of everything. We can hold our heads up and be proud of what we have achieved. That little girl with the rag doll grew up to be smart, strong and beautiful, a good wife and a great mother. And she still has a lot to look forward to. We have a few years left on this earth yet, and we'll make them good ones.

"I've got to go now, Jen. But I'll call you later, yeah? Chin up, old girl. No more tears."

#

A brown–paper envelope arrived by special delivery a few months before my 60th birthday. Fran brought it to me and I held it, unopened, for what seemed like an eternity, though it must only have been minutes. Here was the story of my life. Here were the official records of a 'crime', a court case, and the 17 years of incarceration that followed. Here were the dirty secrets of lies and social injustice that condemned little children, ripped out mothers' hearts and tore homes apart.

I had applied for my file under revised Freedom of Information laws. I was uncertain, now, precisely why, but after reading advice on the Care Leavers Australia Network website, I had signed the form and paid the fee. Now I wasn't at all sure I wanted to know. My hands trembled as I held it and I felt the coldness as the blood drained from my face. Fran stood there expectantly, silent. At last, I tore the flap away and pulled a thin file from the envelope. A dozen pages, maybe. Less than 1,000 words to tell the story of my life. I began to read.

An hour later, I set the file aside. I sat staring silently into space for a long time, struggling to comprehend. Fran picked it up then and read it. I saw the look when she came to that middle page. It had shocked me too.

I wished I had tracked Geoffrey Simms down and murdered him. Ede convinced me that the crime was not his. Perhaps he was a misguided fool when he found me on the riverbank, but the lie four years later was a crime for which he could never be forgiven.

Geoffrey Simms visited my parents just before my 12th birthday. My mother signed the record of interview. They wanted me sent home. Three days later, Geoffrey Simms signed a statutory declaration confirming that he had been unable to find my parents and, in these unfortunate circumstances, I must be retained in care until age 15.[x]

The judge had ordered that I was to be committed to St Patrick's until the age of 12. No order beyond that date. On my 12th birthday, I should have been sent home.

I was stolen twice.

When I read the false claim that I had expressed a strong desire to join the army, the bile rose in my throat and choked me. My eyes watered; my neck and face burnt. I shook with rage. Again there was a false declaration that my parents could not be located. "In these unfortunate circumstances," the social worker had written, "the Commissioner for Child Welfare must sign the consent form in their place."

My father had declined consent, but they had overridden his wishes and lied again.

I could have been a bootmaker. I could have gone home.

The days that followed were a blur. I went mechanically through the motions of living, without feeling and without purpose. I drank too much. I lay awake at night reliving days when the torment seemed unending. I wanted to find Simms and kill him, but I supposed by now he was almost certainly dead.

Finally, I made my resolve.

"I survived the injustice, Fran," I said. "I made a life for myself. I put it behind me. I won't let the reopening of old wounds destroy me. I'm stronger than that. But I want justice."

"How?"

"I'm going to sue the State of New South Wales. False imprisonment. Plenty of people have succeeded with compensation claims for –"

"People falsely accused of a crime, Paul. It's a different situation entirely."

"How? I was charged with a crime. The crime of being a neglected child."

"And how will you prove that you weren't?"

"Eight healthy brothers and sisters raised by loving parents in a happy home. Surely their testimony is enough? And what about the lie when I was 12. If nothing else, I was wrongly incarcerated from age 12 onwards. That's documented. How are they going to argue with that?"

47: THE WHEELS OF JUSTICE

FEBRUARY, 2009

The offices of Thompson, Stanley and Smythe were on the 11th floor of a recently constructed Sydney harbour side tower. Fran and I entered via a marble–tiled lobby, climbing in little glass cells that hovered over the silvery blue harbour. We stepped out on to carpet that swallowed our shoes to approach an extravagantly carved reception counter topped with polished black granite and decorated with elegant stone and brass statuettes. After a brief wait, seated on a soft suede bench in a room filled with original oils by contemporary Australian artists, we were ushered down a long hallway.

In the meeting room, thick velvet drapes were pulled back from huge picture windows overlooking the water and plush leather chairs surrounded a slick, grey-glass and chrome table. I felt conspicuously misplaced surrounded by such opulence, yet attired casually in jeans and open–neck shirt, with Fran beside me in a loose cotton sun frock, sandals and no stockings. We could dress to impress and look quite at home in surroundings like this when it pleased us, but creating an impression of having done well for ourselves was not consistent with today's objectives. Today was about winning sympathy for the battler who survived years of deprivation and abuse.

George Smythe was a dapper little man with a quaint moustache and prominent bald patch in the middle of his scalp. His nose was too big for his face. Thick eyebrows hung low over tiny slits of suspicious eyes always demanding further explanation. His favourite word was 'evidence', and he prefaced every sentence addressed to Fran with 'my dear lady', which irritated me intensely.

"My dear lady, we shall need strong evidence to support a claim that your husband could not reasonably progress a complaint within the time limits provided by statute," he said.

"And it isn't enough that he had no access to information until very recently?"

"My dear lady, well of course that is relevant, but your husband may —"

"With respect, Mr Smythe," I interrupted, "the dear lady's husband is in the room and you may speak to him directly."

Fran kicked me under the table and made a face. We wanted this fellow to represent us pro bono or on a success fee basis. We should be trying to win his favours, not offend him.

"Quite right, Mr Wilson. I do apologise. It's just that all my communication to date has been with your dear lady wife. And not all victims are articulate, let alone sufficiently confident to discuss the legal implications of their situation."

"I'm not a victim, Mr Smythe," I said, slapping the top of the glass table for emphasis. "I was wronged as a child and I believe under International Human Rights Law, which Australia has consented to recognise, I am entitled to reparation."

"Quite right. Quite right, and I shall endeavour to see that it is paid. However, you must understand that the law presents considerable difficulties in cases like this, and the first is timing. We estimate that an application for dispensation to pursue your claim outside the usual time limits will cost $15,000. If you lose, you could face an order to pay the costs the State incurs to defend the application. They will engage the best lawyers available. Money is no object for the N.S.W. Government in matters such as this."

A pasty–faced young woman in a tailored dark-grey pant suit entered just then and took orders for coffee and tea. Before taking her leave, she poured water from a pitcher on a glass–topped sideboard and set a filled glass in front of each of us.

"That's sad," Fran said, "That they will expend taxpayer dollars so freely to obstruct a fair hearing and deny someone justice."

"My dear lady, you must realise that the issue here is precedent—the avoidance of setting one, that is. There may be many care leavers who are eligible to file claims. This firm is currently considering representing more than 40. If the floodgates are opened via a successful case, the State may find itself responding to hundreds of claims. It could become very expensive."

"I am not a 'care leaver', Mr Smythe," I declared emphatically, "and I object to that terminology. I was a stolen white child."

"But you were a child in care, Mr Wilson."

"Hardly! At least not for the first four years of incarceration! I was deprived and abused. There was no 'care' involved!"

"That may well be, Mr Wilson, but you will need strong evidence to support any claim of damages."

"I was snatched from a loving home because my father was never granted his entitlements after serving his country in a theatre of war—losing his youth and his health imprisoned for three long years in a war prison. A callous welfare worker lied to prevent me being returned home four years later, in compliance with the original removal order which applied only until my 12th birthday. I was denied access to my family. I was denied my identity."

"That's quite shocking, I agree. Quite shocking, but I say again, my dear man, you will need evidence to support your claim."

"I have evidence to support my claim that a welfare official lied, costing me my freedom for a further three years and the opportunity to follow a career path of my choosing. Surely you have seen the documents evidencing that lie, Mr Smythe?"

"And what evidence can you present of consequential damages? That is the key question. For example, have you had lasting health issues requiring ongoing medical care?"

I stared at him for a moment, struggling to comprehend. Prisoners didn't need to evidence permanent health damage in order to be compensated for wrongful imprisonment. It was automatic. The damage was quite apparent.

"Can your doctor attest to a history of mental illness?"

I might have leapt across the table then and punched him, but for the soft knock on the door and the girl entering with a tray. She set a fine china cup down before each of us and a platter of biscuits in the centre of the table. She refilled Fran's half–empty water glass and fetched neatly-folded paper serviettes from the sideboard to place beside our cups.

"I thought I made it clear, Mr Smythe," I said, struggling to maintain an even tone. "I am not a victim. I was brought up to be resilient, a survivor. My father taught me never to let anyone or anything get the better of me."

Smythe studied me thoughtfully for a minute, his bushy eyebrows descending even lower over his eyes so they seemed to almost disappear, and his forehead creasing with deep worry lines. He opened a file and closed it again without reading anything from it.

"Unfortunately, courts have little sympathy for survivors, Mr Wilson. We want to show that you endured a lifetime of suffering. Medical records attesting to mental illness, evidence of chronic alcoholism, broken marriages, disturbed children, violent outbursts — criminal behaviour even — these are the sorts of complaints that win public sympathy. But back to the first obstacle. Timing."

"Yes, timing," I said, stirring my coffee vigorously and raising my pitch. "It seems to me, Mr Smythe, that by obfuscating evidence for decades, the State escapes answering for its crimes. All one has to do, apparently, is ensure a victim of crime has no access to the proof of wrongdoing until the statute of limitations expires, and no matter how evil the deed, there can be no penalty and no redress."

"You have to forgive my husband — " Fran began. I glared at her. I didn't need her to make excuses for me, and I had no intention of apologising for my anger at such obvious injustice.

305

"My dear lady," Smythe cut in, "I am quite accustomed to victims being resentful and angry, and, quite frankly, dear, I agree with your husband. The statute of limitations is, in this case, patently unfair. Not to extend the time limit is a denial of natural justice and I shall be arguing accordingly, but you need to understand the risks of embarking on this course. The fact that you and I—and no doubt many citizens of this State—may regard laws as unfair is irrelevant. It is still the law. We have to overcome the time obstacle and then we have to find a way to prove quantifiable damage—damage to which the courts can attach a dollar value, damage the average citizen understands and sympathises with."

I ate a biscuit, sipped my coffee and gazed out over the harbor at the rowboats, motorboats and big, luxury cruisers rocking gently with the waves lapping at their sides, and the sailboats with their sails billowing in the breeze. The Commissioner for Child Welfare would have sat in an office like this one, perhaps not quite so luxurious, but cosy in winter. He would have sat there signing children's lives away and looking forward to taking his own children on weekend boat rides across the harbor while I washed pissy sheets in freezing water and suffered agonising chilblains, hunger pains, bruises and lesions from vicious beatings. And I had to not only evidence lasting damage, but I had to fight for the right to be heard at all, because the good Commissioner concealed evidence until long after the statute expired.

Smythe was still prattling on about the kind of disabilities that might prove I had suffered harm—chronic unemployment, even having been charged with robbery or an act of violence, but being a loony was obviously the most compelling proof.

"Mr Smythe," I said sourly, rising suddenly to leave before he finished his sentence, "Thank you for your time. I appreciate your offer of help, but it seems we are wasting our time. If reparation for wrongdoing is payable only to those who can evidence that they let the wrong destroy them, then I don't qualify. It did me a great deal of harm. It deprived me of my identity and the right to choose my own destiny—took away the right to be me. That caused me a lifetime of pain and suffering, but I would never let the bastards defeat me."

48: ALL BULLSHIT, DAD

JULY, 2010

Ern Stanley, somewhat out of place — and visibly uncomfortable — attired in stiff blue jeans and starched chequered shirt, climbed into the passenger seat of the black Roller Ghost, flicked the air conditioner switch and settled back for a long ride.

Over the past months, he had listened for endless hours while I related parts of my story. We drank vodka and wine. We dined together. Ern took me home and introduced me to his wife and children. We went yachting on the harbour. Ern complimented my resilience, but never patronisingly. He met my brothers and sisters and conversed with them as equals, never condescending. We talked and poured over legal precedents until the small hours of the mornings.

Ern had contacted me three months earlier, having waited a respectable length of time after I had stormed from his partner's office. After suffering George Smythe's affront, I was hesitant to speak with Ern, but a deeply ingrained respect for the rules of courtesy required me to grant a reluctant and resentful hearing.

"Mr Wilson — may I call you Paul, please?"

I didn't answer, but Ern took my silence as consent.

"Paul, I have enormous respect for people who survive adversity as successfully as you did and it disturbs me that my partner may have been patronising and unhelpful."

He paused. Cold silence. Let him sweat — if that's what he's doing. But Ern was remarkably at ease.

"I'd really like to help you, Paul. But more importantly, I'd like to know your full story."

"Thank you for your interest, Mr Stanley," I said, my voice iced with contempt, "but your partner made my position quite clear. I didn't let my childhood turn me into a criminal or a hopeless drunk and I'm not insane. And if the 'effluxion of time' obstructs even entering a courtroom, then my case is hopeless. It's been over 50 years. Most of those who might bear witness — on either side — are dead. And I survived."

Ern was silent for a moment, and for an instant I thought perhaps the line had gone dead.

"The 'effluxion of time' is a challenge, but not insurmountable," he said at last. "There are very good reasons why you could not instigate an action sooner and the State's lawyers will have great difficulty arguing otherwise."

"If I can stump up thousands to buy a hearing, and I'm prepared to risk paying the exorbitant costs the State's fat-cat barristers will bill if I lose."

"We can come to some arrangement. I won't mislead you about the risks, but the obstacle presented by timing isn't insurmountable and I'm willing to go out on a limb to get over that hurdle."

"For what? If I need to show—"

"Would you indulge me, please. Let me get to know you, at least, and make my own assessments. There are many forms of damage. You don't have to have been weak. There is often a high cost to being strong."

"There was a high cost, all right! Every day of my life was a confused struggle. Still is. But I'm not sure I want to relive the saga, Mr Stanley. Just how much reminiscing would be needed for you to make your assessment? Would I have to see a shrink? Pretend to be a loony, maybe?"

Ern laughed. "I'm aware of your distrust of doctors, Paul. And no, pretence is neither necessary nor desirable. A psychologist's report would be helpful, but it will attest to your strength and resilience, and to the fact that you are, quite clearly, perfectly sane and rational. What I seek is an understanding of the type and extent of pain and suffering you endured, both as a child and as an adult, as a consequence of the crimes committed against you, and any economic loss that resulted. Tell me, what kind of reparation do you think would be appropriate?"

"An Aborigine, allegedly 'stolen' and wrongly committed to foster care when his mother 'forgot' she had left a sick baby at a hospital six months earlier, was awarded $525,000 compensation. Compared to his claim—"

"That's not a valid comparison. And there are no real precedents relating to care leavers claiming for abuse."

"It's a valid comparison, Mr Stanley."

"Call me Ern, please."

"Thank you. Ern, I am not claiming for abuse, although I suffered it. My claim is that I was stolen... twice. I was taken from a good home with loving parents, disconnected from my roots and denied contact with my family. I lost my identity and subsequently the freedom to choose a career and my destiny. What's that worth, do you think?"

"Three major criteria are considered in calculating reparation. First, any quantifiable expense or economic loss is considered, then there must be consideration of pain and suffering. And finally, judges consider culpability — to what extent the damage was avoidable and caused by negligence or wrongdoing."

"There was plenty of pain and suffering, and the damage was quite clearly caused by wrongdoing. Lies, Ern. Blatant, outright lies. And negligence. Economic loss? I spent most of my life in shit jobs that paid peanuts, but we got by. Despite all the hardships and setbacks, we are better off now than many retirees, and I guess that would go heavily against me."

"Hmmm," he said, and was silent for a moment. "I can't make assessments until I understand your case better. It's a long, hard road and it will require you to relive your trauma. That can be therapeutic, I'm told, but I'm not the one risking more suffering. It has to be your decision."

"And if I agree to proceed, how would we go forward. "

Ern chuckled. "My methods are regarded as unconventional, to say the least, but I am thorough. After an initial interview session, to extract the critical information, I'd want to take a trip with you. "

"A trip?"

"Down memory lane, but not just in the psychic sense. I want to get to know Paul Wilson, intimately — explore the home you came from, meet your family maybe. I want you to take me back to where you were born and let me inside you to experience your thoughts and emotions while you relive your life."

"What will that cost me?" I put a heavy emphasis on 'that'.

"Nothing initially. If I proceed with your case, we'll discuss costs. Your case might set the stage for actions by others. It could become a class action. If I don't proceed, I'll put the time spent on the trip down to an investment in knowledge and character building. "

Nothing? An investment in character building? Please! The guy was born rich. He's part of the system. What's his real purpose?

"Let me sleep on your proposal, and talk to Fran. I'll get back to you. "

"Please give it serious thought, Paul, and try to trust me. I know that's a tall order, but I really am sincere. "

#

Water–laden clouds blackened large expanses of grey sky and the wind cried and swept the town pavements clean of their litter the day Ern Stanley gathered up the voluminous legal file he had compiled over a month of journeying with me through time, and we drove through the gates of Dubbo airport. Later, Ern would remark that he came to associate the black day with the black story I told. Over a month of travel, listening and observation, I had

309

forced him to confront, full force, the ugly side of the society that fed him, and it scarred him.

We had visited St Patrick's, now a luxury resort. No evidence remained of little children labouring before dawn, washing pissy sheets by hand in freezing water, nor of the dark, dank dormitories where children struggled to tuck bedcovers in with perfect mitred corners, pulling covers tight enough to bounce a coin on. The dusty barren playground was gone, and there was no sign, either, of the worn scrubbing brush that was used to beat the devil out of evil urchins, nor of the sagging timber tank stand on which it had rested.

We visited the town school where I learnt to read and the bakery — now run by the grandson of the man who had kindly saved 'staffies' for hungry waifs.

I ran on the football fields where I had triumphed, suffered the humiliation and terror of being caught stealing a pie, then rejoiced in the kindness and understanding of Father Joseph — one of very few robe–wearing Catholics I had respected — even come to love.

Ohio was now a magnificently restored National-Trust-classified heritage homestead, but the owners kindly allowed me to take Ern on a guided tour of the house and grounds. We stood for an hour in what was once the boot shed. I know Ern cried inside for the little boy who, laboriously welding bits of tyre rubber on to damaged leather soles day after day, had cherished dreams and aspirations that were so cruelly ground to dust.

We visited the site of the old Army Apprentice School at Balcombe, and walked the five miles to the beach on Mornington Peninsula. We walked through an old romni hut in a mini–camp now converted to a tourist site. I saw the folded linen and blankets stacked in perfect symmetry on the beds; the rows of stretchers lined against dark, windowless walls; and the long, open ablution blocks with not the smallest pretence of screening for privacy. Deep in my stomach, something turned. I was again wrapped in an icy shroud of dread, remembering the indescribable horror of returning — after the comparative freedom of Ohio — to total regimentation, constant verbal abuse and bullying, and soul–destroying boredom. I again smelt fear and remembered the unutterable agony of betrayal. I had let down my defences; trusted the Boss; even allowed myself to love him. And the Boss had repaid that love and trust by sending me to be incarcerated again, destroying all ambition and hope, shattering all my dreams.

I showed Ern the spot on the route to school where a hit on the head with a wooden pencil case started a pain that would never heal.

We walked over the property on which the shack my family called home once stood. I pointed to the place where the black car had parked the fateful day Simms drove me home, and to the place where my father laboured with the axe, glistening rivulets of sweat trickling over and between deep carved muscles. For a brief instant, I was a little boy again, trembling in expectation of the sting of my father's belt across my buttocks. But I was spared that brief discomfort, and sentenced, instead, to seven years hard labour in a children's prison and the loss of my freedom for life.

"It was just as the Aborigines describe it, " Ern wrote in his notebook. "He was put in a black car and taken away from everything safe and familiar."

"I was feral before they took me," I said. "I was forced into sterile institutions, to wear uniforms and sleep in barracks, but I belonged in the bush, living off the land and in touch with nature.

"Aborigines talk of one's 'dreaming place'. You may never see it, but you will always long to return to it: the place of your conception; the world you were first born to. My dreaming place was the outback—the 'Never Never' land of blazing suns and blistered red earth, breaking wild horses and herding cattle from waterhole to waterhole and sleeping in a swag under the stars. "

Ern had convinced me to see a shrink. I was reluctant, but I consented.

"The medical reports say you suffer from post–traumatic stress disorder," Ern said, perusing the report that labelled my condition. It reported alcohol abuse, employment issues, lack of confidence to set and pursue life goals, relationship difficulties, anger–management issues—including periodic outbursts of violence—and claimed inability to experience normal feelings and emotions." My laugh—when Ern read it out—was tight with resentment.

"Shrinks love labelling people, don't they. So I'm PTSD, eh, like soldiers who witness horrific brutality in war zones?

"The smells!" I said then, suddenly conscious of the enormous power they had always held over me. "Men who live through the trauma of war are often haunted for ever by memories triggered by the most seemingly insignificant sounds and odours. I used to condemn them for their weakness; regard them with contempt. Later I recognised that contempt as the reaction of a man intensely focused on fighting his own demons, and denying their ability to control him."

A family of travellers shot us a curious glance as they pulled cases towards the terminal. My gaze followed them, granting Ern a moment to surreptitiously pull a handkerchief from his pocket, wipe his face and regain his composure.

"The memory of the smells never left me," I continued. "The disinfectant and floor polish in dormitories. The kitchens, the ablutions blocks, sweaty young men. They controlled me. The institution controlled me. When I came out, I was lost—so thoroughly desensitised that I didn't know how to make a decision. For the rest of my life, the need to make a choice terrified me and I felt cold, nauseous and frightened for ages after. I expected whatever I sought to be snatched away, and I struggled to deny wanting and to prevent anyone from knowing what I longed for or what gave me pleasure."

"How frequently do your senses cause you to relive the trauma, Paul?" Ern asked.

I shrugged. "Not often now. It started to reduce a year or so after I left the army, but every now and then something triggers a bad memory. Honestly, though," I said, composing myself quickly, "It wasn't childhood trauma that hurt me most. You relive the pain often, but you do get past it. The trauma ends and even while reliving it you can remind yourself it's just a memory and it's over. It was the ongoing persecution that did the real damage—the withdrawal of freedom and denial of rights long after I ought to have been allowed to control my own destiny. Bureaucratic bungling and unfair dealings that seemed to go on without end, and my own endless confusion. Outwardly, I appeared capable, controlled and content, but I lived in a constant state of turmoil. When I suffered unfairness—like the wrongful denial of retraining I was legally entitled to—I hadn't the knowledge, the perspective or the confidence to fight for my rights."

I told Ern how vehemently I had hated the army and everything it stood for.

"Yet you wanted to go to Vietman?" Ern said. "There must have been a streak of patriotic fervour somewhere deep inside you?"

"No. I hadn't the slightest inclination to contribute to the defence of a nation that sacrificed my father over something that was happening in Poland, and rewarded his sacrifice by condemning him and his children to a life of misery. Why would I? I wanted to go for money and adventure. If the truth be told, I suspect that's what motivates most modern volunteer soldiers, and was the driving force behind the signatures of any Vietnam vets who weren't conscripted."

Ernest Stanley's cash–register eyes tallied and popped when I told him how Robert Johnson had destroyed Tech Ventures, but I merely shook my head.

"If you took that matter on, you'd get a visit," I said sourly. "Robert Johnson was connected. We were told it was incompetence, but then I did some digging of my own, and what I found was no surprise. Amcorp warned us. We should have run a mile when they mentioned Asian Mafia, but we were floating—hovering somewhere between the top of the clouds and the end of the rainbow, blinded by the gleam of that elusive brass ring."

"So much injustice!" Ern said.

"You know, I never really thought of it that way," I replied. "At least not in relation to my childhood. I was often angry and depressed, but when I thought about it, it was with resignation. It's just how it was. My lot. In many respects,

I had a fortunate life. I didn't go to war. I found a good woman to love, and she loves me. I've got great kids.

"It was that damned Apology that changed my attitude. So many benefits I was denied because I was white. And ultimately I was denied acknowledgement. My childhood never happened. I don't even exist!"

Ern gawked at me. He'd obviously never thought about it that way. Positive discrimination seemed right and proper to the privileged.

"So much injustice," Ern repeated, "but I've always seen it as my mission to address injustice. Mine and my fellow professionals. I'd like to believe we enjoy a measure of success in that endeavour."

I laughed, a sharp, mocking laugh. "I'm sorry, Ernie. Really. But it's such a ludicrous concept, isn't it? You and your fellow professionals are players in a game—a game in which power and money, not righteousness, determines who wins."

"Economic reality is, unfortunately, a significant factor in determining whether or not justice is achievable, Paul," he said, "but we strive hard to ensure that the righteous party prevails as often as possible."

"Economic reality. Yes. That's the justification, but the reality is it's all just a game. And the winners don't care who they persecute during the play," I said, aware my tone was caustic.

"Then we shall play the game to win, my friend," Ern said brightly.

"Win?" I snorted. "There is no win. My father sacrificed his life fighting evil and all he achieved was to prove that it's a lost cause. The corrupt and evil will always prevail. The best men like me can ever hope for is to maybe occasionally put a small dent in their armour."

Ern's little indulgent smile was almost a sneer. "What you can hope for, my friend, is a generous award of compensation—following a no doubt lengthy and immensely satisfying battle of wits that will give all on the legal teams on both sides a handsome feed."

An implacable rattling voice in my head reminded me of the cynical warnings it had issued when I'd acceded to the lawyer's request. I fought the inclination to feel betrayed, but I was dog-weary and aware that my eyes were accusing. Silence hung between us, heavy and awkward.

"So where do we go from here?" I asked at last.

"I go back to my office and compile my notes, and then I prepare and lodge a written claim. And then, my friend, the real journey begins."

"Enjoy the adventure, then," I replied, my tone still acrid. "I'll try my best to enjoy mine."

"What will you do, Paul?" Ern asked.

"With the money, if it eventuates?"

"No. With your life. It's not yet over. You have a great deal of ability. A law suit is a distraction, not an ambition."

"That racing system. I've finally fine–tuned it enough to implement it with confidence, and I have an idea for another invention I think I just might pursue. It's taken longer than I planned, but I'll get rich yet!"

Ern nodded. "Never give up. One day you may just catch that brass ring."

I gave a cynical little chuckle. "Or maybe I'll finally find some way to end the nightmare of confusion and just be me, whoever me may be."

I smiled then, as a curious feeling of satisfaction and relief washed over me. "I got one thing right though, Ern. An achievement few can lay claim to in today's world and certainly not too many waifs or urchins managed. It took a very long time, but I eventually learnt how to love and care. I made a success of marriage and raising kids. My dad once said the only thing we have control over, ultimately, is our attitude to life and the way we treat others. If he could see me today, I think he'd say I did OK. I've had a fortunate life despite all the setbacks. I never let the bastards break my spirit, and I did finally exact my revenge. The sweetest revenge of all: I lived a good life, in spite of all the condemnations and the efforts of so many to break me."

I lifted my case from the boot and checked my watch. A small plane pelted down the runway, skidded, turned into the taxiway, and glided to a halt. Inside the terminal building, the loudspeaker crackled.

"They'll be calling my flight shortly." I swapped my case to my left hand and extended my right. "Drive safely, Ern."

"I will if you return my keys," Ern laughed.

I grinned and fished in my pocket. "Thanks for letting me drive. It's a damn fine car," I said, passing him the engraved silver ring.

The sleek black Roller Ghost slid out of the parking lot, swung on to the main road, and disappeared in a mist of grey and dust. Watching, I felt a familiar emptiness engulf me. A dull, hollow ache started low in my belly and worked its way slowly up to squeeze my chest, dry my mouth and make my forehead pulse.

Black Ghost leaving. Demons finally departing, or Paul once again deposited at the door of a new life, with all the fear, threats, challenges, heartaches, uncertainty and promise that encompassed?

Court rooms. Interrogation. Pompous arseholes in long white wigs slamming gavels to confirm declarations that rupture the fabric of a family's reality, break spirits, kill souls. And Ern Stanley and his cronies, cash–register eyes popping and tallying, contemplating satisfying intellectual battles and fat pay cheques.

Endeavour, frustration, but the ever–enduring hope that, one day, if you play the odds right, that horse your hopes are riding on just might romp home.

And what will you do then? Watch some game–playing arsehole exploit the system to take it all away from you, then pick yourself up and stake your hopes on another.

"It's all bullshit, Dad," I muttered aloud. "You just gotta enjoy the journey and be happy."

ENDNOTES

i.   Official N.S.W. Government records, finally released to "Paul" (not his real name) shortly after his 60th birthday, reveal that the primary reason for his removal was that his family couldn't afford enough blankets for each of their five children to sleep in separate beds.

The legal account of the children's removal begs the question why the social worker didn't assist their father to claim the veteran's pension rightly due to a man who had returned, after three years in a war prison, with shrapnel wounds to his legs, tuberculosis, and no doubt psychological ailments resulting from fear and abuse during incarceration. Despite suffering years of illness, "Fred" went to his grave in his late 60s without ever collecting a cent of his well-earned entitlement. His offspring fought for almost a year before his daughter-in-law finally succeeded in persuading a Federal Government agency to grant his wife a war widow's pension.

While accusing "Paul's" parents of neglect, social workers allowed two baby boys to remain at home in their parents' care, and records indicate that they never followed up to check on the welfare of those children, who, along with six younger siblings born after Paul's removal, grew up healthy, loved and happy and in awe of the parents they adored.

ii.   The name of the child has been changed, but Robbie's story is based on a truthful account told by the author's mother after witnessing a young boy suffering severe punishment for taking a hoe and doing an excellent job of weeding the orphanage gardens.

iii.   It is noteworthy that official records note that the children were charged and convicted of the offence of being neglected, and were sentenced to "be of good behaviour" during a period of incarceration. That record has never been expunged.

iv.   The accounts of conditions in the orphanage were verified from multiple sources, including the author's first-hand observations as a regular visitor, and accounts provided by past employees of St Patrick's, including the stand-in cook who sought to serve milk pudding to the children. Much of what is written here is verified in official records accrued through a Government project that involved interviewing adults who grew up in orphanages and children's homes, and a past employee of St Patrick's.

Unlike children in many Homes throughout the country, residents at St Patrick's did not suffer sexual abuse.

v.   "Father Joseph" is a fictional character, based on a real priest who worked hard to instigate reform at St Patrick's and who showed the children kindness . The story of the girl being beaten for stealing a sip of orange juice is a factual account of an incident in the early '70s, witnessed by the author's mother.

vi.   "Paul" remembered vividly the day the nuns locked the children in the dormitories claiming a prowler presented danger. He recalled seeing the man from a distance, through an upstairs window, but he wasn't close enough to recognise his father. He learnt of his father's visit from a brother about 16 years after the event.

vii.   "Paul" deliberately wiped the negative experiences on the Moree farm from his memory, remembering only that he went with a friend on a farm holiday. He recalled what actually transpired when, in 2008, he was finally allowed to read the (previously legally withheld) official records of his youth in incarceration, and found a section blacked out by authorities who were withholding the information in that section to protect the privacy of third parties.

viii.   "Fran" actually talked with the hawker through a translator, and heard her story just as it is told here. Many years later, when her father-in-law was close to death, he spoke to her for the first time about his war experiences, detailing the girl's remarkable kindness to him and crediting her for saving his life. He wept when "Fran" told him she had met his angel. The story of this remarkable coincidence was first told in a short story titled "SuSu", written by Lorraine Cobcroft when she was in her mid-20s.

ix.   While it is true that "Paul" was cheated out of his deferred pay for the first two years of army service, he actually remained unaware that the State had stolen his pay until, in about 2007, he met up with a man he had served with in Singapore and who had also been an apprentice at Balcombe. When this man mentioned how he had considered investing the lump sum payment he received on graduation, "Paul" was shocked. About a year later, at an army band corp reunion, he asked others for confirmation of the payment. Their responses confirmed, some 30 years after the event, that — by accepting and retaining the payment the army made to the Child Welfare Department as Paul's trustee — the State had robbed him of his pay.

x.   Official records include a notation that the judge ordered "Paul" committed to care until he was 12 years of age. There was no order relating to his care past that date. His file also includes a record of a social worker's interview with his parents shortly before his 12th birthday. That record is signed by his mother. A few pages further on, a Statutory Declaration signed by the social worker declares that his parents could not be located and "in these unfortunate circumstances, the boy must remain in care".

Siblings recall social worker visits, including one made shortly before "Paul" joined the army. They recall his father going raging mad at the suggestion that a son of his might be a soldier, and adamantly refusing consent for him to join. The official records state that the Commissioner for Child Welfare was asked to sign the consent for "Paul" to join the army, because social workers again lied, claiming his parents could not be found.

There has been considerable speculation about the motives for these lies. Ultimately, the conclusion drawn — and supported by a retired social worker who worked in the system at the time — was that the department's budget and thus social workers' jobs depended on retaining as many children as possible in care. Also, children's homes profited from receipt of government support payments for kids in care, by spending far less than the allowance, providing subsistence diets, donated old clothing, and virtually no health or educational benefits. Those running the homes were known to offer generous gifts to social workers — possibly as an incentive to bring in more children, and thus increased Government payments.

GLOSSARY

ANZUK servicemen: Servicemen in the Australian, New Zealand and United Kingdom forces.

Billy: A small, tin bucket with handle, typically hung over a fire to boil water and to make tea.

Boozer (slang): A bar; a place where alcohol is served.

Craybobs: Freshwater crayfish.

Damper: A traditional Australian soda bread prepared by swagmen, drovers, stockmen and other travellers. It consists of a wheat–flour–based bread, traditionally baked in the coals of a campfire.

Holsworthy: A notoriously harsh Australian military prison.

Jack–rabbiting: Running and jumping in a manner similar to a rabbit running from a threat.

Kissing crust: When an unsliced loaf of bread is broken through the centre, the first slice from the middle on each side is uneven but soft. This is referred to as the 'kissing crust' (Otherwise known as the 'fly crust').

Kombi: A panel van/mini bus produced by Volkswagen and introduced in 1950.

Laminex: A plastic–like, washable–surface sheeting typically applied to table tops and kitchen counters.

Linoleum: (informally abbreviated to lino) An extremely durable floor covering made from renewable materials, most commonly on a burlap or canvas backing; popularly used to cover kitchen, bathroom and laundry floors.

Motza (slang): Much, a great deal.

Nappies: Short for napkins, a term used in Australia for babies' diapers.

Removal policies: Social policies that endorsed the removal of children from their family homes by welfare workers who claimed to find evidence of neglect or abuse. Removed children were incarcerated in institutions or sent to foster homes where many suffered severe deprivation and emotional, physical and often sexual abuse. Such policies, which were in effect in Australia from the 1920s to the early 1970s, often resulted in the improper removal (theft) of children from families affected by poverty, illness or temporary incapacity.

Rounders: A game played with a bat and ball, somewhat similar to baseball.

Steelie: A marble made of a silver–coloured metal such as steel, used in a game of marbles.

Six of the best: A term used to refer to a punishment typically inflicted on school–boys in Australia up to the late 1960s. It usually consisted of six strokes of the cane on the open palms, usually three strokes on each hand. On occasions, the cane was applied to the buttocks or a belt, strap or ruler was used.

Stolen Generation: A term controversially used to refer to Aboriginal children stolen from their families, allegedly to integrate them into white society. The term is not typically used in reference to white stolen children. It is not officially recognised that white children were stolen. The wrongful implication that white children were taken for cause, and should blame their parents, compounds the pain stolen whites suffer.

The pictures (as in "into town to the… "): The movie theatre.

Towser: A small boy.

Utility (or ute): A small coupe–style truck.

Yabbies: Another term used for craybobs (freshwater crayfish).the early 1970s, often resulted in the improper removal (theft) of children from families affected by poverty, illness or temporary incapacity.

AUTHOR'S NOTE

When I began to write this book, the man on whom the character Paul Wilson is based recorded this account of his experience:

A Child Welfare Inspector burst into my family home in September 1956.

He burst in like Satan, unannounced and unwelcome, into an idyllic world. He came to tear that world to shreds, destroying my father's pride and strength, parting loved ones, bringing terror and darkness to a world that had known neither.

I didn't understand the persistent explanations or the promises the man made. The significance of the courtroom and the black–robed man with worried brow escaped me, except that it brought indescribable fear. The kindly social worker lady terrified me, and her words confused. I understood only my dad's angry scowls, cursing, spitting and tears; my sisters'[i] sobs, and my own terror.

Weeks of hunger and cold were forgotten. My father's black moods were permanently erased from my memory. Only boyhood adventure, Dad's tall tales and the warmth of my mother's hugs were stamped indelibly on my young mind as a black sedan urged forward, carrying me into a terrifying unknown.

On 8th October 1956, a month before my eighth birthday, two sisters and I were charged in a N.S.W. Children's Court with the crime of being neglected children. I was sentenced to four year's incarceration in a Children's Home.

Twice my sentence was extended as a consequence of a social worker's lies. Ultimately, I was deprived of my freedom for 17 years, and as a consequence, denied the right to choose my career or my destiny.

In April 1974 — aged 26 and a father of two — I found my parents, two brothers I last saw as infants, and six younger siblings I had never known. I was welcomed back into a poor but happy, loving family in which eight children had grown up healthy, happy and emotionally well–adjusted. I learnt to know and deeply love a father who had walked 73 miles each way to try to find me and take me home, only to face cruel lies and be turned away without seeing the little boy who peered, unknowingly, from an upstairs window, at the shadowy figure of his dad.

Forced to suffer the most awful pain life can inflict on a woman, my mother, in her own words, "had other children to care for, so just had to keep on, somehow", but cried herself to sleep every night for 18 years, and probably many nights thereafter, still haunted by misplaced guilt and bad memories. Where did she find the strength and courage to get up every morning?

On February 13, 2008, Prime Minister Kevin Rudd apologised to the so–called Stolen Generation. He didn't apologise to me or to thousands of other stolen Australians. He didn't apologise to my parents for the indescribable agony of being denied all knowledge of the whereabouts or wellbeing of their offspring.

I was stolen—twice. I am a white, native–born, fifth–generation Australian.

I learnt the full extent of bureaucratic bungling and heartlessness on 6th April 2008, when, for the first time, I was permitted to read the records of my youth. I learnt the reason for my removal was that my war–injured father, unaware of veteran pension entitlements and never assisted to secure them—even in his infirm old age—couldn't afford enough blankets to provide each of his five children with their own separate bed.

I inquired about suing the N.S.W. Government for kidnapping and wrongful incarceration. I was advised that it was too late. The effluxion of time would be deemed to have compromised the Government's defence. By withholding records for 52 years, wrongdoers apparently escape all obligations to answer for their crimes and successfully deny their victims the right to redress.

In November 2009, Mr Rudd made a hollow, low–key apology for the abuse and deprivation I suffered while "in care". There was no apology for the greatest hurt of all. On 8th October 1956, I was deprived of a fundamental and essential right of all human beings: the right to be me.

Thousands of white Australians were stolen from families by negligent or misguided child welfare authorities, often for no better reason than because families were poor. Welfare workers not only removed children in preference to implementing other readily–available and cost–effective remedies—such as helping parents access benefits to which they were legally entitled—but often lied to keep children in care. Boosting the number of children in care ensured funds continued to flow to the Government department that kept welfare workers employed. Many workers received generous gifts from the

Homes that operated at substantial profit by depriving children of all but the most basic essentials.

In addition to the many benefits accessible to Aborigines solely on the basis of their race, a formal apology has been made to those Aborigines who claim to have been stolen and to their descendants. Stolen whites have received neither formal acknowledgement nor compensation. In some States, minor compensation has been paid to men and women who suffered abuse as children in institutional or foster care, but those incarcerated in N.S.W. institutions received nothing.

Unlike Aborigines, stolen whites enjoy neither the support of the "mob", nor public sympathy generated by very public outcries about the injustices they suffered. Taught to be ashamed of their past, most kept to themselves and kept their childhood and family history a guilty secret. Generally poorly educated and skilled, and often suffering health issues as a result of childhood abuse and deprivation, they were prevented by financial challenges both from seeking out fellow victims and from pursuing legal remedy. More recently, groups such as CLAN have publicised the abuse many suffered in institutions, but have failed to expose the ugliest truths of past sins against children and have been unsuccessful in persuading governments to make reparation or offer realistic aid. Despite strong recommendations from the Federal Senate, the N.S.W. Government continues to refuse compensation or assistance. CLAN has, however, succeeded in easing the feeling of shame and facilitated reunions of men and women who grew up together and share unique bonds.

Successful legal actions for compensation are virtually impossible due the effluxion of time. Withholding records and poor record keeping by authorities obstructs justice. The literacy and psychological capacity of victims, the emotional strain of reliving their trauma, access to and emotional strain on potential witnesses, and the high costs associated with any attempt to access legal remedies, discourage attempted claims.

Stolen white children, denied healthcare, education, employment opportunities, and permanently damaged by deprivation and abuse, were left to struggle through life without assistance or benefits of any kind—not even recognition. Many who survive are now ageing in poor health due to abuse and deprivation in childhood. Many are desperately poor, and all still struggle with psychological damage caused by the wrongs they suffered.

Although a totally factual biography would be impossible given the effects of trauma on memory and the sensitivities of some of the characters involved, this story was written to expose the ugly truth.

---

i.   Although only one sister is mentioned in this story—at the specific request of the man on whom the character Paul Wilson is based—in fact three children were taken: a boy aged 7, a 9-year-old sister, and a 5-year-old-sister.

www.ingramcontent.com/pod-product-compliance
Lightning Source LLC
Chambersburg PA
CBHW062043080426
42734CB00012B/2541